Women, Sport, Society

During the last four decades women's and gender history have become vibrant fields including studies of attitudes regarding the limited physical and other abilities of females as well as studies of the accomplishments of notable female athletes. We have become increasingly aware that women have made contributions to physical education, dance and sport that go far beyond being teachers, athletes and coaches. They have created and implemented an astonishing variety of programs intended to serve the needs of large numbers of children and youth sometimes organizing student health services, as well as chairing departments of physical education. They have worked as directors of sport, physical education and dance, running playgrounds and recreational facilities and have created and/or served as important officers of a variety of sporting organizations.

This book explores the contributions and achievements of women in a variety of historical and geographical contexts which, not surprisingly opens opportunities for additions, revisions and counter-narratives to accepted histories of physical education and sport science. It seeks to broaden our understandings about the backgrounds, motivations and achievements of dedicated women working to improve health and bodily practices in a variety of different arenas and for often different purposes.

This book was previously published as a special issue of the *International Journal of the History of Sport.*

Roberta J. Park is based at the University of California, Berkeley, USA.

Patricia Vertinsky is based at the University of British Columbia, Canada.

Women, Sport, Society

Further Reflections, Reaffirming Mary Wollstonecraft

Edited by
Roberta J. Park and Patricia Vertinsky

Routledge
Taylor & Francis Group

LONDON AND NEW YORK

First published 2011
by Routledge
2 Park Square, Milton Park, Abingdon, Oxfordshire OX14 4RN

Simultaneously published in the USA and Canada
by Routledge
711 Third Avenue, New York, NY 10017

First issued in paperback 2014

Routledge is an imprint of the Taylor and Francis Group, an informa company

This book is a reproduction of the *International Journal of the History of Sport*, vol. 27, issue 7. The Publisher requests to those authors who may be citing this book to state, also, the bibliographical details of the special issue on which the book was based.

Typeset in Times New Roman by Taylor & Francis Books

British Library Cataloguing in Publication Data
A catalogue record for this book is available from the British Library

ISBN13: 978-0-415-59738-8 (hbk)
ISBN13: 978-0-415-66123-2 (pbk)

Disclaimer
The publisher would like to make readers aware that the chapters in this book are referred to as articles as they had been in the special issue. The publisher accepts responsibility for any inconsistencies that may have arisen in the course of preparing this volume for print.

Contents

CONTENTS

SERIES EDITORS' FOREWORD

On January 1, 2010 *Sport in the Global Society*, created by Professor J.A. Mangan in 1997, was divided into two parts: *Historical Perspectives* and *Contemporary Perspectives*.

These categories will involve predominant rather than exclusive emphases. The past is part of the present and the present is part of the past. The Editors of *Historical Perspectives* are J.A. Mangan, Mark Dyreson and Thierry Terret.

The reasons for the division are straightforward. SGS has expanded rapidly since its creation with over one hundred publications in some twelve years. Its editorial teams will now benefit from sectional specialist interests and expertise.

Historical Perspectives draws on IJHS monograph reviews, themed collections and conference/workshop collections. It is, of course, international in content.

J.A. Mangan
Mark Dyreson
Thierry Terret

SPORT IN THE GLOBAL SOCIETY

Series Editors: J.A. Mangan, Mark Dyreson and Thierry Terret

WOMEN, SPORT, SOCIETY
Further Reflections, Reaffirming Mary Wollstonecraft

Sport in the Global Society: Historical Perspectives

Series Editors: J.A. Mangan, Mark Dyreson and Thierry Terret

Titles in the Series

Gymnastics, a Transatlantic Movement
From Europe to America
Edited by Gertrud Pfister

Post-Beijing 2008
Geopolitics, Sport, Pacific Rim
Edited by J.A. Mangan and Fan Hong

Representing the Nation
Sport and Spectacle in Post-Revolutionary Mexico
Claire and Keith Brewster

Sport in the Cultures of the Ancient World
New Perspectives
Edited by Zinon Papakonstantinou

Sport in the Pacific
Colonial and Postcolonial Consequencies
Edited by C. Richard King

Sport Past and Present in South Africa
(Trans)forming the Nation
Edited by Scarlet Cornelissen and Albert Grundlingh

The Beijing Olympics: Promoting China
Soft and Hard Power in Global Politics
Edited by Kevin Caffrey

The Politics of the Male Body in Sport
The Danish Involvement
Hans Bonde

The Rise of Stadiums in the Modern United States
Cathedrals of Sport
Edited by Mark Dyreson and Robert Trumpbour

The Visual in Sport
Edited by Mike Huggins and Mike O'Mahony

Women, Sport, Society
Further Reflections, Reaffirming Mary Wollstonecraft
Edited by Roberta Park and Patricia Vertinsky

Sport in the Global Society
Past SGS publications prior to 2010

Fringe Nations in Soccer
Making it Happen
Edited by Kausik Bandyopadhyay and
  Sabyasachi Malick

From Fair Sex to Feminism
Sport and the Socialization of Women in
  the Industrial and Post-Industrial Eras
Edited by J.A. Mangan and Roberta J.
  Park

Gender, Sport, Science
Selected Writings of Roberta J. Park
Edited by J.A. Mangan and Patricia
  Vertinsky

Globalised Football
Nations and Migration, the City and the
  Dream
Edited by Nina Clara Tiesler and João
  Nuno Coelho

Italian Fascism and the Female Body
Sport, Submissive Women and Strong
  Mothers
Gigliola Gori

Japan, Sport and Society
Tradition and Change in a Globalizing
  World
Edited by Joseph Maguire and
  Masayoshi Nakayama

Law and Sport in Contemporary Society
Edited by Steven Greenfield and Guy
  Osborn

Leisure and Recreation in a Victorian
  Mining Community
The Social Economy of Leisure in
  North-East England, 1820–1914
Alan Metcalfe

Lost Histories of Indian Cricket
Battles off the Pitch
Boria Majumdar

Making European Masculinities
Sport, Europe, Gender
Edited by J.A. Mangan

Making Men
Rugby and Masculine Identity
Edited by John Nauright and Timothy J.
  L. Chandler

Making the Rugby World
Race, Gender, Commerce
Edited by Timothy J.L. Chandler and
  John Nauright

Militarism, Hunting, Imperialism
'Blooding' The Martial Male
J.A. Mangan and Callum McKenzie

Militarism, Sport, Europe
War Without Weapons
Edited by J.A. Mangan

Modern Sport: The Global Obsession
Essays in Honour of J.A.Mangan
Edited by Boria Majumdar and Fan
  Hong

Muscular Christianity and the Colonial
  and Post-Colonial World
Edited by John J. MacAloon

Native Americans and Sport in North
  America
Other Peoples' Games
Edited by C. Richard King

Olympic Legacies – Intended and Unin-
  tended
Political, Cultural, Economic and Educational
Edited by J.A. Mangan and Mark Dyr-
  eson

Playing on the Periphery
Sport, Identity and Memory
Tara Brabazon

Pleasure, Profit, Proselytism
British Culture and Sport at Home and
  Abroad 1700–1914
Edited by J.A. Mangan

Rain Stops Play
Cricketing Climates
Andrew Hignell

Reformers, Sport, Modernizers
Middle-Class Revolutionaries
Edited by J.A. Mangan

Rugby's Great Split
Class, Culture and the Origins of Rugby
  League Football
Tony Collins

Running Cultures
Racing in Time and Space
John Bale

Scoring for Britain
International Football and International
  Politics, 1900–1939
Peter J. Beck

Serious Sport
J.A. Mangan's Contribution to the His-
  tory of Sport
Edited by Scott Crawford

Shaping the Superman
Fascist Body as Political Icon – Aryan
  Fascism
Edited by J.A. Mangan

Sites of Sport
Space, Place and Experience
*Edited by John Bale and Patricia Ver-
  tinksy*

Soccer and Disaster
International Perspectives
*Edited by Paul Darby, Martin Jones and
  Gavin Mellor*

Soccer in South Asia
Empire, Nation, Diaspora
Edited by Paul Dimeo and James Mills

Soccer's Missing Men
Schoolteachers and the Spread of Asso-
  ciation Football
J.A. Mangan and Colm Hickey

Soccer, Women, Sexual Liberation
Kicking off a New Era
Edited by Fan Hong and J.A. Mangan

Sport: Race, Ethnicity and Indigenity
Building Global Understanding
Edited by Daryl Adair

Sport and American Society
Exceptionalism, Insularity, 'Imperialism'
*Edited by Mark Dyreson and J.A.
  Mangan*

**Sport and Foreign Policy in a Globalizing
  World**
*Edited by Steven J. Jackson and Stephen
  Haigh*

Sport and International Relations
An Emerging Relationship
*Edited by Roger Levermore and Adrian
  Budd*

Sport and Memory in North America
Edited by Steven Wieting

Sport, Civil Liberties and Human Rights
*Edited by Richard Giulianotti and David
  McArdle*

Sport, Culture and History
Region, Nation and Globe
Brian Stoddart

Sport in Asian Society
Past and Present
Edited by Fan Hong and J.A. Mangan

The Games Ethic and Imperialism
Aspects of the Diffusion of an Ideal
J.A. Mangan

The Global Politics of Sport
The Role of Global Institutions in Sport
Edited by Lincoln Allison

The Lady Footballers
Struggling to Play in Victorian Britain
James F. Lee

The Magic of Indian Cricket
Cricket and Society in India, Revised
    Edition
Mihir Bose

The Making of New Zealand Cricket
1832–1914
Greg Ryan

**The 1940 Tokyo Games: The Missing
    Olympics**
Japan, the Asian Olympics and the
    Olympic Movement
Sandra Collins

The Nordic World: Sport in Society
*Edited by Henrik Meinander and J.A.
    Mangan*

The Politics of South African Cricket
Jon Gemmell

The Race Game
Sport and Politics in South Africa
Douglas Booth

**The Rise of Stadiums in the Modern
    United States**
Cathedrals of Sport
*Edited by Mark Dyreson and Robert
    Trumpbour*

The Tour De France, 1903–2003
A Century of Sporting Structures,
    Meanings and Values
Edited by Hugh Dauncey and Geoff Hare

This Great Symbol
Pierre de Coubertin and the Origins of
    the Modern Olympic Games
John J. MacAloon

Tribal Identities
Nationalism, Europe, Sport
Edited by J.A. Mangan

**Women, Sport and Society in Modern
    China**
Holding up More than Half the Sky
Dong Jinxia

Prologue: Reaffirming Mary Wollstonecraft! Extending the Dialogue on Women, Sport and Physical Activities

Roberta J. Park

In *A Vindication of the Rights of Woman* (1792) Mary Wollstonecraft (often referred to as 'the first great feminist writer') declared: 'Let us then, by being allowed to take the same exercise as boys, not only during infancy, but youth, arrive at perfection of body, that we may know how far the natural superiority of man extends.' [1] The treatise contains several statements that remain of consequence today regarding the importance of exercise and playful sports for females.

Sarah Pomeroy opened the section entitled 'Physical Education' of her recent book *Spartan Women* (2002) with the observation: 'There is more evidence, both textual and archeological, for athletics than for any other aspect of Spartan women's lives. Furthermore, there is more evidence for the athletic activities of Spartan women alone than for the athletics of all the women in the rest of the Greek world combined.' [2] Only recently have historians begun turning their attention to the importance that sport and other physical activities have had for women in many societies. It is being found that these have been of more consequence than usually has been recognized.

Reflecting the same sentiments to be found in Wollstonecraft's *Vindication of the Rights of Woman*, Elizabeth Cady Stanton, a major force in the 'woman's rights movement' that emerged in the United States during the nineteenth century, had written in 1850: 'We cannot say what the woman might be physically, if the girl were allowed all the freedom of the boy in romping, swimming, climbing, and playing hoop and ball. ... Physically as well as intellectually, it is use that produces growth and development.' [3] There were many other women who expressed similar views. For example, la Duchesse d'Uzès declared in the preface to *Pour bien faire du sport* (1912): 'Oh my sisters, do not be afraid to develop your biceps a bit, and have ... hands capable of seizing a carbine or directing a horse.' This now little-known book, prepared as part of the Femina-Bibliothèque collection, set forth techniques and other information regarding 30 sports for women (and included records that women had achieved in 20 of these). [4] Halfway around the world Chinese feminists Qiu Jin and Chen Jiefen were insisting that 'the way forward lies with physical education'. [5]

When asked today what sport and other physical activities have done to bring about advances for women, most individuals are likely to focus upon such things as the number who have become involved in major sporting events. These increases certainly have been remarkable. For example, 611 female athletes participated at the 1960 Rome Olympic Games. By the 2008 Beijing Olympics, where they comprised 42 per cent of the participants, the number had risen to 4,746. [6] However, focusing only on accomplished athletes does not enable one to comprehend the range of what some women have been able to achieve in and through sport and related physical activities. Fortunately, in recent years a growing number of insightful historical accounts have begun to bring forth much more extensive and comprehensive understandings regarding this important story. *From 'Fair Sex' to Feminism: Sport and the Socialization of Women in the Industrial and Post-Industrial Eras*, which was published 1987, [7] did much to lay down the foundations for studies that would follow.

Several things had brought about these developments. One was the 'new social history' (which drew upon insights from fields such as sociology and anthropology) that rose to prominence in the 1960s. The decade of the 1960s also witnessed the emergence of feminist movements in a number of countries. The ensuing field of 'women's history', which became formalized in the 1970s, encouraged more studies regarding women and their place in history. *Clio's Consciousness Raised: New Perspectives on the History of Women*, which was published in 1973, opened with the statement: 'Women's history is developing into a new research area at a particularly exciting time. It has been stimulated by two related but essentially independent developments: the maturation of social history and the appearance of a renewed women's movement.' [8]

Initially the focus had been upon such things as women's political struggles, their enfranchisement and economic independence. Attention then turned to biological and medical matters, especially those relating to reproduction and presumed weaknesses and disabilities – both intellectual and physical – that had rendered women the inferior 'second sex'. [9] Although this approach attracted a great deal of attention, by the 1990s it was becoming evident to some scholars that focusing on 'weakness and disabilities' obscured many aspects of a complex story. Especially missing were studies of women whose lives were guided by physical as well as intellectual vigour.

Much of the 'debilitating' approach had been fostered by new ways of thinking about 'the body', which also had emerged during the 1960s and 1970s. Especially influential were the writings of the French sociologist and historian Michael Foucault regarding how 'power' is related to the body and sexuality. [10] As they sought to better understand the social construction of gender and how societies had exerted control over women's bodies and minds, many feminists turned to his assertion that 'the body' functions as the primary target of power and to matters dealing with 'representation' and 'identity'. Many books and articles dealing with such matters appeared. *Embodied Practices: Feminist Perspectives on the Body* (1997) and *Ambiguous Embodiment: Construction and Deconstruction of Bodies in Modern German Literature and Culture* (2000) [11] are two of several that now contain at least a chapter dealing with sporting or otherwise physically active bodies – a reflection of the growing interest in these matters.

The tendency on the part of many scholars had been to deal mostly with theoretical or abstract conceptions of 'the body' and to try to interpret what these presumably might have meant. While this approach may have its uses, an excessive reliance upon 'theory' can cause one to overlook the actual contexts in which events took – and take – place. As Kathy Davis points out in her introduction to *Embodied Practices: Feminist Perspectives on the Body*, 'bodies are not simply abstractions'. They are 'embedded in the immediacies of everyday, lived experience'. Therefore, such matters need to be examined in 'concrete social, cultural, and historical contexts'. [12] A similar admonition has been set forth by Paula Fass, a noted contributor to the history childhood, in a 2003 issue of the *Journal of Social History*: '[W]hat historians are most in need of today is not so much unfettered imagination as disciplined imagination.' They need more 'devotion to hard work in primary sources ... explicit connections between the theory and the historical behavior ... [and] showing the reader how the conclusions were drawn from the evidence'. [13]

Perspectives set forth by sociologist Raewyn W. Connell in *Masculinities* (1995) also need to be considered. The author points out that the modern world's thinking about the body is informed by two approaches. The biological defines the body as a machine that is governed by the laws of physics and chemistry. The social sciences tend to hold that 'the body is more or less a neutral surface or landscape on which a social symbolism is imprinted'. [14] Both approaches merit attention. Moreover, we remain far from adequately understanding how, and under what circumstances, the two relate. Perhaps nowhere are these two perspectives more intricately entwined than in the quadrennial Olympic Games, where 'visions' of an athlete can easily slide from the cellular and sub-cellular perspectives of an exercise physiologist to the almost transcendental imagery of an athlete 'soaring' over hurdles in the 400-metre race. [15]

When in 1996 Ann Hall observed that although female bodies now had a central place in feminist writing, she accurately noted that these were not the strong and capable bodies of women who engaged in sports and other physical activities. [16] It is encouraging that in addition to *From 'Fair Sex' to Feminism: Sport and the Socialization of Women in the Industrial and Post-Industrial Eras*, books such as *Women's Sports: A History* (1991) and *Coming on Strong: Gender and Sexuality in Twentieth-Century Women's Sport* (1994) had begun to offer a much needed different approach. [17] Fan Hong's informative *Footbinding, Feminism and Freedom: The Liberation of Women's Bodies in Modern China* (1997), which deals with the social, cultural and political contexts of 'women's exercise in China between 1840 and 1949' quickly ensued. A decade earlier, in *The Female Tradition in English Physical Education, 1880–1890*, Sheila Fletcher had been the first to devote much needed attention to the still sparsely analysed subject of women who successfully carved out careers in physical education. [18] Her book remains a classic in the study of female physical education.

A new milestone was set in 2001 with the appearance of *Freeing the Female Body: Inspirational Icons*. The women who comprise its ten chapters all were involved, in a variety of ways, with promoting sport, organized exercise and/or physical training. All saw in such activities ways in which women could identify themselves as achievers, utilize their intellectual and organizational as well as physical skills and make valuable contributions to their societies. In a variety of ways they challenged the prejudices and conventions of their times, and in so doing created greater opportunities for other women as well as children, youths and even sometimes men. Some became accomplished athletes, as did Trebisonda Valla, holder of the Italian woman's records in the 80-metre hurdles and the high jump, who would become both 'a political instrument of fascist purpose' as well as an agent of the emancipation of Italian women. [19] Dedicated to achieving equal opportunities for females, physician Alice Profé (born in the Prussian province of Posen), studied medicine in Switzerland, the only nineteenth-century European country that willingly offered women this opportunity. She was relentless in challenging unproven assertions about female weakness, conducted health and physical training courses, and was a coach for the German team at the 1930 Women's Olympic Games in Prague. She also acquired authorization to practice 'sports medicine' at a time when that emerging field was dominated by men. [20]

Margaret Stansfeld had learned the Swedish system of gymnastics from Martina Bergman-Osterberg, who created what became a very influential physical training college for women following her arrival in England. Stansfeld became founder of Bedford Physical Training College and served as its principal for more than 40 years. She also fostered a variety of physical education programmes for children and youth. Although not a feminist, Stansfeld had a significant role during the first half of the twentieth century in shaping physical education as a profession for women and increasing women's opportunities to engage in sport and leisure activities. Alexandrine Gibb, who was for many years a reporter for the *Toronto Star*, served as manager of the Canadian track team that competed at Stamford Bridge in 1925 and made a number of other contributions to women's sports. At the same time that she was convinced that women should be allowed to coach and administer their own sports, she also insisted upon adhering to prevailing notions of feminine decorum. [21] As these and other chapters of *Inspirational Icons* attest, the emancipation of women has been considerably advanced by those who were involved in a variety of ways, not only with sporting performances but with physical education, medical aspects of physical activity, recreational activities, a variety of clubs and organizations and much more. Another striking example of what researchers recently have brought to the fore is Dong Jinxia's insightful study of women, sport and society in China during the second half of the twentieth century. [22]

In his epilogue to *Freeing the Female Body* J. A. Mangan made a number of significant observations. One was that viewing women as a single category is both simplistic and limiting. Indeed, much more attention needs to be directed to the distinct, and sometimes contradictory, views that different women held and the actions that they took. Another is that more attention needs to be directed at relationships that were created between women and men. The two sexes were not, as much of the feminist literature often suggests, always at odds with each other. There were occasions in the past when women and men worked together quite amicably to advance a variety of projects and organizations. One such instance was the honorary organization the American Academy of Physical Education, in which women were elected, and held leadership positions, much earlier than is usually recognized. [23]

Not only did women create and implement a variety of programmes that served the needs of large numbers of children and youth, males as well as females; they functioned as directors of playground and recreational programmes and departments of physical education and performed important roles for student health services. As educators, club women, philanthropists, missionaries or community leaders they have been a significant influence in the creation and development of local, national and international organizations concerned with sport and/or physical education. Some have engaged in research that has contributed to the physical, social, and psychological well-being of children, youth and sometimes adults, thereby extending knowledge in exercise physiology and other sport sciences. Even if their role has not always been numerically equal to that of men, in physical education women have held leadership positions much more often than has been the case in other professional organizations.

Of course it was not always men who 'determined the identity of women' or 'dictated what was desirable and undesirable'. This significant observation also is set forth in the epilogue to *Freeing the Female Body*. [24] Indeed, women often made their 'own demands of other women', and sometimes of men. This certainly was the case with regard to physical education, where women in a number of countries supported themselves by establishing professional careers at a time when few other such opportunities existed. Much more remains to be known about these matters – and especially how they have related to race and social class. For example, in an insightful article entitled 'Enter Ladies and Gentlemen of Color', Gwendolyn Captain has observed that African American Inez Patterson, who had been a field hockey player, track star and record-setting distance swimmer while attending high school in Philadelphia during the 1920s, went on to organize 'athletic clubs and provided athletic training for aspiring black youth in New Jersey and New York'. [25]

This collection, then, is concerned with the activities, experiences, contributions and successes of women who devoted some, or all, of their lives to sport, physical education, recreation, dance, the sport sciences, medicine as it relates to exercise and health and much more. It seeks to broaden our awareness and understandings of the backgrounds, motivations and achievements of dedicated women working to improve health and bodily practices in a variety of different arenas and for often different purposes. These are examined within relevant social, cultural, historical and geographical contexts. Four observations that appear near the end of a 2004 *Journal of Women's Studies* article by Gerda Lerner, who has been fondly called 'the mother of women's history', are especially relevant: (1) Many groups still remain undocumented and uninterpreted; (2) There is a need to focus on the activities, thoughts, and experiences of women, not just representations; (3) Careful attention needs to be given to 'differences among women'; (4) 'We might, to begin with, challenge the ahistoricity of some influential feminist theories ... of the structuralists and post-structuralists, and of those theories that construct psychology without regard to social context'. [26] It is hoped that this collection will open opportunities for more additions, revisions and counter-narratives to these growing and important aspects of the past.

Notes

[1] Wollstonecraft, *A Vindication of the Rights of Woman*, 138.
[2] Pomeroy, *Spartan Women*, 12.
[3] [Elizabeth Cady Stanton] writing under the pseudonym 'Sunflower' in the feminist newspaper in *The Lily*, 1 April 1850.
[4] Duchesse d'Uzès, 'Preface', viii–ix.
[5] The contributions of these two, and many other women are set forth in Fan Hong's *Footbinding, Feminism and Freedom*.
[6] See http://in.answers.yahoo.com/question/index?qid=20081007201411AASCxpU, accessed Aug. 2009.
[7] Mangan and Park, *From 'Fair Sex' to Feminism*.
[8] Hartman, 'Preface', xii.
[9] See for example, Davis, 'Embodying Theory', 14–15.
[10] A great deal has been written about Foucault's influence. See for example, Frank, 'How Images Shape Bodies'. Frank is citing a 1996 article by Nick Crossley, 'Body-Subject/Body Power'.
[11] Davis, *Embodied Practices*; Wilke, *Ambiguous Embodiment*.
[12] Davis, *Embodied Practices*.
[13] Fass, 'Cultural History/Social History'.
[14] Connell, *Masculinities*.
[15] See for example, Park, '"Cells or Soaring?"'
[16] Hall, *Feminism and Sporting Bodies*.
[17] Guttmann, *Women's Sports*; Susan Cahn, *Coming on Strong*.
[18] Fan Hong, *Footbinding, Feminism and Freedom*; Fletcher, *The Female Tradition in English Physical Education*.
[19] Gori, 'A Glittering Icon of Fascist Feminity'.
[20] Pfister, 'Breaking Bounds'.
[21] Smart, 'At the Heart of a New Profession'; Hall, 'Alexandrine Gibb'.
[22] Mangan, 'Prospects for the New Millennium'.
[23] See for example, Park, '"An Affirmation of the Abilities of Woman"'.

[24] Mangan, 'Prospects for the New Millennium'.
[25] Captain, 'Enter Ladies and Gentlemen of Color'.
[26] Lerner, 'US History'.

References

Cahn, Susan. *Coming on Strong: Gender and Sexuality in Twentieth Century Women's Sport.* New York: Free Press, 1994.

Captain, Gwendolyn. 'Enter Ladies and Gentlemen of Color: Gender, Sport, and the Ideal of African American Manhood and Womanhood During the Late Nineteenth and Early Twentieth Centuries'. *Journal of Sport History* 18 (1991): 81–102.

Connell, R.W. *Masculinities.* Berkeley, CA: University of California Press, 1995.

Crossley, Nick. 'Body-Subject/Body Power: Agency, Inscription and Control in Foucault and Merleau-Ponty'. *Body and Society* 2, no. 2 (1996): 99–116.

Davis, Kathy. 'Embodying Theory: Beyond Modernist and Postmodernist Readings of the Body'. In *Embodied Practices: Feminist Perspectives on the Body: Feminist Perspectives on the Body,* edited by Kathy Davis. London: Sage Publications, 1997.

Dong, Jinxia. *Women, Sport and Society in Modern China: Holding Up More than Half the Sky.* London: Frank Cass, 2003.

Duchesse d'Uzès, La [Mortement]. 'Preface'. In *Pour bien faire du sport.* Paris: Pierre Lafitte and Co., 1912.

Fan Hong. *Footbinding, Feminism and Freedom: The Liberation of Women's Bodies in Modern China.* London: Frank Cass, 1997.

Fass, Paula. 'Cultural History/Social History: Some Reflections on a Continuing Dialogue'. *Journal of Social History* 37, no. 1 (2003): 39–46.

Fletcher, Sheila. *The Female Tradition in English Physical Education, 1880–1890.* London: The Athlone Press, 1984.

Frank, Arthur W. 'How Images Shape Bodies'. *Body and Society* 4, no. 1 (1998): 101–12.

Gori, Gigliola. 'A Glittering Icon of Fascist Feminity: Trebisonda "Ondina" Valla'. In *Freeing the Female Body: Inspirational Icons,* edited by J.A. Mangan and Fan Hong. London: Frank Cass, 2001: 173–195.

Guttmann, Allen. *Women's Sports: A History.* New York: Columbia University Press, 1991.

Hall, M. Ann. *Feminism and Sporting Bodies: Essays on Theory and Practice.* Champaign, IL: Human Kinetics, 1996.

Hall, M. Ann. 'Alexandrine Gibb: In "No Man's Land of Sport"'. In *Freeing the Female Body: Inspirational Icons,* edited by J.A. Mangan and Fan Hong,. London: Frank Cass, 2001: 149–72.

Hartman, Mary S. 'Preface'. In *Clio's Consciousness Raised: New Perspectives on the History of Women,* edited by Mary S. Hartman and Lois Banner. New York: Harper & Row Publishers, 1974.

Lerner, Gerda. 'US History: Past, Present, and Future'. *Journal of Women's Studies* 16, no. 4 (2004): 24–5.

Mangan, J.A. 'Prospects for the New Millennium: Women, Emancipation and the Body', In *Freeing the Female Body: Inspirational Icons,* edited by J.A. Mangan and Fan Hong, 237–250. London: Frank Cass, 2000.

Mangan, J.A. and Roberta J. Park, eds. *From 'Fair Sex' to Feminism: Sport and the Socialization of Women in the Industrial and Post-Industrial Eras.* London: Frank Cass, 1987.

Park, Roberta J. '"Cells or Soaring?": Historical Reflections on "Visions" of the Body, Athletics, and Modern Olympism'. *Olympika: The International Journal of Olympic Studies* 9 (2000): 1–24.

Park, Roberta J. '"An Affirmation of the Abilities of Woman": Women's Contributions to the American Academy of Kinesiology and Physical Education'. *Quest* 58 (2006): 6–19.

Pfister, Gertrud. 'Breaking Bounds: Alice Profé, Radical and Emancipationist'. In *Freeing the Female Body: Inspirational Icons*, edited by J.A. Mangan and Fan Hong. London: Frank Cass, 2001: 98–118.

Pomeroy, Sarah. *Spartan Women*. Oxford: Oxford University Press, 2002.

Smart, Richard. 'At the Heart of a New Profession: Margaret Stansfeld, a Radical English Educationalist'. In *Freeing the Female Body: Inspirational Icons*, edited by J.A. Mangan and Fan Hong. London: Frank Cass, 2001: 119–148.

Wilke, Sabine. *Ambiguous Embodiment: Construction and Deconstruction of Bodies in Modern German Literature and Culture*. Heildburg: Synchron, 2000.

Wollstonecraft, Mary. *A Vindication of the Rights of Woman, With Strictures on Political and Moral Subjects*. New York: W. W. Norton and Co., 1967 [1792].

From Physical Educators to Mothers of the Dance: Margaret H'Doubler and Martha Hill

Patricia Vertinsky

Margaret H'Doubler and Martha Hill were American physical educators who played pioneering roles in the debate over the place of modern dance in higher education. In establishing the first university degree programme in dance education in the women's physical education department at the University of Wisconsin in 1927, H'Doubler has been credited with challenging the way Americans thought not only about dance and female physicality but also higher education for women. Rivalling the reach and influence of H'Doubler in the promotion of dance education in higher education, however, was Martha Hill, a former student of H'Doubler. In a markedly different approach to the teaching of dance, Hill and her modern dance colleagues at Bennington College reoriented the nature of college dance during the 1930s towards a vocational and professional model, reshaping dance as an arts-based discipline. In my discussion I examine the relative contributions of H'Doubler (who was not a dancer) and Hill (who was a dance performer) to these opposing developments in dance education in the academy during the first half of the twentieth century; trace the rise and fall of dance's importance within women's physical education programmes; and discuss the equivocal nature of H'Doubler and Hill's legacies to feminism and the gendering of the body.

Introduction

Intimate histories of dance in the American university, writes Elliot Eisner, are extremely rare. [1] Yet anyone who has studied the history of dance education knows that Margaret H'Doubler established the first dance major in higher education in the United States – and perhaps in the world. [2] Fewer realize that the innovative programme was nurtured within the Department of Physical Education by a female physical educator who was initially far more interested in basketball than expressive movement. From a physical education perspective, Ellen Gerber did not consider physical educator Margaret H'Doubler sufficiently important to include her among the leading innovators and institutions in the world history of physical education, although Jessie Bancroft's Posture League is included, as is Elizabeth Birchenall's contribution as founder of the American Folk Dance Society in 1916 and Margaret Streicher's leadership in developing 'revolutionary' *Natürliches Turnen*, in Austria. [3] Similarly, in the world of professional dance H'Doubler has not been evaluated or assessed as a model for connoisseurs of the art form, although she has been recognized and applauded as a remarkable teacher. Yet in establishing the first university degree programm in dance education at the University of Wisconsin, dance scholar Janice Ross claims that Margaret H'Doubler changed the future of dance education and female physical education in America, challenging 'the way Americans thought about not only dance and female physicality, but also higher education for women'. [4]

Rivalling the reach and influence of H'Doubler in the promotion of dance education in higher education, however, was Martha Hill, a former student of H'Doubler. In a markedly different approach to the teaching of dance, Hill and her modern dance colleagues at Bennington College during the 1930s reoriented the nature and focus of liberally based college dance towards a vocational and professional model, seeding the future of dance as an arts-based discipline and reshaping the academic world of dance. This paper examines the relative contributions of H'Doubler and Hill to these developments in dance education in the academy during the first half of the twentieth century, traces the rise and fall of dance's importance within physical education programmes and discusses the equivocal nature of H'Doubler and Hill's legacies to feminism and the gendering of the body.

Margaret H'Doubler

In her recent biography of H'Doubler, Ross tells the story of how dance education entered the twentieth century university. She likens H'Doubler to the Gibson girl, Charles Dana Gibson's prototype of the turn-of-the-century modern woman, athletic yet graceful, strong but not overly muscled, adventurous while decorous – in short, a figure of accommodation to past and present. H'Doubler entered the University of Wisconsin as a student in 1906 at a time when middle- and upper-class women were beginning to gain entry to higher education in greater numbers and when state universities such as Wisconsin were identifying with progressive ideas and the notion of service to the community. [5] H'Doubler's upbringing was conducive to this ethos. She was born in Deloit, Kansas, in 1889 to a prosperous and reform-minded Swiss immigrant family and after a comfortable rural childhood, where she was encouraged to study and be physically active, she moved with her family to Madison and graduated from high school there. At school she participated enthusiastically in basketball, field hockey and attended eurhythmic classes before entering the University of Wisconsin in 1906. [6] As a biology major enrolled in required physical education courses for women, she tells in her own words her delight at participating in sports and gymnastics and coming home to announce 'I'm going to be a gym teacher'. She showed a special talent in basketball and in team coaching, and it was for the latter that she was hired by the newly established women's physical education division in 1910. 'So there I was', said H'Doubler, 'and could go on to what I loved to do' – teaching apparatus work and coaching basketball and baseball. She was obviously an excellent coach; records from the student newspaper of the time pointed out that women's basketball was so popular that there was standing room only at some of the women's games. [7]

Blanche Trilling and H'Doubler at Wisconsin

When Blanche Trilling arrived at the university in 1912 to join Clarke W. Hetherington, director of physical education', and take charge of the women's physical education division, she developed a working partnership with H'Doubler that lasted for decades. Hetherington was viewed as one of the early giants of physical education, a philosopher committed to 'play as nature's method of education', a path to character development and spontaneous living. [8] Strongly influenced by John Dewey's concepts of mind-body unity and the ideas of G. Stanley Hall at Clark University, he had worked assiduously to 'naturalize' physical education as well as to solidify gender differences in sport by substituting play days for athletic competition for girls. This accorded nicely with maternalist physical educators' vision of what manner of activities was appropriate for women – a viewpoint with which both Trilling and H'Doubler concurred. Trilling found a ready ally in Hetherington in developing her programmes for women along progressive lines. 'Her position on fitness and sports was expansively optimistic, braided through with notions of morality, good citizenship, and inclusiveness.' [9] It was also a conservative standpoint, for she was resolutely opposed to competition in female sport and the perceived unseemly and unhealthy aspects of over-exertion and unladylike behaviour, noting that exposure to the 'evils of commercialization and exploitation of outstanding girl athletes often leads to the danger of nervous breakdown'. [10] As one of the leading female physical educators of the day she eschewed competition in favour of participation and collaboration, with the goal of getting as many women as possible involved in a wide variety of 'appropriate' physical activities. Indeed, she played an important role in fostering the Athletic Federation of College Women as well as sitting on the executive committee of the Women's Division of the National Amateur Athletics Federation (NAAF), convened in 1923 by Mrs Hoover, president of the Girls Scouts of America and wife of the future President Hoover. It was this committee that defined the prevailing wisdom for women's physical education for the next 30 years – a sport for every girl and every girl in a sport. [11]

H'Doubler goes to Columbia University

Trilling was committed to expanding the scope of the women's physical education programme so that when her young teacher H'Doubler requested leave from the physical education department to go to Columbia University to further her studies in philosophy and aesthetics she was enthusiastic. [12] Trilling, herself a dance educator certified in the Chalif method, also saw this as an opportunity for H'Doubler to use her stay in New York to 'look into dance suitable for college women' as a future teaching possibility at Madison. [13] H'Doubler was understandably reluctant to investigate the subject, let alone teach it instead of the team sports that she loved, but she agreed to try. 1916, the same year that H'Doubler attended Columbia, was also the year that John Dewey published his influential *Democracy and Education* and it was likely that H'Doubler attended classes with both him and William Heard Kilpatrick. During the time she was in New York she never did complete her degree. Nor is it clear how far she was influenced by Dewey's progressive views on education and creativity. [14] She was certainly increasingly unhappy about Trilling's charge to seek out 'new dance' possibilities and complained about the dreary elementary ballet classes she saw in New York. On a visit to Boston to visit her brother she stopped in at the Sargent School, only to find that 'they didn't have the slightest idea of what I was talking about'. [15] A trip to Wellesley College was equally unpromising. Back in New York, it was only when she viewed the movement classes of music teacher Alys E. Bentley at Carnegie Hall that she believed she had found what she was looking for. [16] 'I could see it right away. And I thought, yes, get a technique worked out that is based on the body structure, the structural responses first and know body technique, and then you can have the knowledge of how to develop your own style.' [17]

The Role of Dance in Women's Physical Education

It was not the case that there was no dance taught at the time in women's physical education programmes in schools and colleges. H'Doubler herself had participated in folk, ballroom and Chalif-method dance classes during her undergraduate studies – though she claimed they were quite disagreeable. German gymnastic clubs introduced forms of gymnastic dance into the United States in the second half of the nineteenth century and the first women's colleges all offered some forms of music and movement along with social dancing. Indeed, Madison had a thriving Turner society as well as an Academy of Dancing and Deportment for middle-class patrons – re-named more commercially 'Professor Kehl's Palace of Pleasure and Education' in 1899. [18]

A major influence that helped bring dance into schools and colleges were the ideas of two Europeans: François Delsarte, who developed a system of expression through the body after he damaged his voice through opera singing, and Émile Jaques-Dalcroze, whose system of eurhythmics filtered into German modern dance through the work of Rudolf Laban and his pupil Mary Wigman as well as throughout Europe and across the Atlantic. The Delsartian system also made its way into the vocabulary of German expressive dance but more obliquely through strands of American-style Delsartism brought back to Europe by American modern dancers, Isadora Duncan, Loie Fuller and Ruth St Denis, and harmonic gymnastics advocates Bess Mensendieck and Hedwig Kallmeyer. [19] Both systems (and their offshoots) provided the impetus for the development of a complex array of expressive movement forms that were taken up in the late nineteenth and early twentieth centuries in various educational and recreational contexts and would become an important stimulus to the professional and educational thrust of the work of Margaret H'Doubler.

Delsarte claimed that his system was a fully scientific approach to the body, and though it was designed to accompany oratory and focus on 'gesture', Delsartism became a highly popular form of gymnastics and expressive movements for young ladies in private schools and colleges. [20] They succeeded those of Dio Lewis who had successfully introduced his own system of light exercises for girls and women in the 1860s and 1870s. [21] Delsartism was initially introduced by Steele Mackaye, an American who studied with Delsarte in France before returning to America and promoting a form of harmonic gymnastics. [22] Mackaye's system ultimately developed into a broad popular movement for middle- and upper-class women focused on expressive dance led by Genevieve Stebbins, who amalgamated some of his ideas with those she had learned from Delsartean practitioners on her visits to France. Stebbins also acknowledged the influence of yoga, Swedish Ling gymnastics and Dudley Allen Sargent's exercise system in her prolific writings, including *The Delsarte System of Expression* (1885) which went through six editions by 1902, *Dynamic Breathing and Harmonic Gymnastics – A Complete System of Psychical, Aesthetic and Physical Culture* (1893) and *The Genevieve Stebbins' System of Physical Training* (1913). 'Delsarte', she praised, 'has given the aesthetics and Ling the athletics of a perfect method.' [23]

In her approach to expressive movement and the making of 'harmonious bodies' Stebbins focused on the sacred dances of the Orient and the art of ancient Greece, orchestrating poses derived from Greek statuary. Both were themes which were typically attributed to American-born modern dancer Isadora Duncan, who danced to much wider audiences than Stebbins, [24] but they were also taken up in the burgeoning physical education movement and taught, for example, in William Anderson's Chautauqua School of Physical Education and at women's colleges at Elmira, Rockford and Smith. [25] Portland, Maine, dance teacher Melvin Ballou Gilbert also developed a system of aesthetic gymnastics from Delsarte theories as a substitute for regular gymnastic work for women and to meet Sargent's complaint that dancing did not develop the arms and trunk. The Gilbert method gradually became known as aesthetic dance, which was modified by Sargent and others to become gymnastic dancing. [26] H'Doubler was most likely exposed to Delsarte through Genevieve Stebbins's popular manuals, though as Ross points out, her direct experience with Delsarte's methods remains speculative. What was important was that the dissemination of American Delsartism through widely popular manuals was particularly useful in helping to support middle- and upper-class women in socially acceptable forms of expressive physical movement, clothing reform and their entrance into public life – including the profession of physical education. [27]

Stebbins's manuals also reached into the Settlement House Movement as an instrument of social reform. [28] At Hull House in Chicago and New York's Henry Street Settlement, female settlement workers introduced aesthetic dance practices to working-class immigrants. Having attended Delsarte classes with Stebbins, the Lewisohn sisters began club and class work in dance and drama at Henry Street in 1905 and taught Dalcroze-inspired rhythmic dance to teenage girls, leading to a series of seasonal dance festivals. These festivals became extremely popular well beyond the settlement houses as Americanizing rituals while also providing some respect for immigrants' own traditions through expressive dance. [29] At Hull House, forms of dance were introduced by Mary Wood Hinman alongside activities in the gymnasium and playground, and, in order to overcome middle-class anxieties about the temptations of commercial dance halls, Hinman travelled to Europe to collect folk dances, view Dalcroze's eurhythmics and study English country dancing. On her return she taught gymnastic dancing and folk dancing to children, not only at Hull House but at schools throughout Chicago and later at Columbia University summer school. In 1904 the Hinman Normal School was launched to train women to teach a wide variety of dance forms, including pageantry and festivals. [30]

Folk dancing became increasingly popular in the settlement houses and in schools, partly, suggests Tomko, because Delsarte movements remained focused upon middle- and upper-class women, while folk dancing 'effectively operated to inscribe working-class identity on immigrant girls' bodies'. [31] Especially influential in introducing folk dance to physical education was Elizabeth Burchenall who graduated from the Sargent Normal School in 1898 before attending Gilbert's Normal School of Dancing. Appointed as an instructor at Columbia University, she began research into folk dances that spanned a lifetime. Her work caught the attention of Luther Gulick, director of physical training for the schools of New York and founder of the Academy of Physical Education, who was an ardent promoter of folk dance for girls and women as an alternative to athletics viewed as more suitable for males. Together they established folk and 'national' dancing as part of the city's physical education programme. [32]

Like American Delsartism, Dalcroze eurhythmics informed and stimulated the thinking of many early-twentieth-century dancers and physical educators, for both fit well with the tenets of progressive education and an approach to pedagogy that encouraged aesthetic attention to the body. Émile Jaques-Dalcroze was clearly influenced by Delsarte in seeking movement forms with a new dynamic and freedom, though unlike Delsartism, eurhythmics did not achieve such widespread popularity in the United States, at least directly. By introducing the importance of music and rhythm to expressive movement forms, however, Dalcroze's influence travelled back and forth across the Atlantic well into the twentieth century and reached into physical education and expressive dance and gymnastics practices in varied and lasting ways.

Among the American female physical educators who studied Dalcroze methods were Gertrude Kline Colby, who spent three years studying eurhythmics. Colby had been a graduate of the Boston Normal School of Gymnastics and a student of Gilbert in aesthetic dance before going on to teach 'natural movement' at the Speyer School (the progressive demonstration school for Columbia Teachers College) in 1913 and later at Teachers College itself. [33] Colby's views on natural dance were in a sense a portrait of educational dance in transition, linking folk and 'national' dances to new views on expressive movement forms likely influenced by Isadora Duncan. As she described it,

> At Teachers College, Columbia University we have adopted the name 'natural dancing' feeling that this term expresses more nearly the thing for which we are working. It is based on such free natural movements as walking, skipping, running, leaping etc., By making ourselves free instruments of expression, rhythmically unified ... we dance ideas not steps. [34]

Colby's teaching ideas were taken up by one of her pupils Bird Larson, who further developed them in her educational programme of natural rhythmic expression and dance pageantry at Barnard College on the Columbia University campus in 1914. [35] This was an important step, conjectures Hagood, for by introducing aesthetic notions of dance into the curriculum, it began the process of individuating dance education from its more utilitarian sister activities in physical education, including folk and national dances. [36] It was also an important link to the work of H'Doubler who must have come into contact with both during the time that she studied for her master's degree at Columbia and as a part-time teacher there between 1916 and 1918. And, while H'Doubler did not directly acknowledge Delsartism, she did take classes in the Jaques-Dalcroze method in New York, albeit reporting the experience as somewhat disappointing. [37]

Reflecting on her sojourn in New York, H'Doubler made little mention of Colby and Bird, or others working in the small circle of nationally recognized dance educators at that time, in her oral histories or written materials. [38] She attended at least one seminar course taught by Dewey, and although she later claimed that she was 'not a bit' influenced by his ideas, much of the language and thinking of her later writings closely paralleled Dewey's views on education and creativity. Her biographers have mixed views about the extent of Dewey's influence on the development of the 'Wisconsin dance idea'. Ross sees H'Doubler's writings on dance as derivative of Dewey's theories on experience, learning and art but suggests that she missed the subtlety in his thinking about expression in art. [39] Wilson suspects that H'Doubler never really tried to translate and utilize Dewey's theories into dance methods but rather selected whatever seemed most suitable for her in practice. 'Truth be told', he cautions, 'H'Doubler was a sponge when it came to new ideas but she was not a rigorous scholar ... she rarely paused in her thinking to record a source thoroughly ... and her class and reading notes are long gone.' [40]

'Miss Huh-Dee' at Wisconsin – 'Won't You Share in the Joy of Dance with Me?' [41]

Nevertheless, once back at the University of Wisconsin H'Doubler began to put into practice her developing ideas on dance education with strong support from Blanche Trilling and her students who nicknamed her 'Miss Huh-Dee'. In 1921 she published her first textbook, *A Manual of Dancing*, incorporating her ideas on self-expression through movement and proclaiming that 'if dancing is to hold a place of importance in an educational curriculum ... those teaching this activity should believe in its values, not as performance but as an educational influence of the finest type'. [42] Indeed, one of dance's virtues was that it was to be a personal, non-competitive, democratic activity in line with the prevailing female physical educators' vision where participation and enjoyment trumped a focus on skill development and performance. 'In dancing', she continued,

> the student should be taught that she may give expression to her own reactions, and not those of another ... there should be no imitation or memory so far as set movements and gestures are concerned. How can there be if we adhere to our definition of dancing – self expression through movement. [43]

In dance, therefore, the student was to be her own textbook, laboratory and teacher.

It was a model increasingly adopted by other female college educators, leading to the demand for trained teachers in expressive dance and the development of a minor in dance education at Wisconsin in 1923. Even before this, notes Mary Lou Remley, alumnae from Wisconsin were teaching 'Miss H'Doubler's dancing' at Northwestern University, the University of Washington, Michigan State Normal School, the University of Texas, Illinois State Normal University, North Carolina College for Women and Wellesley College. [44] In 1927, H'Doubler and Trilling persuaded the university to adopt a specialized major in dancing within the course in physical education for women in the Faculty of the College of Letters and Science. A master of arts in physical education with a specialization in dance followed swiftly. Thus, dance entered the realm of structured learning 'through the door provided for it by its association with physical education'. [45] Interpretive dance had become established as an academic discipline in American higher education by a committed female physical educator who 'never studied dance seriously, never performed and only rarely demonstrated'. [46] Indeed it appears that H'Doubler never particularly enjoyed dance as an art form and could be quite critical of the performances of female modern dancers.

Once H'Doubler discovered dance she never left it, says Ross. 'She steadily moved away from women's sports until she was exclusively a teacher of dance.' [47] Among the classes she developed and taught were three levels of interpretive dance, the theory and technique of dancing, rhythmic form and analysis, dance composition and philosophy of dance. She remained in her position until retirement in 1954 and throughout these years hewed to her philosophy of dance as personal 'feminine' expression and certainly not performative.

Orchesis

The one exception to this philosophy was the development of *Orchesis* clubs which started as a result of students requesting extra dance classes. It became in many ways a student club, a sort of extra laboratory for movement exploration rather than a site of choreography and performance. [48] In spite of this, public *Orchesis* presentations did become popular around Madison until closed down by the university president worried about the propriety of being known in the press as 'a dancing school', and H'Doubler seems to have readily acquiesced to his anxieties. The concept of *Orchesis*, however, spread rapidly to other universities and colleges and lasted well beyond the 1950s, serving as a basis for the development of dance major programmes in a number of universities and colleges. Roberta Park, for example, describes the success of *Orchesis* in the Department of Physical Education on the University of California Berkeley campus. It was stimulated by Lucile Czarnowski, who began teaching there in 1923 before taking graduate work with H'Doubler and returning to promote the Wisconsin dance idea at Berkeley. H'Doubler herself visited Berkeley in 1929 during which visit she gave several lectures and taught a two-week extension course for local teachers. [49] According to Park, by 1931 Berkeley's senior *Orchesis* had an active membership of 17 and another nine young women were working in junior *Orchesis* to develop end-of-term productions. A year later *Orchesis* hosted German modern dancers Mary Wigman and Harald Kreutzberg at formal teas and dinners, and in 1936 Martha Graham was feted at a reception, followed by a dance symposium for several northern Californian colleges, including Stanford, Berkeley and Mills College. [50] The extremely popular annual dance symposia continued well into the 1950s and it was only towards the end of that decade that interest in competition – rather than participation – became dominant among the students. Participation in *Orchesis* slowly diminished at Berkeley during the turmoil of student revolts in the 1960s and new imperatives related to the emerging 'academic discipline' of physical education leading to the disbanding of the group and the eventual relocation of dance production to the Department of Dramatic Art in 1969–70. [51]

Here, as elsewhere, the core elements of H'Doubler's philosophy of dance education and her arguments against melding educational goals with professional standards were slowly overcome by the evolution of the discipline of dance and its growing desire to define itself in higher education through association with the other fine arts rather than physical education. Though H'Doubler constantly maintained that the dance experience was educational rather than performance-based, the line between the two revealed an obvious tension. Indeed, modern dancer Ruth St Denis took issue with H'Doubler over her claim that the stimulus for the emerging curricular field of dance education had come from a scholarly interest in physical education. 'Let us not forget', she said, 'that art leads, and education follows.' [52]

H'Doubler obviously disagreed, though this debate continued throughout the twentieth century, the contentious issue being whether physical educators could claim dance education as part of their professional repertoire or whether dance was to be ensconced as a performing art. Ironically, suggests Ross, 'H'Doubler got what she wanted – a new course in dance education – and also what she did not want, namely the eventual establishment of dance as a fully theatrical art form in academia'. [53] 'Over time the subjective, aesthetic nature of dance found itself at odds with the utilitarian, objective desires of physical education. Both turned away, one from the other, towards allied areas of study in the face of external questions and doubts raised about each other as an academic discipline.' [54]

Martha Hill and the Bennington Experience: Moving Dance from a Sport to an Art Form

Among those involved in this evolution and shaping the future of dance as an arts-based discipline was a former student of H'Doubler, Martha Hill, whose contribution to the 'Bennington experience' was particularly significant in taking dance education in this new and more professional direction. [55] Hill initially attended Dr Kellogg's Normal School of Physical Education at Battle Creek, Michigan and became dance director there before leaving to take up a variety of teaching assignments. [56] In 1926 she enrolled in the undergraduate physical education programme at Teachers College, Columbia University and at the same time, entranced by the New York dance performances of Martha Graham, began to study dance with Graham. That was it, she said, 'it was an instant conversion'. [57] 'Coming from East Palestine, Ohio' (after her Bible Belt childhood) 'I found this beautiful thing in dance. ... Instead of the body being a carnal thing it was a beautiful instrument.' [58] She also took time to take a summer course with H'Doubler in Wisconsin, though 'they didn't quite gel very well' according to one of H'Doubler's students. [59] Hill found the experience dismal and H'Doubler's views conservative and constraining. 'That summer confirmed my belief in Martha Graham', she said. 'At Wisconsin they never used anything below their waists. Everything was arms. No torso. That would be too erotic!' [60]

Hill's next job was in the physical education department of the University of Oregon where she developed her ideas on dance education before returning to Teachers College in 1929 to complete her degree. At the same time she entered the professional dance world, performing for two years with Martha Graham at the Dance Repertory Theatre in New York until it closed down. She changed her stage name to Martha Todd, 'sensing that her "white gloved professors" (such as H'Doubler) disapproved of the wicked ways of the village artists with whom she conspired'. [61] Like many other aspiring modern dancers of the period, she returned to teaching in order to make a living, and became director of dance at New York University before agreeing to spend part of her time at Bennington College, a new women's college which opened in Vermont in 1932. Founded on progressive educational theories in the middle of the Depression, it offered a bachelor of arts degree with a concentration in dance, becoming the first such college degree to emphasize a focus on dance as a performing art. [62] Reminiscing about her contributions to the programme, Hill said: 'Taking dance out of the PE Department, from a sport to an art form, that was the big accomplishment of 1932.' [63] Two years later, Bennington School of the Dance offered summer sessions in dance production that rivalled H'Doubler's summer courses for dance teachers and provided a locus for some of the leading modern dancers in America to teach and perform (among them Martha Graham, Hanya Holt, Doris Humphrey and Charles Weidman.) Here, Hill excelled in facilitating collaborative ventures in modern dance at a time in the early 1930s 'when the modern dancers were young, headstrong, running like wild things through the streets of tradition' [64] and also frequently out of work. At the same time, the main clientele at Bennington were still female physical educators who took back the modern dance ideas they learned there to their college programmes and often invited leading dancers to bring modern dance performances to their campus. [65] By 1935, a modern-dance-based touring schedule known as the 'Gymnasium Circuit' was set up by Hill to take dance performances to college gymnasia, providing a source of income for modern dancers but also visibly exacerbating the debate about the scope and nature of modern dance in physical education. At Bennington's summer school session held at Mills College in Oakland in 1939, Doris Humphrey ruefully conceded the importance of the 'despised physical education department. It is something like a combination of a circus and a drugstore. It keeps you healthy and occasionally provides amusement.' [66] She was quite correct in realizing the importance of female physical education in providing work and audiences for modern dancers, and indeed at Bennington dance training fit well into the agenda set for women students. Yet ultimately the pressure of competitive groups of dancers and differing political and artistic agendas in the shadow of Franco's Spain, European fascism and the Second World War led to shifting priorities and some federal support for the arts, leading away from physical education to arts-based programmes in higher education:

> The debate over the place of modern dance in the physical education program sparked by Bennington and the 'Gymnasium Circuit' helped set the stage for the eventual shift of studies in dance from their traditional academic home in programs of physical education to alliance with programs in the fine and performing arts. [67]

In Hill's view, good dance was good dance, not to be watered down by education.

H'Doubler visited Bennington in 1934 and again for the last time in 1938 as a guest lecturer, but she found the approach to dance distasteful, especially the popularity of angular movements stemming from the pelvis which were a hallmark of Martha Graham's dancing style. [68] She objected to Bennington's focus on skilled performance and professionalism which she believed neglected the practical necessities of the physical education environment and an emphasis on participation, and she documented her views at length in her third and most widely referenced tract, *Dance: A Creative Art Experience*. 'If we can think, feel and move, we can dance', she wrote, and 'if dance is to be brought into universal use, if it is to help in the development of a more general appreciation of human art values it must be considered educationally'. [69]

Both physical educators, though working in very different environments, the views of Martha Hill and Margaret H'Doubler diverged even as they worked together with the American Physical Education Association (APEA) to organize dance education on a national level. In 1931 they were both involved in successfully petitioning the APEA to create a National Section on Dancing – H'Doubler and her students having previously provided a dance demonstration at the Midwest Society of Women Physical Educators (MWSWPE) meeting in Milwaukee to highlight the educational potential of dance. [70] Essential to their success was the assistance of physical educator Mabel Lee, who assumed the presidency of APEA in 1931, the first woman to do so. H'Doubler was a member of the Dance Section's first executive committee but for some reason declined her election as National Section chair in 1933, relinquishing a leadership role. Martha Hill assumed leadership of the Eastern District of the APEA and successfully organized a series of conferences and dance symposia. By the late 1930s, however, there were growing signs of obvious dissatisfaction with dance being so closely aligned with physical education; during the war years the work of the National Section was curtailed and the post-war years brought transformative changes to society that necessarily affected the role of dance education in higher education. [71]

Gender Legacies

Although she never mentions either Margaret H'Doubler's unique dance education developments at the University of Wisconsin or Martha Hill's contribution to the Bennington experience in *Dancing Class*, Linda Tomko suggests that among the several legacies left by new progressive-era dance practices, the gender legacies remained distinctly equivocal. 'Dance activity', she says, 'won reconsideration and recasting of received views on the body-woman-dance linkage ... asserted women's claims to dance innovation and direction ... and set the profession [of dance teaching] on its way to becoming a female occupational domain.' [72] Furthermore, she demonstrates in a number of ways how progressive dance practices worried urgent issues of class, ethnicity and immigration, though these were never central concerns of H'Doubler in her long career at the University of Wisconsin. H'Doubler was committed to college women and the democratic ideology of the expression of self through an original movement form, but there is little in her biographies, reminiscences or papers to suggest she had much interest in rebelling against social conditions and she rejected certain forms of dance popular among working class girls (folk, popular and theatrical) as not being worthy of a university campus. In a critique of Ross's description of H'Doubler,

Blumenfeld-Jones says that 'we find a woman who is neither a product of her times nor a perfectly free individual ... flawed, ignoring important possible congenial developments in dance ... and misinterpreting her most important theoretical influence, John Dewey'. [73]

Yet to physical educators who had flocked enthusiastically to experience H'Doubler's dance education methods over a 40-year period 'she was in a class by herself ... an educator rather than an artist ... an intellectual giant'. [74] 'I never thought of Marge [H'Doubler] in the context of dance', said one of her former students in a group discussion. 'I always thought of her in the context of movement.' Elizabeth Hayes said that

> there was a wonderful flow to her classes and after each class we'd go away saying wasn't that a wonderful class. ... We were too enthralled with the words and ideas she gave us to pause and question what we were learning. ... We were thrilled to have encouragement to pursue our love of dancing. [75]

In this respect, Ross's view that H'Doubler's classes were a sort of assertiveness training for women is apposite – albeit training in keeping with the white, middle-class and gendered origins of her movement forms. [76] And if charisma and ability to connect with students personified H'Doubler, it also characterized Martha Hill, who reflected that 'If I have to name the one accomplishment I'm proudest of I think its probably achieving collaboration. I like to say my major is people. That's my talent.' [77] Indeed Hill's unique influence lay in spotting opportunities for development and orchestrating opportunities for others to develop their particular talents in dance.

H'Doubler was christened 'the thinking dancer' by her students for the ways in which she approached her craft – a sort of guided learning – but it is not clear how far she thought about dance as a medium for radical negotiations around gender. By making dance education acceptable in higher education at a time of women's suffrage, and enabling women to learn about and enjoy their physicality, one could say she advanced a feminist agenda. But maintaining dance as part of women's physical education feminized dance and perpetuated gender divisions just as it prolonged the gender divide in faculties and departments of physical education in higher education. Although dance education provided an avenue for women's professional advancement in society opening greater (although still limited) opportunities for female physicality in an era of educational progressivism, it also led in the long run to a subordinate status for female dance educators. Long after her retirement, H'Doubler's students and followers belittled the advances of female equality in sport set in motion by Title IX in 1972, implying that dance had been set back by the effects of the law. 'For that, I am very angry with Title Nine' said Elizabeth Roberts in group discussion about H'Doubler's legacy. 'The sports people are taking over ... no movement and no consideration of movement.' [78] The rest of the group all agreed with this anti-sport view – one that had been clearly articulated by Celeste Ulrich in 1964, who pointed out that 'in a sense dance permits and encourages the sort of body expression that sports activities only allow in rigid and stratified patterns'. [79]

Martha Hill pushed further along a feminist agenda, embracing dance as a way to fulfil new female demands for expressive outlets on stage as well as in educational arenas. She personally defied conservative middle-class views of dance performances as decadent or tawdry by going on the stage, and she worked effectively with leading modern dancers to find new ways to advance their art form. She helped pave the way to a new agenda for dance as art in higher education, creating the dance division at the Juilliard School and developing the 'conservatory model' paradigm on which most tertiary training is now based. Especially, she understood the necessary tension between individual identity and communal harmony which lay at the core of the new modern dance performance. [80] 'It seems to me', she said upon receiving an honorary degree from Bennington College, 'I'm sort of a catalyst – pushing things ahead.' [81] She was, concludes McPherson in her recent biography of Martha Hill, 'the secret in the middle' for being an initiator and pioneer in the field of dance, moulding the field's emerging academic persona and shaping the artistic landscape for American modern dance while remaining largely behind the scenes and constantly facilitating opportunities for others. [82] Some complained that her vision of a conservatory approach to classical modern dance training remained stuck in the modernist era, closing the door to the new wave of artistic changes that emerged during the 1960s and 1970s, though time validated the sustainability of Hill's formalist approach as Juilliard became known as the Harvard of the dance world. [83]

Yet even while pushing ahead with different visions, both Hill and H'Doubler remained very much the lady. Their many students remembered them as impeccably dressed, striding down hallways or across campus, Hill coiffed with her signature asymmetrical topknot, H'Doubler always fashionably attired in a form-fitting tailored dress, never slacks, and wearing a silver bracelet on either wrist. Both Hill and H'Doubler married later in life. At the age of 45, H'Doubler surprised everyone by marrying Wayne Claxton, a music teacher 13 years her junior. [84] Rumour had it that English teacher Gertrude Johnson, who had long been her roommate, was so shocked she took to her bed. [85] In 1952, Hill married her lifelong love, Thurston 'Lefty' Davies, director of New York's Town Hall, though he died within a decade. Neither bore children but both are survived by legions of their 'dance children' who maintain the grand narratives of dance education history and edify the woman-body-dance linkage.

Notes

[1] Ross, *Moving Lessons*, back cover.
[2] Wilson *et al.*, *Margaret H'Doubler*, xv. Ross suggests it was the first in the world (see *Moving Lessons*, ix); Hagood points out that Teachers College Columbia had the first dance education program led by Gertrude Colby (see Hagood, *A History of Dance*, 70).
[3] Gerber, *Innovators and Institutions*.

[4] Ross, *Moving Lessons*, ix. See, for example, the oral history archives of the American Association for Health, Physical Education and Recreation dated 8 Oct. 8, 1972 – the official AAPHER interview was also submitted to the Oral History Archive of the Library and Museum of the Performing Arts, New York Public Library at Lincoln Centre.

[5] Struna and Remley, 'Physical Education for Women.'

[6] Women had been allowed to study in the Normal Department at the University of Wisconsin since 1863 and in 1866 all departments and colleges at the University were opened to women as well as men. Except for a brief period, this access continued and a formal course of physical training for women was established by Miss Clara Ballard from Boston in 1889. At first, 'the women's programs generally consisted of performances of the "Pizzicati Dumb-bell Chorus" and an exhibition of 'Americanized Delsarte' in addition to marching and fancy Indian club swinging routines (see *The Daily Cardinal*, 28 Feb. 1896). A wide variety of sports and swimming classes were added and Lathrop Gymnasium was opened for women in 1910. For a full description of women's physical activities to 1913 see Struna and Remley, 'Physical Education for Women'.

[7] Wilson *et al.*, *Margaret H'Doubler*, 18.

[8] Hetherington was honored by being made Fellow number 1 at the Academy for Physical Education, an organization generally considered to have been his brainchild. Gerber, *Innovators and Institutions*, 396.

[9] Hartman, 'Health and Fun', 8.

[10] 'Athletics Blamed for Nervous Ills', *New York Sun*, 5 Oct. 1927.

[11] Saunders, *The Governance of Intercollegiate Athletics*. See also Trilling, 'History of Physical Education for Women at the University of Wisconsin'.

[12] The role of Teachers College at Columbia University concerning the broad role of physical education in society was extremely important, but H'Doubler did not leave many records concerning her studies there.

[13] Chalif, *The Chalif Text Book of Dancing*.

[14] In her reminiscences she said that she was not at all influenced by him.

[15] Taken from an interview with Margaret H'Doubler commissioned for the Oral History Archives of the American Association for Health, Physical Education and Recreation by Mary Alice Brennan, 8 Oct. 1972. Now held in Oral History Archive of the Library and Museum of the Performing Arts, New York Public Library at Lincoln Center.

[16] Remley, 'The Wisconsin Idea of Dance'.

[17] Ibid., 5.

[18] See Ross, *Moving Lessons*, 80.

[19] Ruyter, *The Cultivation of Body and Mind*, 71; Ruyter, 'American Delsartism'. Martin points out that 'modern dance developed as a very complex matrix of appropriations of different movement sources', and it was clear that Duncan had learned from the movement systems of Delsarte, as had St Denis who explored musical theatrical dance (Martin, *Critical Moves*, 152). See also Thomas, 'Physical Culture, Bodily Practices'.

[20] Gerber, *Innovators and Institutions*, 203; Geraldy, *Delsarte System*, 562.

[21] For a detailed study of the gymnastics system of Dio Lewis see Todd, *Physical Culture*; Chisholm, 'Incarnations and Practices'.

[22] Ruyter, 'American Delsartism', 424.

[23] Stebbins, *Delsarte System*, 406.

[24] It was Stebbins, according to Ruyter, who was the real inventor of American modern dance but she was an educator rather than a performer, lacking the wider international audiences of Duncan and St Denis (See *The Cultivation of Body and Mind*, 127). When she married Ted Shawn they set up the renowned Denishawn School of Dance in Los Angeles in 1915 which successfully combined Delsarte exercises with Dalcroze eurhythmics, helped create a new

audience for dance among middle-class audiences and shifted more attention towards the expressive (Segel, *Body Ascendant*, 85). Ted Shawn reassembled what he considered the authentic Delsarte method in his book, *Every Little Movement*.

[25] Ainsworth, *The History of Physical Education*, 9, 25, 26, 51. Jowitt notes that the new image of woman as dancer invented by Isadora Duncan was widely imitated by both amateurs and professionals. 'She can't of course be held responsible for all the pageants and Greek games in American college theater and physical education departments for the well meaning girls in bare feet and bunchy tunics tripping over Midwestern grass flourishing scarves, garlands and sacrificial bowls that were by 1914 indispensable in displays of "natural" or "interpretive dancing".' (Jowitt, 'Images of Isadora', 28).

[26] Kraus *et al.*, *History of the Dance*, 297. Gilbert began a teaching association with the Boston Normal School of Gymnastics in 1898 and his students offered dance instruction at normal schools and settlement houses throughout the area (Tomko, *Dancing Class*, 175–7). For his system of aesthetic dance which utilized some ballet techniques see Gilbert, 'Classic Dancing' and Spears, *Leading the Way*, 69–70.

[27] Ross, *Moving Lessons*, 21.

[28] Thomas, 'Physical Culture', 199.

[29] Tomko, *Dancing Class*, 79–122; Dalcroze often had his students participate in civic festivals where they illuminated the text and music in the eurhythmic group arrangements he designed.

[30] Hinman, 'Educational Possibilities'.

[31] Tomko, *Dancing Class*, 171.

[32] Gulick, *The Healthful Art*. Although Gulick was the founder of the early short-lived Academy, the one that exists today was begun in 1926 and formally founded in 1930.

[33] Colby, *The Conflict*; Colby, *Natural Rhythms*.

[34] Colby, *Natural Rhythms*, 7–10.

[35] Larson eventually left education and developed her own dance studio in New York before dying at a young age following childbirth.

[36] Hagood, *A History of Dance*, 77.

[37] Ross, *Moving Lessons*, 22.

[38] Hagood, *A History of Dance*, 49; H'Doubler, *The Dance*; H'Doubler, Dance: *A Creative Art Experience*.

[39] Ross, *Moving Lessons*, 129–34

[40] Wilson *et al.*, *Margaret H'Doubler*, 326.

[41] Betty Toman in 'Two Students Remember Miss Huh-Dee', in Wilson *et al.*, *Margaret H'Doubler*, 116.

[42] H'Doubler, *A Manual of Dancing*, 12.

[43] Ibid., 8, 11. H'Doubler's philosophy was further extended in *Dance and Its Place in Education* (1925), the published version of her thesis that constituted the research for her master's degree at the UW-Madison, and the *Manual of Dancing* and *Rhythmic Form and Analysis* (1932) as well as *Dance: A Creative Art Experience*, 1940.

[44] Remley, 'The Wisconsin Idea of Dance', 190.

[45] Hagood, *A History of Dance*, 100.

[46] Ross, *Moving Lessons*, 16.

[47] Ibid., 168.

[48] Students began a Women's Athletic Association in 1902 which for more than 50 years served as an umbrella organization to organize and promote women's activities.

[49] From the Dance Files at Hearst Gymnasium (see Park, 'Creating', 79).

[50] Park, 'Creating', 81, discusses 'Orchesis tea for Mary Wigman', Spring 1932; 'Tea Complimenting Miss Martha Graham and Mr. Louis Horst', *Daily Californian*, 26 March 1936. (Horst was Martha Graham's mentor).

[51] Park, 'Creating from Minds and Bodies', 82.

[52] St Denis, 'The Creative Impulse', 15.

[53] Ross, 'Institutional Forces', 121.

[54] Hagood, *A History of Dance*, 100.

[55] McPherson, *The Contributions of Martha Hill*.

[56] From 1923 to 1926, she was the director of the Women's Department of Physical Education at Kansas State Teachers College in Hays, Kansas.

[57] Soares, *Louis Horst*, 61.

[58] Topaz, 'Martha Hill, 1900–1995', 116.

[59] Hermione Sauthoff Davidson's reminiscences, in Wilson *et al.*, *Margaret H'Doubler*, 153.

[60] Soares, 'Barnard's 1932 and 1933 Symposium', 193.

[61] Ibid., 194.

[62] Kreigsman, *Modern Dance*, 6.

[63] See note 6 in Ross, *Moving Lessons*, 246.

[64] Topaz, 'Martha Hill, 1900–1995', 117.

[65] Robert Leigh, the first president of Bennington College, originally wanted to make the college coeducational but was persuaded that parents would be less willing to take risks (of dance training) with their sons' education than their daughters (see Foulkes, *Modern Bodies*, 114.)

[66] Humphey, quoted in Foulkes, *Modern Bodies*, 116.

[67] Hagood, *A History of Dance*, 120. The Bennington experiment was so successful that it continued for nine years, eight at Bennington and one at Mills College in California.

[68] Marion Van Tuyl noted that H'Doubler found the curve more beautiful than the angle: see Ross, *Moving Lessons*, 203.

[69] H'Doubler, *Dance: A Creative Art Experience*, ix–x.

[70] Beiswanger, 'National Section', 23.

[71] For a discussion of the debate during the 1930s in the physical education journals and APEA, see Hagood, *A History of Dance*, chs 6 and 7. In 1999 leaders in the National Dance Association finally separated from the American Association of Physical Education, Recreation and Dance to create a new National Dance Education Organization, but those left behind retained a National Dance Association associated with AAPHERD.

[72] Tomko, *Dancing Class*, 216.

[73] Blumenfeld-Jones, 'Partial Stories'.

[74] Wilson *et al.*, *Margaret H'Doubler*, 159.

[75] Elizabeth Hayes interview, National Dance Academy, 2007, 178. In Porter Hearn and Crabtree 'Preserving our Legacy for Future Generations of Educators', 18–23.

[76] Ross, *Moving Lessons*, xi.

[77] Topaz, 'Martha Hill, 1900–1995'.

[78] Elizabeth Roberts, quoted in Wilson *et al.*, *Margaret H'Doubler*, 161. The women's intercollegiate athletic programme was officially created at the University of Wisconsin in 1974 after a complaint had been filed against the university for flagrant violation of Title IX. Hartman 'Health and Fun', 19–20.

[79] Ulrich, 'Dance As An Art', 15.

[80] Foulkes, *Modern Bodies*, 2.

[81] Topaz, 'Martha Hill, 1900–1995'.

[82] Hagood, Review, 314.

[83] Coe, 'Old School Tights', 72.

[84] They met at a riding stable where they both rented horses for recreational riding.

[85] Wilson *et al.*, *Margaret H'Doubler*, 74.

References

Ainsworth, Dorothy. *The History of Physical Education in Colleges for Women*. New York: A.S. Barnes, 1930.

Beiswanger, Barbara Page. 'National Section on Dance: Its First Ten Years'. *Journal of Health, Physical Education and Recreation* (May–June 1960): 23.

Bentley, Alys. *The Dance of the Mind*. New York: Sherwin Publishing, 1933.

Blumenfeld-Jones, Donald S. 'Partial Stories: An Hermeneutic Account of Practicing History'. *International Journal of Education and the Arts* 2, no. 10 (2001), available online at http://www.ijea.org/v2n10/index.html, accessed 26 June 2009.

Chalif, Louis H. *The Chalif Text Book of Dancing*. New York: Isaac Goldman Coy, 1916.

Chisholm, Ann. 'Incarnations and Practices of Feminine Rectitude: Gymnastics for US Women'. *Journal of Social History* 38, no. 3 (2005): 737–63.

Coe, Robert. 'Old School Tights'. *The Village Voice*, 19 March 1972, 72.

Colby, Gertrude K. *The Conflict: A Health Masque in Pantomime*. New York: A.S. Barnes, 1930.

Colby, Gertude K. *Natural Rhythms and Dances*. New York: A.S. Barnes and Co., 1922.

Dewey, John. *Democracy in Education*. New York: Macmillan, 1916.

Foulkes, Julia L. *Modern Bodies: Dance and American Modernism from Martha Graham to Alvin Ailey*. Chapel Hill, NC: University of North Carolina Press, 2002.

Geraldy, Marie Dèlsarte. *Delsarte System of Oratory*, 4th edn. New York: Edgar S. Werner, 1893.

Gerber, Ellen W. *Innovators and Institutions in Physical Education*. Philadelphia, PA: Lea and Febiger, 1971.

Gilbert, Melvin Ballou. 'Classic Dancing'. *American Physical Education Review* 10 (June 1905): 145–154.

Goold, Florence E. 'The Eurhythmics of Jaques-Dalcroze'. *American Physical Education Review* 20 (Jan. 1915): 35–37.

Gulick, Luther. *The Healthful Art of Dancing*. Garden City, NY: Doubleday, Page & Co., 1910.

Hagood, Thomas K. Review of Elizabeth McPherson, *The Contributions of Martha Hill to American Dance and Dance Education, 1900–1995*, *Research in Dance Education* 9, no. 3 (Nov, 2008): 313–15.

Hartman, Chris. 'Health and Fun shall Walk Hand in Hand: The First 100 Years of Women's Athletics at the University of Wisconsin, Madison', available online at http://archives.library.wisc.edu/uw-archives/exhibits/athletics/athletics01intro.html, accessed 26 July 2009.

H'Doubler, Margaret Newell. *A Manual of Dancing: Suggestions and Bibliography for the Teacher of Dancing*. Madison, WI: Tracy and Kilgore, 1921.

H'Doubler, Margaret Newell. *The Dance and its Place in Education*. New York: Harcourt, Brace and Company, 1925.

H'Doubler, Margaret Newell. *Rhythmic Form and Analysis*. Madison, WI: Kramer Business Services, 1932.

H'Doubler, Margaret Newell. *Dance: A Creative Art Experience*. New York: F.S. Crofts, 1940.

Hagood, Thomas K. *A History of Dance in American Higher Education*. Lewiston, ME: The Edwin Mellen Press, 2000.

Hinman, Mary Wood. 'Educational Possibilities of the Dance'. *The Journal of Health and Physical Education* 5 (April 1934): 14–15, 62–63.

Jaques-Dalcroze, Èmile. *The Eurhythmics of Jaques-Dalcroze*. Introduction by M.E. Sadler. London: Constable and Company, 1912.

Jowitt, Deborah. 'Images of Isadora: The Search for Motion'. *Dance Research Journal* 17, no. 2 (1985): 21–9.

Kraus, Richard, Sarah Chapman Hisendager and Brenda Dixon. *History of the Dance in Art and Education*. Englewood Cliffs, NJ: Prentice Hall, 1991.

Kreigsman, Sali Ann. *Modern Dance in America: The Bennington Years*. Boston, MA: G.K. Hall, 1981.

Martin, Randy. *Critical Moves: Dance Studies in Theory and Politics*. Durham, NC, and London: Duke University Press, 1998.

McPherson, Elizabeth. *The Contributions of Martha Hill to American Dance and Dance Education, 1900–1995*. Lewiston, ME, and New York: The Edwin Mellen Press, 2008.

Mensendieck, Bess. *Korperkultur des Weibes: Praktisch hygienishche und praktisch asthetitische winke [Women's Physical Culture]*, 3rd edn. Munich: F. Bruckmann, A-G, 1906.

Park, Roberta J. 'Creating from Minds and Bodies: The Spring Dance Concert'. *Chronicle of the University of California: A Journal of University History* 6 (2004): 77–88.

Porter Hearn, Colleen and Kacey E. Crabtree. 'Preserving our Legacy for Future Generations of Educators'. *Journal of Physical Education, Recreation and Dance*, 74, no. 4 (2008): 18–23.

Remley, Mary Lou. 'The Wisconsin Idea of Dance: A Decade of Progress, 1917–1926'. *Wisconsin Magazine of History* 58, no. 3 (1975): 179–195.

Ross Janice. *Moving Lessons: Margaret H'Doubler and the Beginning of Dance in American Education*. Madison, WI: The University of Wisconsin Press, 2000.

Ross, Janice. 'Institutional Forces and the Shaping of Dance in the American University'. *Dance Chronicle* 25, no. 1 (2002): 115–24.

Ruyter, Nancy Lee Chalfa. 'American Delsartism: Precursor of an American Dance Art'. *Educational Theatre Journal* 25, no. 4 (1973): 421–35.

Ruyter, Nancy Lee Chalfa. *The Cultivation of Body and Mind in Nineteenth Century American Delsartism*. Westport, CT: Greenwood Press, 1999.

St Denis, Ruth. 'The Creative Impulse and Education'. *Denishawn Magazine* 1, no. 4 (1925): 14–16.

Saunders, Katherine. *The Governance of Intercollegiate Athletics*. Madison, WI: University of Wisconsin, 1977.

Segel, Harold B. *Body Ascendant: Modernism and the Physical Imperative*. Baltimore, MD: The Johns Hopkins Press, 1998.

Shawn, Ted. *Every Little Movement: A Book about Francois Delsarte*, 2nd edn. New York: Dance Horizons, 1974.

Soares, Janey Mansfield. *Louis Horst: Musician in a Dancer's World*. Durham, NC: Duke University Press, 1992.

Soares, Janet Mansfield. 'Barnard's 1932 and 1933 Symposium: Bringing Dance to the University'. In *Proceedings, Reflecting on our Future: Society of Dance History Scholars*, compiled by Linda L. Tomko. University of California Riverside, 1997.

Spears, Betty. *Leading the Way: Amy Morris Homans and the Beginnings of Professional Education for Women*. Westport, CT: Greenwood Press, 1986.

Spiesman, Mildred, C. 'Dance Education Pioneers: Colby, Larson and H'Doubler'. *Journal of Health, Physical Education and Recreation* 31 (Jan. 1960): 25–7, 76.

Stebbins, Genevieve. *Delsarte System of Expression*, 6th edn. New York: Dance Horizons, 1977 [orig. pub. 1902].

Struna, Nancy and Mary Lou Remley. 'Physical Education for Women at the University of Wisconsin, 1863–1913'. *Canadian Journal of History of Sport and Physical Education* 4, no. 1 (1973): 8–26.

Thomas, Helen. 'Physical Culture, Bodily Practices and Dance in Late Nineteenth Century and Early Twentieth Century America'. *Dance Research: The Journal for the Society for Dance Research* 22, no. 2 (2004): 195–204.

Thomas, Helen. *The Body, Dance and Cultural Theory*. New York: Palgrave Macmillan, 2003.

Todd, Jan. *Physical Culture and the Body Beautiful: Purposive Exercise in the Lives of American Women, 1800–1875*. Macon, GA: Mercer University Press, 1998.

Tomko, Linda J. *Dancing Class: Gender, Ethnicity and Social Divides in American Dance, 1890–1920.* Bloomington, IN: Indiana University Press, 1999.

Topaz, Muriel. 'Martha Hill, 1900 –1995'. *Dance Magazine* 70, no. 2 (Feb. 1996): 116–17.

Trilling, Blanche. 'History of Physical Education for Women at the University of Wisconsin, 1898–1946'. Unpublished MSS in UW Madison Archives.

Ulrich, Celeste. 'Dance as an Art Form in Physical Education: A Symposium by Selected Educators'. *Journal of Health, Physical Education and Recreation* (Jan. 1964): 15.

Wilson, J., T. Hagood and M.A. Brennan. *Margaret H'Doubler: The Legacy of America's Dance Education Pioneer.* Youngstown, NY: Cambria Press, 2006.

The Physical is Political: Women's Suffrage, Pilgrim Hikes and the Public Sphere

Jaime Schultz

In the first decades of the twentieth century, American women held swimming com-petitions, scaled mountains, piloted aeroplanes and staged large-scale parades in their quest for the right to vote. In effect, they spectacularized suffrage by positioning their bodies in the public sphere rather than confining their mission to the parlours and meeting-halls of their more conservative sisters. In this essay, I examine two suffrage hikes that took place in the second decade of the twentieth century. The first was the 12-day, 170-mile 'Hike to Albany' in 1912. The second hike involved the 'Army of the Hudson' march on Washington, DC, which departed from Newark, New Jersey in 1913. Thirteen women (joined intermittently by others who completed various segments of the journey) completed the entirety of the arduous, often treacherous 225-mile route in just 16 days. In the end, Woman Voter *estimated that the hikes resulted in $3 million worth of advertising for the cause and declared that 'no propaganda work ... had ever achieved such publicity'. As the suffragettes occupied city streets and rural roads, their message reached the eyes, ears and collective consciousness of what often seemed an insulated or uninterested public. Moreover, the women staked a symbolic claim on the polity, interweaving the democratic technologies of the right to assemble and speak freely with the incongruity of their denial of full citizenship. They engaged in what I call 'physical activism' – the articulation of physical activity and political activism – striking simultaneous blows to the myths of women's physical and political inferiority.*

> *Gleanings*
> There is a method in the madness of the hiking suffragettes,
> There's a harvest from their sowing, they're the fish within their nets.
> They are stirring up the natives on their journey tempest tossed.
> They are getting advertising at a very trifling cost.
> Now the hike along the Hudson seemed a foolish trip and vain,
> But it gave them advertising from Los Angeles to Maine.

All the sport that many writers made of Colonel Rosa Jones
Added fibre to their muscles, added marrow to their bones.
To secure the right of suffrage is the purpose and intent
Of the women who are hiking to the seat of government.
Since the female is so stubborn when she will we know she will,
Let us give the ballot to her, and then ask her to keep still.

Introduction

Published in the 5 March 1913 issue of *Woman's Journal*, the official organ for the National American Woman Suffrage Association (NAWSA), the poem 'Gleanings' depicted the second of two hikes or 'pilgrimages', as they were most frequently called. Organized by Rosalie Jones and Ida Craft, two suffragettes from New York, the first of these endeavours was the 1912 'Hike to Albany' from New York City in which several women walked 12 days, covering approximately 170 miles, to present their suffrage petition to the governor-elect. In the second hike, 13 women made up the core of the 'Army of the Hudson' that traversed 250 miles from New York to Washington, DC in just 16 days. Upon reaching the nation's capital, the hikers joined the parade of over 5,000 women scheduled to take place the day before President Woodrow Wilson's 1913 inauguration. In the end, *Woman Voter* estimated that the hikes resulted in $3 million worth of advertising for the movement and declared that, 'no propaganda work … had ever achieved such publicity'. [1]

A closer look at 'Gleanings' yields several significant insights into the ideological implications of these hikes. First, though their actions may have appeared to be 'madness' or 'foolish and vain', the women walked with the purpose of securing their right to vote. Second, although many journalists mocked their efforts, the fact that they covered the pilgrims' progress with interest and regularity ensured important advertising that the campaign would not have otherwise received. Finally, the poem refers to the pilgrims as 'suffragettes', a term typically associated with British, often militant women who worked for the ballot, as opposed to the more conservative American 'suffragists'. Yet Rosalie Jones was clear to emphasize that she considered her politics aligned with the first classification: 'I want you to understand that there is a distinction between the suffragette and the suffragist. The former is one who wants to get votes for women and works for it. The latter is one who thinks about it, but hasn't time to work for it.' [2] While her judgement of this distinction might give the wrong impression, it nevertheless highlights the importance of combining work – in this case physical activity – with the desire for the franchise. Ultimately, the 'hiking suffragettes' eschewed both the cultural mores of acceptable feminine behaviour and the prevailing cautions against arduous exercise and female over-exertion in their endeavours to win the ballot.

During the second decade of the twentieth century, tactics that took women 'out of the parlours and into the streets' proved to be controversial but effective means of re-energizing the campaign for suffrage. [3] These 'stunts', as they were sometimes described, allowed the women not only to voice their message but to stake a symbolic claim on the polity, interweaving the democratic technologies of the right to assemble and speak freely with the incongruity of their denial of full citizenship. Women who occupied the city streets and rural roads to win their right to vote did so with a sense of ownership and entitlement. They were not temporarily passing through the public sphere but were *in it* in order to be *of it*. The pilgrimages possessed the added dimension of strenuous, sustained physical activity, further debunking the myth of female frailty that had been used to argue against their enfranchisement. But while their spectacular efforts succeeded in drawing attention, reactions to and media coverage of their hikes often resulted in ridicule, disgust and insult towards the women and their efforts.

Historian Catriona Parratt argues that by 'broadening our conception of sport', we might begin to construct more nuanced understandings of women's history. [4] To that end, several scholars have suggested a (re)turn to 'physical culture', defined by Jennifer Hargreaves and Patricia Vertinsky as 'those activities where the body itself – its anatomy, its physicality, and importantly its forms of movement – is the very purpose, the raison d'être, of the activity'. [5] Such definitions, however, tend to preclude events such as 'physical-activity-based fund-raising events (or "thons")'. [6] The 2,610-mile torch relay from Seneca Falls, New York to Houston, Texas before the start of the 1977 National Women's Conference, or 90-year-old Doris 'Granny D' Haddock's 14-month cross-country trek to advocate campaign finance reform are similarly disqualified. While the term 'physical culture' provides dilation from 'sport', it discounts myriad forms of active corporeality in which the socio-political *cause* sounds the clarion call for human movement. As such, 'physical activism', or the articulation of physical activity and political activism, may provide a new categorization, for while the political is the impetus for human movement, the physical is no less important; indeed, the act would lack the same resonance if the statement had been expressed in any other way.

Making A Spectacle of Suffrage

In the years before the country's Civil War, American women began a campaign for the vote that lasted until the 1920 ratification of the Nineteenth Amendment of the Constitution. The United States government has classified white women as citizens since the advent of the republic, but in terms of both duties and obligations, notions of citizenship had always been, and continue to be, inherently gendered (as well as racialized, class-based and heteronormative). Without the right to vote many suffragists argued that women were little more than members, subjects or denizens of the United States. Indeed, an 1890 article outlining the meaning of citizenship in the US distinguished 'active citizens, the voting and office-holding class' from that of 'passive citizens, the class of women and minors'. [7] Accordingly, feminists defined the right to vote as central to citizenship and trusted that the franchise would be the wellspring from which other rights and privileges might flow.

Just before her 1873 trial for casting an illegal ballot, American feminist Susan B. Anthony delivered a series of speeches, asserting that voting constituted 'the one [privilege] without which all the others are nothing'. [8] It was 'the right and duty of woman', wrote Anthony's colleague, Elizabeth Cady Stanton in the 1848 *Declaration of Sentiments and Resolutions*, 'to promote every righteous cause by every righteous means ... by any instrumentalities proper to be used, and in any assemblies proper to be held', yet in the decades that followed, this defiant energy seemed to wane towards 'a period of unrelieved "doldrums"' for the suffrage movement. [9] During her 1909 tour of the United States, British suffragette Emmeline Pankhurst criticized Americans for their 'curious state of quiescence' and Harriet Stanton Blatch, Stanton's daughter, returned to the US after living in England and declared the movement 'completely in a rut. ... It bored its adherents and repelled its opponents.' [10]

These critiques were, in large part, aimed at the leadership of the National American Woman Suffrage Association (led at the time by Anna Howard Shaw and Carrie Chapman Catt), who lobbied for the vote on a state-by-state basis as opposed to working towards women's enfranchisement through federal constitutional amendment. As Catt wrote in a letter to the *New York Tribune*, she believed in 'evolutionary rather than revolutionary methods for obtaining reforms'. [11] Their campaign was conservative and made up of 'virtually educational bodies' confined to annual conventions and social events, a 'partial feminization of male political style'. [12] Yet, by 1900 only four states had granted women the ballot and the lethargy of the movement, as well as the transatlantic exchange of suffrage tactics, inspired the germination of a 'suffrage renaissance' and a period of 'stunning political experimentation' in the early decades of the twentieth century. [13]

At the helm of these shifts was a new generation of women largely influenced by their more active, sometimes militant, British sisters who pledged themselves to 'deeds not words'. These deeds included a variety of exploits designed to capture media, and thereby national, attention for their cause. 'Sandwichettes' (women wearing sandwich boards with pro-suffrage slogans) laboured through the streets; suffragists staged pageants, tableaux and parades that 'carnivalized' urban spaces and forced 'the feminine trooping into public life'. [14] Women made open-air speeches on street-corner soapboxes, from the backs of horse-drawn wagons and chauffeured automobiles, from interurban trolley cars, astride horses and while ferried on the flats of canal boats. In short, they made spectacles of themselves and of suffrage.

Physical Activism

Writing for the magazine *Women's Home Journal* in 1923, Glenna Collett remarked that, 'American women, in the first quarter of the twentieth century, have won two rights: the right of exercising the suffrage and the right of participation in sport', yet there has been little scholarly articulation of voting rights and physical culture. [15] If academics have neglected to unite the two, there are indications that suggest that turn-of-the-century feminists did not. Suffragettes spoke at boxing matches and encouraged supporters to attend baseball games in 'the hope of winning from the fans some of the enthusiasm they show for the national game to the support of the votes-for-women cause'. [16] Historian Joyce Kay, noting that 'historians who have written extensively on the battle for the vote … have failed to make any connection with sport and leisure', brings to light several instances upon which women made use of prominent sportscapes to advertise their cause, including vandalizing golf courses, boathouses and cricket clubs, among other venues. Perhaps the best known of these incidents involved suffragette Emily Davison, who died from injuries she sustained after throwing herself in front of a horse belonging to King George V at the 1913 Epsom Derby. Women orchestrated these efforts, seen as outlandish acts of militancy at the time, as occasions upon which the public could not help but consider the issue of the ballot. [17]

At other times, women have vigorously propelled and navigated their bodies through time and space in order to dispel notions that they were physically, and thereby socially, inferior to men. [18] In 1876, for example, Britain's Agnes Beckwith attempted to cross the English Channel, proclaiming 'I'll swim to France to win votes for women'. [19] Later, suffragettes sailed up the Thames shouting 'Rise Up Women' as they passed near the Parliament building; in 1908, balloonist Muriel Matters flew over that same building dropping flyers that read 'Votes for Women'. Three years later, American mountain climber Annie Smith Peck ascended Peru's Mount Coropuna at the age of 61 and unfurled a 'Votes for Women' banner at the summit. [20] That same year, a faction of 'athletic girls' from Columbia University's physical education programme, carrying tennis rackets and basketballs, joined the parade of 3,000 to 5,000 women who marched down New York's Fifth Avenue demanding the right to vote. [21]

America's bicycle craze of the 1890s provided another way in which physical activity influenced, and was influenced by, the women's movement. Susan B. Anthony felt that the vehicle had 'done more to emancipate women than anything else in the world', while Elizabeth Cady Stanton declared: 'Woman is riding to suffrage on the bicycle.' Following her 15-month, round-the-world bicycle tour, Annie Cohen Kopchovsky, who rode under the name 'Annie Londonderry', declared: 'I am … a "new woman", if that term means that I believe I can do anything any man can do.' [22] Thus, the bicycle facilitated women's physical mobility, freedom and autonomy in both literal and symbolic ways.

Swimming provided another activity that women used to insist upon enfranchisement. In 1915, approximately 20 members of the National Women's Life-Saving League staged a 'suffrage feat' in which they dubbed a mannequin 'Aunty Anti-Suffrage', described by the *New York Times* as being 'fully clothed and hampered alike by her garments and her principles, being an old-fashioned woman who does not believe it is ladylike to swim'. Aunty Anti-Suffrage was 'taken out in a boat and flung violently in the water' but was 'saved from a watery grave' by the suffragists who raced to her rescue. [23] Rather than passively waiting for the ballot, these women declared themselves (physically) active in its pursuit.

During the Progressive Era, American women began to more fully enjoy the benefits of physical culture than they had at previous times in history. As Victorian ideologies concerning women's ethereal frailty, weakness and delicacy began to wane a new, more athletic version of femininity started to take hold. For working-class girls and women, organizations such as the Playground Association of America, the Young Women's Christian Association (YWCA) and industry-sponsored recreation programmes offered forums for physical culture. Those of the wealthier classes enjoyed athletic prospects in the forms of conspicuous leisure and sporting opportunities, while others took advantage of increased opportunities in higher education, where they were exposed to physical education classes away from the 'prying eyes of the public'. [24] Medical and physical education leaders espoused a philosophy of moderation, in which physical training was designed to promote reproductive health and hygiene, and prepare women for the future demands of motherhood and domestic service.

Some publications, such as *Outing* magazine, advocated long-distance walking for women, reporting on Wellesley College's physical education programme where 'girls think nothing of walking from five to ten miles once a week', and pointed to a group of women 'eighty years young' striding over similar distances. [25] Several British and North American pedestriennes drew large crowds during the late 1800s and suffragists viewed the athletes' accomplishments as symbols for women's rights, applauding them for dispelling beliefs in women's innate frailty. Yet the general consensus was that the efforts put too great a strain on women's mental and physical well-being, as well as to their appropriately gendered subjectivity. [26] Although the 'New Woman' shook up the traditional gender order by engaging in traditionally male pursuits at the turn of the twentieth century, females were warned that their engagement in politics and sport, twin male preserves, would have pernicious, masculinizing effects on their bodies, minds and spirits. These sentiments undoubtedly influenced those in the suffrage movement, making the hikes of 1912 and 1913 all the more significant.

On to Albany, 1912

Rosalie Jones, like many on the front lines of the American suffrage movement, came from a wealthy, socially prominent Eastern family. During a trip to Europe following her graduation from Adelphi College, Jones encountered French and British suffragettes who piqued her interest in the cause. [27] Around 1911, Jones began to participate in open-air meetings with prominent feminists such as Inez Milholland, Alva Belmont, and Harriot Stanton Blatch. Though it was reported that the assembled crowds received the women with a volley of eggs and soft tomatoes, they continued their efforts undaunted and unabated. Jones then joined with Elisabeth Freeman, an English-born feminist, to tour Long Island in a horse-drawn wagon. During their 250-mile journey, as well on as a subsequent trip through Ohio, the women distributed literature and gave speeches from the platform of the wagon adorned with 'Votes for Women' signs.

In 1912, Jones became president of the Nassau County, New York, branch of NAWSA, a position she held for two years. It was during this time that she hatched the idea of a suffrage hike. [28] 'The object of the pilgrim army', announced Jones, 'is not merely to make a sensational march on Albany, but to meet the people along the way and talk suffrage to them.' [29] At a congress of seven large New York suffrage societies, members composed a message that the pilgrims would deliver to the state's governor-elect before his inaugural address: 'The Suffrage hopes of the Empire State send greetings and renewed congratulations to Governor William L. Sulzer; and express an earnest hope that his administration may be distinguished by the speedy passage of a Woman Suffrage Amendment.' [30] The message, 'signed by the presidents of the various New York suffrage organizations, engraved on parchment and hand illumined by Miss Jones', was ceremoniously sealed in an envelope in preparation for the journey. [31]

On the morning of 16 Dec. 1912, 26 women set off from the New York City corner of 242nd Street and Broadway. Uniformly adorned with sashes and stoles emblazoned with 'Votes for Women', they carried knapsacks similar to those of the Boy Scouts which were, as reported, 'made of khaki and ... of the right suffrage color, which is yellow'. Each pilgrim carried a walking staff, 'cut from Long Island forests' and 'decorated with 'Votes for Women' streamers and a notch ... cut on those for every town through which the Pilgrims pass'. [32] The two leaders of the march, 'General' Rosalie Jones and 'Colonel' Ida Craft, wore their 'suffrage parade hats' as they led the others towards their north-western destination. Emergency supplies, donated by the nurses of the Henry Street Settlement, included a medical kit on which they had inscribed 'First Aid Is All Right for Bruises, but Nothing Will Save Us but Votes for All'. [33] Through the use of multiple signifiers – their bodies, their physical labour, their words, their costumes and their accoutrements – the women expressed their solidarity with one another and to their pledge to stamp out the injustices of unequal citizenship (Figures 1 and 2).

Jones and company combined religious and militaristic discourse to emphasize the fervour and dedication they felt for their cause. Joining the ranks were 'Corporal' M.N. Stiles, 'Private' Sybil Wilbur, and 'Surgeon General' Lavinia Dock. With Jones and Craft, they comprised the five women who hiked the entire 170 miles to Albany, averaging around 14 miles a stretch in just over 12 days. [34] Also in attendance were Mr Alphonse Major, who piloted the commissary automobile, Mrs Olive Schultz, who preceded the procession by car as the 'official scout', Miss Lillian D. Rockefeller as 'aide de camp' and Mrs. Jessie Hardy Stubbs – the official 'war correspondent'. [35] Stubbs sent regular reports to *Woman's Journal*, but the pilgrims were joined by such a mass of journalists as they made their way to the state's capital that, as she wrote, 'So consistent is the steady flow from the versatile pens of our army of special correspondents now at the front, that it is scarcely

Figure 1. From left, Rosalie Jones, Jesse Hardy Stubbs, and Ida Craft. The women wear sashes reading, 'Votes for Women.' Craft's satchel reads, 'Votes for Women Pilgrim Leaflets.' George Grantham Bain Collection, Library of Congress, Prints and Photographs Division, Reproduction Number LC-DIG-ggbain-11099.

necessary for the war correspondent of the marching body to write one line for publication.' [36] Even the often derisive *New York Times* began regularly reporting on the hike, confessing that it would 'provide the material for many an interesting narrative'. [37]

The pilgrims' troupe temporarily swelled as others joined along the way. Walking between ten and 22 miles per day, the delegation stopped periodically for lunch, dinner and tea, and to give both impromptu and scheduled speeches. They were usually greeted at the outskirts of town and escorted to a hospitable venue where they were the guests of the local suffrage organization. As they made their way through the countryside, they 'talked suffrage' to residents and handed out buttons and literature – what they called their 'ammunition' – to any takers they might encounter. Journalists wrote that inhabitants of factories and schools often rushed from their confines to cheer on the hikers. As the mayor of Poughkeepsie welcomed the group: 'You would never have aroused such enthusiasm or had the chance to speak in the places you have if you had adopted the more conventional method of carrying the message.' [38] Thus the unconventionality of women tramping through New York's countryside obliged even the most disinterested and unaware to consider the issue of the franchise for women.

Figure 2. Jesse Hardy Stubbs and Rosalie Jones. George Grantham Bain Collection, Library of Congress, Prints and Photographs Division, Reproduction Number LC-DIG-ggbain-10996.

The north-eastern winter made their journey even more difficult, and therefore more newsworthy. It was reported that 'the pilgrims had plodded along roads almost knee-deep in snow and slush'. [39] Other days, they waded over muddy byways, trolley tracks, hill and dale, battling wind, fog, injury and fatigue. Yet in the face of such adversity they reached Albany on the afternoon of 28 Dec. where, according to the writers of the 1922 *History of Woman Suffrage*, 'Whistles blew,

Figure 3. 'Suffrage Hikers.' George Grantham Bain Collection, Library of Congress, Prints and Photographs Division, Reproduction Number LC-DIG-ggbain-12622.

bells rang, motor cars clanged their gongs, traffic paused, windows were thrown up and shops were deserted while Albany gazed upon them and large numbers escorted them to the steps of the capitol where they lifted their cry "Votes for Women".' [40] Three days later, they were granted a meeting with Governor-elect Sulzer, who commended the women on their journey and pledged his allegiance to their cause.

The 1913 Army of the Hudson

It was during the march on Albany that Jones devised the idea of a second hike to Washington, DC that would dovetail with the massive suffrage parade scheduled to take place the day before President Woodrow Wilson's inauguration. With thousands of tourists in town, the pilgrims were sure to draw a crowd and their second trek in as many months would generate even greater media excitement. This time they carried an appeal, signed by NAWSA president Anna Howard Shaw, urging Wilson to advocate equal suffrage to his constituents. Once more, Olive Schultz piloted the automobile that would survey the road conditions and Elisabeth Freeman accompanied the group in a wagon adorned with a sign that read 'Criminals and the insane can't vote, neither can I, what about it?' Again in attendance was a coterie of journalists who constructed accounts of the women's exploits.

Figure 4. 'Rosalie Jones's Army.' George Grantham Bain Collection, Library of Congress, Prints and Photographs Division, Reproduction Number LC-DIG-ggbain-15122.

Of the 200 who embarked on the morning of 12 February 1913, only 60 persevered through lunchtime and when they had finished their hike that first day, the Army of the Hudson had dwindled to just 16. The remaining band persisted on, their numbers inflating and deflating as others joined and left what was meant to emulate General George Washington's historic voyage across the Delaware River during the American Revolutionary War. This symbolic gesture had to be jettisoned when ice floes thwarted their journey. Instead, the pilgrims re-routed, which Jones claimed 'was not quite the same ... but that she considered the movement of women to obtain their belated rights of as much importance to this country as Gen. Washington's celebrated crossing'. [41] Their alternative path proved a difficult one, as the women had to make their way through heavy clay and mud that significantly slowed their pace.

The pilgrims' basic protocol remained the same, though this time they agreed to wear long, brown hooded capes, purchasable for $1 (Figures 3 and 4). Not a negligible sum, the majority of participants were primarily wealthy women who could afford the time required to march, as well as the additional estimated expense of $2 per day. [42] At the same time, many of the pilgrims did express a strong sense of class-consciousness that set them apart from other NAWSA members, making such declarations as 'there will be no diamonds worn in the "Pilgrims' Hike"' for they perceived such extravagance to be in 'bad taste'. [43] More significant was Jessie Hardy Stubbs's letter to *Woman's Journal* upon arriving in Albany in 1912 stating that

> We all of us realized and have repeated over and over again, that we were not walking any more or even as much as the longest 'hike' that thousands of American working women walk everyday to their jobs. ... The only difference [is that] while the great army of women in the industrial world are carrying all kinds of burdens and standing on their feet twelve and fourteen hours a day, there is no popular acclaim for them, but a perpetual drudgery and, in many cases, barely a living wage. [44]

By diminishing the arduousness of their trek in comparison with the struggles of their working-class sisters, the pilgrims demonstrated the ways in which physical expressions might draw attention to multiple socio-political causes of the day.

They also showed somewhat greater sensitivity to the 'color question' than did the national board, though they had been warned by two southern businessmen, who claimed to represent thousands of others, that 'if you advocate votes for negro [sic] women you will indeed find that your way to Washington lies through enemy's country'. [45] The racialized controversy especially came to the fore as NAWSA officials prepared for the Washington parade, as many southerners objected to black women's suffrage, as well as their marching shoulder to shoulder with their white peers. The pilgrims, on the other hand, were joined, if only for a mile, by a contingent of African American women 'carrying a banner with the inscription, "Votes for Negro Women"'. [46] Later, when asked if the Colored Women's Suffrage Club would accompany them into Washington, Jones replied '"Yes they will", with an accent upon the first and last words'. [47] She fell short of endorsing black women's suffrage, however, stating 'that has to do largely with certain States. The men and women of those States must solve their own problems.' [48] Moreover, there is no evidence to suggest that the pilgrim army did anything to solicit support from, or to reach out to, African Americans.

This second hike provided further opportunities and challenges. To celebrate the pilgrims' arrival, the Wilmington, Delaware, city council declared a half-day holiday. Yet as they prepared to march out of the city the next morning, 'two youths distributed to the pilgrims several suspicious-looking packages labeled "Handle with care." Opening them carefully, the suffragettes found they contained black sticks marked "dynamite."' It turned out to be a hoax – the sticks were merely made of carbon, but the prank rattled the women, who undoubtedly felt less than safe from the start. [49] Supporters packed the streets to greet them in Philadelphia and in Baltimore 'they were received by Cardinal Gibbons in his mansion, an extraordinary courtesy, as they were not Catholics,' relayed *The History of Woman Suffrage*. [50] Perhaps because of her unfamiliarity with the rituals of Catholicism, Rosalie Jones greeted His Eminence not with the traditional kneel and kiss of his ring, but instead 'rushed forward and grasped the [him] by his hand', asking 'How do you do?' and shocking onlookers. 'This sensation was further accentuated', reported the *Washington Post*, 'by Miss Elizabeth Freeman, official orator of the marchers, who smoked a cigarette before 150 men ... who entertained the hikers at a luncheon'. Even her fellow suffragists found this unsuitable and asked her to stop. When she refused, the man beside her plucked the offensive item from her fingers and extinguished it himself. Her smoking, an activity deemed masculine at the time, was mocked in the press and stoked the sentiments of those who believed women's pursuit of male privileges a foolish and comical prospect.

Contrasting the suffragettes with what he called 'the noble and modest women who have devoted their lives to the sisterhood and the service and uplift of the poor', the Cardinal stated

> Here we have true women, women who know their place. Then look at the other picture in contrast. On the one hand we see good accomplished in a quiet, modest way. On the other we see the noisy, clamorous and spectacular way of other women, and as an example of this I point to the hikers who were among you a few days ago.

He further declared that 'I am not in favor of suffrage now, nor was I when I received the hikers'. When asked 'Do you think the hiking method has aided the cause of woman suffrage?' the Cardinal replied 'Oh, I am sure it has not.' [51] In all, it seems as though the 'noisy' and 'spectacular' efforts of women who did not 'know their place' did little to convince Baltimoreans to support the crusade for the ballot.

In Laurel, Maryland, approximately ten miles from the capital, Jones received a telegram from NAWSA officials: 'Board voted to have message presented by officers and Congressional Committee. Letter following.' [52] In other words, the pilgrims would no longer be permitted to deliver the message to President Wilson they had carried for 240 miles; instead, the officers of the national organization would execute the mission in what they felt to be a more 'formal' manner. It was terribly upsetting news to the hikers, though Jones complied, telling the press 'I am a soldier who obeys orders.' Trying to soothe things over, NAWSA officials communicated that they would allow the hikers to accompany the congressional committee and the officers of the association and 'expressed regret that there had been a misunderstanding'. Jones, however, refused: 'I am through', she said. 'I was asked to give up the message I had received in New York to deliver to President Wilson. I did so. It is now out of my hands, and so far as I am concerned that ends the matter.' [53] Citing the 'cold reception' they received 'after the long walk', several hikers returned home in protest rather than completing the march. [54]

As the remaining party descended on the nation's capital, 'Gen. Jones halted her command and ordered the hikers' into formation with military-like precision. [55] They had navigated their way through four states, walking as far as 27 miles in one stretch. The crowd amassed for their arrival, according to reporters, seemed 'enthusiastic, but for the most part it was merely attracted by curiosity'. [56] There would be yet another slight from NAWSA when the pilgrims learned that their group had been assigned to the back half of the much-anticipated pre-inauguration parade. Even so, they joined the immense and impressive ensemble, replete with patriotic imagery, allegorical pageants, elaborate costumes and aesthetic staging. Chaos broke out when the DC police force failed to control the mob that began to harass, and then physically attack the demonstrators. The journalists in attendance quickly publicized the assaults, the reports of which were condemned by papers around the country. Even in anti-suffragist papers, editorials rebuked the attackers for violating the women's civil rights, which won the suffragettes the public's sympathy, if not support, bringing the promotion of their cause to an even greater level. [57]

Press Coverage: A Double-Edged Sword

In the early years of the twentieth century, NAWSA and the popular press shared an ambivalent relationship. While there were those suffragists who did not wish to draw immodest or inappropriate attention, others believed that public exposure would advance their agenda. Speaking at the 1912 Mississippi Valley Suffrage Conference on the topic of 'Methods of Reaching the Press', Mrs Edna Cutler urged women to 'create news worthy of display under big headlines and calling for photographs. Be spectacular', she continued, 'which is possible without being outlandish. Do the things that will force the indifferent to read of suffrage.' [58]

The leaders of NAWSA had initially dismissed such strategies as 'unfeminine and therefore obnoxious and ridiculous', and refused to speak at the first open-air meeting in New York in 1907. [59] It was soon apparent, however, that the tactics garnered much-needed support. As Ellen Carol DuBois writes, following the 1907 meeting, 'Newspaper coverage increased immediately; by 1908 even the sneering *New York Times* reported regularly on suffrage. The more outrageous and controversial the event, the more prominent the coverage.' [60] Suffragettes and suffragists alike continually danced upon the razor-thin lines between spectacular and outlandish, ridiculous and controversial, as they experimented with the most effective ways to further their campaign.

Such was the case for the pilgrimages of 1912 and 1913, for they were joined by journalists not just from the New York newspapers but from periodicals, weeklies and dailies from around the country. 'The newspapers of California', read one letter to the *Woman's Journal*, 'are giving an extraordinary amount of space to the suffrage pilgrimage … large pictures and whole columns, day after day. No suffrage topic outside of California has had such an amount of publicity.' [61] Nationwide coverage was a crucial technology in soliciting support for a constitutional amendment. Concurrently, the pilgrims' presence in the public sphere generated displeasure that undercut their cause. Specifically, the press reported on three different types of peril the women faced, all of which coalesced to insinuate that their hike was foolhardy and that their task was not one to be taken seriously: women put the domestic sphere in danger by devoting their energies to suffrage; by making those energies visible to the public sphere, these women faced danger from others; by exerting those energies, in any sphere, the women were a danger to themselves.

In the first instance, crowds chastised the women because their participation meant their disregard for home and family or, perhaps worse, that they had wholly rejected such roles. One woman exhorted Jones to 'go home and mend your husbands' clothes'. Another admonished Craft: 'You ought to settle down and have a home of your own.' When a spectator was asked if she favoured their cause, she responded that she was 'too domestic to go in for that sort of thing'. [62] In another example, the poet and historian Frank Prentice Rand penned a piece titled 'The Voteless Volunteers' for the *New York Times*, assembling vignettes in which the pilgrims' absence left their homes, as well as the traditional gender order, in disarray:

> Oh, mother, we can't do a thing with this flour;
> We cannot recall how much lard to allow;
> And, Sis, we do wish you were here for an hour
> To guess what your baby is howling for now.
> Jack is sweeping the floor, in a frantic endeavor
> To stifle his sobs, though they somewhat persist;
> For his sweetheart declared she would marry him never,
> And, tossing her head, hurried off to enlist.

Mothers, sisters and sweethearts depicted in the poem – those 'Militant maidens of Rosalie Jones' – abandoned their children and beaus, oblivious to all but their potential enfranchisement. [63]

Second, journalists implied that women needed protection from the public sphere, as evidenced by the threats of hostile crowds, unfamiliar creatures, inclement weather and treacherous terrain. At various points in the hikes, encounters with cows, turkeys and snakes caused panic among the hikers, if one is to believe the press accounts. In Newark, Delaware, it was reported that a group of young boys released mice at the feet of the hikers who, according to the *Washington Post*, reacted with overblown hysteria. Elsewhere, they were assailed with rockets, gunshots and rocks. In Leiperville, Pennsylvania, the hikers were assaulted with stones and 'snow-balled ... by a crowd of small boys'. No serious injuries were reported and before hostilities escalated the cavalry from the nearby Chester Military College rode in and broke up the attack. [64] There were rumours of plans to kidnap Jones. In College Park, Maryland, they 'encountered more insults and rowdyism ... than at any time during the 240-mile hike from New York.' There, 200 male students from the Maryland Agricultural College (now the University of Maryland) attacked them verbally and physically, the *New York Times* reported:

> Two women were jostled, and one was knocked down. Students in uniform by their hooting compelled Gen. Jones to stop speaking. They pushed against one of the automobiles. They then tore the pennant off the baggage automobile, and tried to get the baggage from the machine. The great [suffrage] banner was stolen. [65]

These persistent accounts – written for both serious and comedic effect – suggested that women's delicate natures required they be shielded from both outdoor exposure and politics.

Finally, the exertion of the hikes, according to the media, ravaged the women's bodies and their psyches. The women, it was written, 'suffered untold agony'. One had 'crawled nearly a mile on her hands and knees' to reach her destination. Another was 'in a raving hysteria for several hours' and even General Jones's 'slight, delicate frame' and 'face show[ed] the strain of the march'. [67] Most common, however, were the unrelenting reports of maladies of the feet that included disintegrating shoes and badly sprained ankles. The feet of 'Surgeon General Dock', the *Times* related, were 'blistered, though she has been spending almost every minute of rest treating them they were in bad condition when she started out this morning'. [66] Later, writers recounted that

> Col. Craft's physical condition is such that Gen. Jones and her staff have begged her to give up the hike. Col. Craft will not give up. Her feet are bleeding and so swollen that she cannot fasten her shoes. When Col. Craft reached the inn, she had to be assisted into the house. [67]

Official 'war correspondent' Jessie Hardy Stubbs tried to dismiss much of these accounts as inaccurate and facetious. 'Lest there be any anxious acquaintances of the Pilgrims', she wrote,

> who believe all they read about 'our feet', let it be stated for all time – it is the one huge newspaper joke! We are all so well, so happy, so keen, a real physician would starve on the job. Most of our feet are so hard knives would not cut them.

She continued by stating that 'The modern newspaper reporter is a rapid fire fiction artist, who is paid for working his or her risibles' and composed a poem to that effect entitled 'the new Pilgrim cry':

> Rah, rah rah, who are we?
> We are the Pilgrims,
> Don't you see!
>
> What are we doing?
> Don't ask us.
> Buy any paper,
> They make the fuss! [68]

Certainly, both Stubbs and the rest of the press corps had their own agendas for portraying the hikers in a particular light. Stubbs meant to paint a strong and valiant picture while newspaper reporters demonstrated tones of derision and pity. The discrepancies between the two representations also demonstrate the fallibility of relying on media accounts as primary source material. But regardless of the *way* in which the media covered the pilgrims and their hikes, the fact that they covered them at all was vastly significant.

Conclusion

Alice Stone Blackwell, editor of *The Woman's Journal*, declared the 1913 'suffrage pilgrimage … a great success. It got the public's attention', she wrote. 'It proves anew that there is no need to do anything lawless to arrest attention. All that is needed is something novel.' [69] The ways in which the hikes effectively engaged Americans' notice is important, but they should not be reduced to '"media events" staged solely for the benefit of the press'. Instead, cautions historian Michael McGerr, 'such public demonstrations gave participants a sense of pride, solidarity, and power'. [70] Considering the hundreds of miles the women logged and hundreds of hours spent with one another in devotion to suffrage, to dismiss their efforts as publicity stunts would do them a tremendous disservice.

Women continued their fight for the right to vote for several years. With the 1914 outbreak of the First World War and eventual US involvement, many abandoned their suffrage work and dedicated themselves to war efforts. Others, such as the Congressional Union, kept up their pressure on President Wilson, though it seems the public and other suffragists viewed their tactics as unpatriotic during times of national crisis. The controversy they created ensured that suffrage would remain present in American consciousness while the temporary service work of others hastened the cause. By 1917, New York became the 14th state to give women the ballot and President Wilson voiced his support for a federal constitutional law that would grant women the franchise. In 1920 the requisite 36 states voted to ratify the Nineteenth Amendment to the US constitution, thus marking the end of a long, hard-fought battle brought about by the articulation of multiple, at times discordant, strategies.

Writing in 1986, philosopher Monique Canto-Sperber argued that 'Feminist politics is real only if women, together with their bodies, their works, their labor, and their voice, are present in a place where everyone can see them'. [71] Nearly a century earlier, a faction of women fighting for enfranchisement made sure that their cause was visible, audible and physical in ways that could not be ignored. This essay examined just one of many ways in which the physical, and physical activity, can be central to political statements and campaigns. It was not just an issue of being in the public sphere, but that the pilgrims moved their bodies through that space in a spectacular way. At a time when few thought women capable of strenuous and prolonged activity, the miles they accrued by the persistence of their steps and commitment to their cause made the physical political. Pierre Bourdieu notes that, 'There are a great many things we understand only with our bodies.' [72] There are also a great many things that can be communicated only with the body, through motion, form, and appearance, in the occupation and navigation of space, by engagement and interaction, as ideological manifestation. Of all the tools available to groups and individuals in a given society, the body seems the most fundamental and perhaps the most underestimated possibility for enacting change. The concept of physical activism may help bring to bear those situations through which to consider the power of corporeal action.

Acknowledgements

The author wishes to thank Patricia Vertinsky, Roberta Park, and Andrew Riley for their generous assistance with this project.

Notes

[1] 'The Hike to Washington', *Woman Voter*, March 1913, 10.
[2] 'Will Lead Her Army Here', *Washington Post*, 10 Jan. 1913.
[3] DuBois, 'Working Women, Class Relations, and Suffrage Militance', 56.
[4] Parratt, 'About Turns', 9.
[5] Hargreaves and Vertinsky, *Physical Culture, Power, and the Body*, 1.
[6] King, *Pink Ribbons, Inc.* The notion of 'thons' refers to events that often combine physical activity with raising funds for and public awareness of a particular cause, such as walk-a-thons, skate-a-thons, bowl-a-thons, bike-a-thon and marathons.
[7] Richman, 'Citizenship of the United States', 105. See also Smith, 'Modern Citizenship', 108.
[8] Stanton *et al.*, *History of Woman Suffrage*, vol. 2, 638, emphasis in original.
[9] Flexner, *Century of Struggle*, 72.
[10] Blatch and Lutz, *The Challenging Years*, 92.
[11] Quoted in Ibid., 203.
[12] Kraditor, *The Ideas of the Woman Suffrage Movement*, 226; McGerr, 'Political Style and Women's Power', 870.
[13] Graham, *Woman Suffrage and the New Democracy*; McGerr, 'Political Style and Women's Power', 869.
[14] In Tickner, *The Spectacle of Women*, 58.
[15] Collett, 'Sports for Women', 21.
[16] 'News Items Gathered from All Quarters', *Sporting Life*, 17 May 1913, 32.
[17] Kay, 'It Wasn't Just Emily Davison!', 1338; Kay, '"No Time for Recreations till the Vote is Won"?'
[18] See, for example, Borish, '"The Cradle of American Champions"'; Todd, *Physical Culture and the Body Beautiful*; Vertinsky, *The Eternally Wounded Woman*.
[19] 'I'll Swim to France To Win Votes for Women', *Washington Post*, 26 Oct. 1913.
[20] Hymowitz and Weissman, *A History of Women in America*, 278.
[21] 'Women Parade and Rejoice at the End', *New York Times*, 7 May 1911.
[22] Quoted in Zheutlin, 'Annie Londonderry's Extraordinary Ride', 2.
[23] 'Brave Suffragists Save "Anti" from Sea', *New York Times*, 18 July 1915.
[24] Park, 'Sport, Gender and Society in a Transatlantic Victorian Perspective', 86–7.
[25] Marks, 'Outdoor Life at Wellesley College', 121; 'Outdoor Men and Women'; Mullett, 'Country Walking for Women'.
[26] Kenney, 'The Realm of Sports and the Athletic Woman', 124–6; Shaulis, 'Pedestriennes'.
[27] Naylor, 'General Rosalie Jones', 4. Her family, which included a staunch anti-suffrage mother and sister, felt she had 'disgraced her family'. Upon returning home, she littered an acre of her land with women's suffrage signs and slogans, to which one neighbour remarked: 'We always used to think Miss Rosalie was a lady.'

[28] Demonstrating the transatlantic suffrage network and exchange of ideas, just one month earlier *Woman's Journal* published an article about a group of women who walked 400 miles from Edinburgh to London 'holding meetings and collecting signatures to a suffrage petition all along their route': '"Brown Women" Finish March', *Woman's Journal*, 23 Nov. 1912.

[29] *Woman's Journal*, 4 Jan. 1913.

[30] Harper, *The History of Woman Suffrage*, 452.

[31] 'Suffragists Plan Albany Pilgrimage', *New York Times*, 10 Dec. 1912.

[32] 'Pilgrims Tram to Albany', *Woman's Journal and Suffrage News*, 21 Dec. 1912.

[33] In 'Pilgrims Weren't Like This', the *New York Times* attempted to discount the applicability of the word 'pilgrimage' for what the suffragettes had planned. I found no explanation for the use of the usually religious term, though it seems to be one selected by Jones and not one assigned to her or her mission: *New York Times*, 11 Dec. 1912.

[34] *The Woman's Journal* (12 Dec. 1912) published their itinerary in advance of the hike. From New York City, the pilgrims would stop on Monday 17 Dec. in Irvington, on Tuesday in Ossining, Wednesday in Peekskill, Thursday in Fishkill-on-the-Hudson, Friday in Wappingers Falls, Saturday in Poughkeepsie, Sunday 23 Dec. in Rhinebeck and Monday in Germantown. The pilgrims would then spend Christmas in Hudson before travelling to Stuyvesant Falls the following day. There was one final layover in Rensselaer before arriving in Albany on 31 Dec. 1912, the day before Governor Sulzer's inauguration.

[35] Other Pilgrims or 'sergeants' included, at one time or another, Mrs Edward Van Wyck, Mrs James Lees Laidlaw, Miss Miller, Mrs William M. Ivins, Miss Gwynne Peake, Miss Beeker, Miss Margerie Cullum, Mrs Cora Perry Hamilton, Mrs Martha Wentworth Suffren, Mrs Velma Swanston Howard, Mrs Anna Ross Weeks, Mrs H.D. Holbert, Mrs Lang, and Mrs Sylbil Wilbur.

[36] Jessie Hardy Stubbs, 'Pilgrims March Bravely Onward', *Woman Journal*, 28 Dec. 1912.

[37] 'Pilgrims Weren't Like This', 12.

[38] 'Girls Desert Mill to Follow Hikers', *New York Times*, 2 Dec. 1912.

[39] 'Automobile Upset Almost Ends Hike', *New York Times*, 28 Dec. 1912.

[40] Stanton *et al.*, *History of Woman Suffrage*, 452.

[41] 'Suffragette Army Balked by Delaware', *New York Times*, 16 Feb. 1913.

[42] 'Lack of Peanuts "Hikes" Only Peril', *New York Times*, 15 Dec. 1912.

[43] Ibid.

[44] 'Sulzer Swears Aid To Cause', *Woman's Journal*, 4 Jan. 1913.

[45] 'Gen. Jones Dodges the Color Question', *New York Times*, 20 Feb. 1913.

[46] 'Message To Wilson Taken from Hikers', *New York Times*, 28 Feb. 1913.

[47] 'Suffrage Hikers Send Wilson A Flag', *New York Times*, 27 Feb. 1913.

[48] 'Gen. Jones Dodges the Color Question'. Years later, as Spinzia writes, Jones, who leased out part of her estate to tenants, 'refused to rent to a black family, just as she had refused to allow the 'Negro Suffragists' to march with her contingent to Washington, DC, in 1913': Spinzia, 'Women of Long Island', 5.

[49] 'Mice Scatter Army', *The Washington Post*, 21 Feb. 1913.

[50] Stanton *et al.*, *History of Woman Suffrage*, 453.

[51] 'Hikers Clamorous, Says Gibbons, Who Opposes Suffrage', clipping dated 1 March 1913 from 'Faithfully Yours, An Interactive Scrapbook of Elisabeth Freeman: Suffragette, Civil Rights Worker, and Militant Pacifist', available online at www.elisabethfreeman.org, accessed 13 Mar. 2009.

[52] Quoted in 'Message To Wilson Taken from Hikers', *New York Times*, 28 Feb. 1913.

[53] 'Army Ends Its Hike', *New York Times*, 1 March 1913.

[54] 'Pilgrims Quit "Army"', *Washington Post*, 2 March 1913.

[55] 'Army Ends Its Hike'.
[56] Ibid.
[57] Lumsden, 'Beauty and the Beasts'.
[58] 'Wants Women Spectacular', *New York Times*, 22 May 1912.
[59] Lumsden, *Rampant Women*, 87.
[60] DuBois, 'Working Women', 56.
[61] Alice Park, letter to the editor, *The Woman's Journal*, 4 Jan. 1913.
[62] 'Suffragette Army Balked by Delaware', *New York Times*, 16 Feb. 1913.
[63] Frank Prentice Rand, 'The Voteless Volunteers', *New York Times*, 18 Feb. 1913.
[64] '"Army" Escapes Rout', *Washington Post*, 18 Feb. 1913.
[65] 'Message to Wilson Taken from Hikers', *New York Times*, 28 Feb. 1913.
[66] 'Weary, Aching Hikers', *Washington Post*, 22 Feb. 1913.
[67] 'Col. Craft Walks On, But Hikers Protest', *New York Times*, 23 Feb. 1913.
[68] 'Pilgrims March Bravely Onward', *Woman's Journal and Suffrage News*, 28 Dec. 1912.
[69] Alice Stone Blackwell, *The Woman's Journal*, 4 Jan. 1913.
[70] McGerr, 'Political Style and Women's Power, 1830–1940', 879.
[71] Canto, 'The Politics of Women's Bodies', 339.
[72] Bourdieu, 'Program for a Sociology of Sport', 160.

References

Blatch, Hariot Stanton and Alma Lutz. *The Challenging Years: The Memoirs of Harriot Stanton Blatch*. New York: Putnam's, 1940.

Borish, Linda. '"The Cradle of American Champions, Women Champions … Swim Champions": Charlotte Epstein, Gender and Jewish Identity, and the Physical Emancipation of Women in Aquatic Sports'. *International Journal of the History of Sport* 21 (2004): 197–235.

Bourdieu, Pierre. 'Program for a Sociology of Sport'. *Sociology of Sport Journal* 5 (1988): 153–61.

Canto, Dominique. 'The Politics of Women's Bodies: Reflections on Plato'. In *The Female Body in Western Culture: Contemporary Perspectives*, edited by Susan Rubin Suleiman. Cambridge, MA: Harvard University Press, 1986.

Collett, Glenna. 'Sports for Women'. *Woman's Home Companion*, Sept. 1923, 21.

DuBois, Ellen Carol. 'Working Women, Class Relations, and Suffrage Militance: Harriot Stanton Blatch and the New York Woman Suffrage Movement, 1894–1909'. *Journal of American History* 74 (1987): 56.

Flexner, Eleanor. *Century of Struggle: The Woman's Rights Movement in the United States*. Cambridge, MA: Belknap Press, 1975.

Graham, Sara Hunter. *Woman Suffrage and the New Democracy*. New Haven, CT: Yale University Press, 1996.

Hargreaves, Jennifer and Patricia Vertinsky. *Physical Culture, Power, and the Body*. London: Routledge, 2007.

Harper, Ida Husted, ed. *The History of Woman Suffrage, vol. VI, 1900–1920*. New York: J.J. Little and Ives Company, 1922.

Hymowitz, Carol and Michaele Weissman. *A History of Women in America*. New York: Bantam Books, 1978.

Kay, Joyce. '"No Time for Recreations till the Vote is Won"? Suffrage Activists and Leisure in Edwardian Britain'. *Women's History Review* 16 (2007): 535–53.

Kay, Joyce. 'It Wasn't Just Emily Davison! Sport, Suffrage and Society in Edwardian Britain'. *International Journal of the History of Sport* 25 (2008): 1338–54.

Kenney, Karen. 'The Realm of Sports and the Athletic Woman, 1850–1900'. In *Her Story in Sport*, edited by Reet Howell. West Point, NY: Leisure Press, 1982.

King, Samantha. *Pink Ribbons, Inc.: Breast Cancer and the Politics of Philanthropy*. Minneapolis, MN: University of Minnesota Press, 2006.

Kraditor, Aileen S. *The Ideas of the Woman Suffrage Movement, 1890–1920*. New York: W.W. Norton, 1981.

Lumsden, Linda J. *Rampant Women: Suffragists and the Right of Assembly*. Knoxville, TN: University of Tennessee Press, 1997.

Lumsden, Linda J. 'Beauty and the Beasts: Significance of Press Coverage of the 1913 National Suffrage Parade'. *Journalism and Mass Communication Quarterly* 77 (2000): 593–611.

McGerr, Michael. 'Political Style and Women's Power, 1830–1940'. *Journal of American History* 77 (1990): 864–85.

Marks, Jeannette A. 'Outdoor Life at Wellesley College'. *Outing* 32, no. 2 (1898): 117–24.

Mullett, Mary B. 'Country Walking for Women'. *Outing* 38, no. 4 (1901): 443–7.

Naylor, Natalie A. 'General Rosalie Jones (1883–1978): Oyster Bay's Maverick Suffragist'. *The Freeholder* 12 (2007): 3–7.

'Outdoor Men and Women', *Outing* 46, no. 4 (1905): 728–835.

Park, Roberta J. 'Sport, Gender and Society in a Transatlantic Victorian Perspective'. In *From 'Fair Sex' to Feminism: Sport and the Socialization of Women in the Industrial and Post industrial Eras*, edited by J.A. Mangan and Roberta J. Park. London: Frank Cass, 1987.

Parratt, Catriona M. 'About Turns: Reflecting on Sport History in the 1990s'. *Sport History Review* 29 (1998): 4–17.

Richman, Irving Berdine. 'Citizenship of the United States'. *Political Science Quarterly* 5 (1890): 104–23.

Shaulis, Dahn. 'Pedestriennes: Newsworthy but Controversial Women in Sporting Entertainment'. *Journal of Sport History* 26 (1999): 29–50.

Smith, Rogers M. 'Modern Citizenship'. In *Handbook of Citizenship Studies*, edited by Engin F. Isin and Bryan S. Turner. London: Sage, 2002.

Spinzia, Judith Ader. 'Women of Long Island: Mary Elizabeth Jones and Rosalie Gardiner Jones'. *The Freeholder* 11 (Spring 2007): 3–7.

Stanton, Elizabeth Cady, Susan B. Anthony and Matilda Joselyn Gage, eds. *History of Woman Suffrage, vol. 2*. New York: Arno, 1969.

Tickner, Lisa. *The Spectacle of Women: Imagery of the Suffrage Campaign. 1907–14*. Chicago: University of Chicago Press, 1988.

Todd, Jan. *Physical Culture and the Body Beautiful: Purposive Exercise in the Lives of Women, 1800–1875*. Macon, GA: Mercer, 1998.

Vertinsky, Patricia A. *The Eternally Wounded Woman: Women, Doctors, and Exercise in the Late Nineteenth Century*. Urbana, IL: University of Illinois Press, 1994.

Zheutlin, Peter. 'Annie Londonderry's Extraordinary Ride'. *Women in Judaism: A Multidisciplinary Journal* 5 (2008). Available online at http://wjudaism.library.utoronto.ca/, accessed 13 Mar. 2009.

From Alice Milliat to Marie-Thérèse Eyquem: Revisiting Women's Sport in France (1920s–1960s)

Thierry Terret

Alice Milliat (1884–1957) and Marie-Thérèse Eyquem (1913–1978) were two female sport leaders whose institutional actions had important consequences for women's sporting participation. This contribution examines the extraordinary careers of both of these women in the context of the broader history of women's sport in France. Milliat's and Eyquem's lives and the institutional battles they fought on behalf of women were similar in a number of respects although they took place in different time periods: during the 1920s for Milliat and in the 1940s and 1950s for Eyquem. In pursuing their goals through opportunistic means, both challenged the gender order during periods of war and their aftermath: Milliat in the First World War period, and Eyquem in the Second. In spite of their similarities and differences, the two sport leaders were nevertheless representative of two distinct forms of feminism: one more strictly militant, the second more political.

Introduction

Alice Milliat (1884–1957) and Marie-Thérèse Eyquem (1913–1978), whose influence covered the period from the 1920s to the 1960s, were two female sport leaders whose institutional actions in France and at an international level had important consequences for women's participation in sport. There is less collective memory about Alice Milliat than there is of Marie-Thérèse Eyquem. However, both individuals remain relatively unknown in spite of their importance in the history of sport and the large number of contemporary works in which their names have appeared. [1] A pioneering article published in 1977 in the *Journal of Sport History* explored the role of Alice Milliat in the creation of the Fédération Sportive Féminine

Internationale (FSFI). [2] However, one had to wait nearly 30 years to learn more about her impact at a national level when two dissertations [3] were completed and a book, dedicated entirely to her, was written by French historian André Drevon. [4] The work of Marie-Thérèse Eyquem is even less known because, apart from the brief essay of the French sports historian Laurence Munoz, her career still remains surrounded by secrecy that is probably due in part to her work with the French collaborationist state of Vichy during the occupation of France by the Nazis, [5] as well as to her sexual orientation at a time when she was working within Catholic circles. Nonetheless, her later actions as president of the International Association of Physical Education and Sport for Girls and Women (IAPESGW) between 1961 and 1965 moved her more into the public eye. [6]

It is quite surprising that there has been little analysis of the work of these two sports leaders. Their careers had much in common; and in their most important work they followed each other in succession. Alice Milliat's activities and contributions took place from the 1920s to the mid-1930s; Marie-Thérèse Eyquem's initiatives began with her first responsibilities within the Catholic women's sport movement during the mid-1930s and continued throughout the following three decades. An examination of these two extraordinary careers enables us to revisit the broader history of women's sport in France from the 1920s to the 1960s.

Social Trajectories

Alice Joséphine Marie (née Million) was born in a *petite-bourgeoisie* family [7] in the French city of Nantes in 1884. Her father was a business employee, her mother a seamstress. In this environment, achieving a better social status depended mainly on school success and Alice Million became a primary school teacher. She then went to England, where she married a compatriot, Joseph Milliat. The 20 year-old woman probably discovered rowing while in London and practised it regularly but never excelled at the sport. Her husband died early in 1908, and she decided to travel through Europe and the United States. During her journeys she developed various language skills and eventually became a translator upon her return to France during the First World War. Upon moving to Paris she became a member of the oldest women's athletic sport club, Fémina sport, [8] although with a relatively limited sporting involvement. She died in 1957 in relative professional and social anonymity.

To some extent, Marie-Thérèse Eyquem's social milieu was similar to that of Alice Milliat's. Born in 1913 in a village of south-eastern France named La Teste-de-Buch (30 years after the birth of Alice Milliat), Eyquem also belonged to the provincial *petite-bourgeoisie*. Her father was a baker and later became an insurance employee; her mother was a primary school teacher but gave up that role to dedicate herself to the education of her children. [9] In 1925, the family moved to Paris, where Eyquem received a religious education. She then left school at the age of 14, took courses by correspondence, and ended up getting a degree in classics. During the 1920s, in a

Catholic society benevolent to young people, she discovered gymnastics and sports, including badminton, tennis and basketball, but never competed. In 1931, at the age of 18, she sought out Sister Bouvier, the head of the women's works of St Vincent de Paul, to help her find a job. She was appointed secretary of a Catholic sports association that had been founded in 1919 and at the time covered mainly the Paris area: the Rayon Sportif Féminin. [10] Later, she assumed various responsibilities within ministerial institutions in political regimes as diverse as those of Vichy France (1940–45), the Fourth Republic (1945–59) and the Fifth Republic (after 1959).

Both Alice Milliat and Marie-Thérèse Eyquem made conscious decisions to terminate their respective connections with the world of sport. Disgusted by the dirty tricks of the International Olympic Committee, the International Association of Athletics Federations and the French Federation of Athletics (Fédération Française d'Athlétisme), Milliat gave up her efforts in 1936 and disappeared completely from the sport scene. Eyquem remained committed to a career as politician and feminist militant until 1965, a date that corresponded with the end of her term as president of the International Association of Physical Education and Sport for Girls and Women, and then ceased all efforts in the direction of sport. [11]

Married for four years only, Alice Milliat remained single until the end of her life and had no children. The same relative isolation was partly the case with Marie-Thérèse Eyquem, although everything indicates that her celibacy – she never married – was rather an assumed consequence of her hidden homosexuality. Both women shared a relationship with the provincial *petite-bourgeoisie* and a rather liberal education (in a more secular way for Alice Milliat and in a more Catholic one for Marie-Thérèse Eyquem) which allowed them to work and quickly acquire financial autonomy. Although both had relatively limited sporting experiences, each performed a leading role at the institutional level.

Their careers were thus quite similar, but with one major difference. In contrast to Marie-Thérèse Eyquem, Alice Milliat was never a feminist in any formal way and never belonged to any movement struggling for the emancipation of women or for their right to vote. In this sense she was a political militant, whereas Marie-Thérèse Eyquem was a feminist at both a personal and political level.

Leading Women's Sport: The Institutional Battles

In 1914 women's sport in France was still in its infancy. [12] Only an unassuming French Union of Women's Gymnastics (UFGF) existed. The UFGF had been established by a man, Mr Podesta, with six companies in Lyon in 1912, as a reaction to the reluctance of the powerful male-dominated Union des Sociétés de Gymnastique de France (USGF). The main sports federation in the country, the Union des Sociétés Françaises de Sports Athlétiques (USFSA) was not ready to recognize and accept the presence of women, promoting instead a hegemonic masculinity. [13] During the Great War, however, the absence of men (who were required on the Front) accelerated a movement that previously had been barely perceptible. The first French championship of athletics for women was held between the three major Parisian women's sport clubs in July 1917: Académia, En Avant and Fémina-Sport. [14] In December of the same year, two men, Pierre Paysse from Fémina-Sport and Albert Pelan from En-Avant, decided to create the Fédération des Sociétés Féminines Sportives de France (FSFSF). The FSFSF became an official organization in January 1918 with Dr. Baudet, a male surgeon, as president. It was in this context, at the end of the Great War, that Alice Milliat underwent her first experiences as a sports leader. Indeed, in the very same month of January 1918, Pierre Payssé offered her the presidency of Fémina Sport, which he had founded in 1911; he also proposed her name as treasurer of the FSFSF. In June 1918, she was named general secretary of the FSFSF and in March 1919 took over the presidency in the place of Dr Baudet.

Under her jurisdiction the federation stimulated the development of women's sports in the country. Within three years, the membership had grown from 14 clubs in 1920 to 70 in 1921 and 130 in 1922. [15] The circumstances had been favourable enough for the FSFSF in 1919 to have received the approval of a male institution par excellence, the Ministry of War. The patronage of the president of the Republic was given the following year. Alice Milliat then was regularly invited to the various committees in charge of the development of physical education and sport. She was supported by a very influential politician, Henry Pate, known as the first instigator of sport policies in France, [16] who accepted the honorary presidency of the FSFSF. The female federation also had the support of Adolphe Chéron, another member of parliament who was favourable to physical activities and the very active president of an influential federation linked to the army: the Union des Sociétés d'Education Physique et de Préparation Militaire. [17] Alice Milliat was even called upon to participate in the inter-allied congress held at the Sorbonne in April 1919, where she presented a report on the organization of physical education and sports for women. The following year she was invited by the Minister of Social Hygiene to take part in the inter-ministerial commission in charge of the study of the organization of sports and physical education in the country.

Despite her early successes, Alice Milliat had, from the beginning, to fight against the negativity of the sports press. [18] The newspaper *L'Auto* eventually tried to destabilize her, establishing a rival federation in 1925 which did not last long. Not only did the FSFSF have to face the reactions of the sports movement itself at a time when most of the sports federations were in their early stages, [19] Milliat's idea that sport should be open to women with the same regulations and conditions as men shocked the more conservative women who were members of a rival federation, the Fédération Française Féminine de Gymnastique et d'Éducation Physique (FFFGEP). Influenced by the patriarchal norms of French society, the FFFGEP had more success than Alice Milliat's federation with more than 500 clubs in 1928 – a level never reached by the FSFSF.

In May 1935, at the age of 51, Milliat left the presidency of the FSFSF – which in 1922 had been renamed Fédération Française Sportive Féminine – citing ill-health as the reason for her departure. For 15 years her activism had been directly responsible for both the development of female basketball, football and athletics in France and the institutionalization of women's sport at the international level.

Although supported by different networks, the work of Marie-Thérèse Eyquem can be seen partly as a continuation of that of Alice Milliat. When, in March 1937, the Catholic sports association called Rayon Sportif Féminin became the Fédération Catholique d'Education Physique Féminine and enlarged its influence throughout the whole country, Marie-Thérèse Eyquem remained the general secretary of the new structure just as she had been in the former organization. An ardent proponent of women's sports in the Catholic movement, she multiplied the number of members in the federation by ten within four years. [20] In 1939, she joined the Ministry of Information, taking a position of senior writer for the Presidency of the Council within the General Commissariat of Information. The political circumstances of the time – the beginning of the Second World War – quickly enhanced her position. After a few months of the *Blitzkrieg*, the new government of Marshal Pétain was located in the southern part of France in Vichy in 1940. A *Commissariat* for 'General Education and Sport' was immediately created. Its head was the former tennis champion Jean Borotra, who needed a writer for the department of information and propaganda. Marie-Thérèse Eyquem had the right profile: professionally, she could claim a similar experience at both the Ministry of Information and the Rayon Sportif Féminin; moreover, her Catholic education provided guarantees for a government whose human and ideological links with the traditional church were extremely strong. Under these circumstances the position evolved and Jean Borotra immediately appointed the 27-year-old Marie-Thérèse Eyquem as director of women's sports for France on 17 August 1940. [21] Following the replacement of Jean Borotra by Colonel Jep Pascot in April 1942 in order to tighten the policies of the regime, she became a special assistant for women's physical education and sports. During these four years, she was extremely active in implementing the ideas of the Commissariat for General Education and Sport for women. She developed the collaboration between the various women's sport federations. She created training courses through which 6000 female physical education instructors were trained during a single year. She was at the head of initiatives for propaganda such as the Sports Festival on 5 July 1942, which brought together almost 50,000 gymnasts throughout the country. [22]

It would probably be incorrect to consider Marie-Thérèse's actions as the single cause of the considerable evolution of women's participation in sport in France during the Vichy period. French historian Jean-Louis Gay-Lescot has argued with conviction that the success of sport at this time could be explained by sport's capacity to provide people a temporary feeling of freedom and the possibility of escaping the unbearable pressures of everyday life. [23] However, one has to note that, with a hundred new clubs created every month, [24] women's sports increased more than men's sports. There were 14,000 women in 2250 clubs in 1939, and the numbers grew to 26,700 women in 3,700 clubs by 1943. Between 1938 and 1946, the number of members increased from 1,000 to 18,000 in basketball and from 1,500 to 6,000 in athletics. It took almost 20 years to observe a similar dynamic in France.

Yet Marie-Thérèse Eyquem had to accept the merger of the Rayon Sportif Féminin with FGSPF by order of the Vichy government, meaning the end of the very last female sport federation in France. However, the beneficial effects of her actions allowed her to escape from the sanctions thaht were served upon the collaborators of the Vichy regime at the Liberation. [25] On 1 May 1945 she was nominated inspector in the new General Direction of Youth and Sport which replaced the former structure. She kept this position until 1961, when she was promoted to Principal Inspector of Youth and Sport. She then took advantage of her institutional position to further promote women's sports in the country, departing from this path during the 1960s to focus upon militant feminism and political action within the Socialist Party.

Sport and the Gender Order in France

Despite the differences between the two periods under consideration, the comparison between the struggles of these two female sport leaders is made possible by the continuation of strong patriarchal values and the efforts of both women on behalf of female sport in France between the 1920s and the 1960s. Despite the feminist achievements of both at political and social levels, [26] the continuities are more important than the ruptures, as has been highlighted in several works exploring gender issues during this long period. [27] In other words, with the exception of the two brief periods, 1918–22 and 1940–44, during which the contradictory feeling of vulnerability and the euphoria of post-war could have encouraged certain initiatives, Alice Milliat and Marie-Thérèse Eyquem both worked in a rather conservative context where men generally remained the masters of the game.

A good illustration of these continuities is reflected in the famous formula of Dr Maurice Boigey, who worked at the Military School of Joinville-Le-Pont, the institution which, in France, was officially in charge of the definition of physical education in the 1920s: 'The nature of women is not to fight, but to procreate.' [28] The sentence, first published in 1922, was used once more in the book of the *Méthode Française* in 1925, which remained the official guide for all schools until the mid-1960s in the country. [29]

Examples of discourses strongly criticizing sportswomen were as numerous in the 1950s as they were in the 1920s. The ideal role of woman was still seen as mother and housewife. She was viewed as physically under-developed and therefore unable to train or exercise too intensely. Only measured, methodical and controlled physical activities were recommended for her, far from the excesses of sport. The best practices were walking, skipping, racket games, fencing and swimming, not football and athletics. For Boigey, competitive sports for women were not only unnecessary but also risky, because 'every exercise with clashes, shocks and shakings is dangerous for the uterus'. [30]

During the 1920s, while female homosexuality became more visible through styles of dress and behaviours, these representations reflected also the conservative fear of an inversion of gender codes. [31] The model of the flapper scared society. [32] Female sport brought on suspicions of inverted sexuality and androgyny. Even the federations that were less hostile to the participation of sporting women adopted the assumption of the natural vulnerability of women and invented regulatory devices to limit their participation and reduce the physiological and moral risks. Women should play *barrette* rather than rugby, i.e. a game for children in which physical contact was lower. [33] Rather than football, they should engage in a ball game played on a smaller field with a smaller ball, more rests and special regulations restricting contact. [34] Water polo was replaced with 'push-ball' [35] In athletics, women could run 100 metres, but not 800 metres; they could practise high jump but not pole vaulting; they could throw a weight of 4 kilos but not one of 7.257 kilos. Conversely, the champions of the inter-war period were seen as exceptional phenomena who could not serve as models, as confirmed by the discourses accompanying the exploits of tennis player Suzanne Lenglen, the swimmer Suzanne Wurtz or the pilots Hélène Boucher and Maryse Bastier. [36]

These conceptions remained largely unchanged in France during and after the Second World War. [37] The 'national revolution' that Marshal Pétain called for directly affected gender identities. France was asked to 'return' to her traditional values. Men should be more virile, women healthier. Masculinity even became perceived as the real backbone of General Education and Georges Hébert's 'natural method' the main reference of physical education. It was also the basis for the implementation of *chantiers de jeunesse* (youth camps) by General de la Porte du Theil in 1940. He took inspiration from both the army and the Scouts to create a structure in which all young men should proceed after the army to become tougher through obligatory exercise. [38] As for the women, sport was officially expected to develop their natural qualities of womanhood and motherhood. For them, according to historian Hélène Eck, 'the project of the Révolution Nationale … built a symbolic and ideal universe of motherhood, family and home'. [39] Dance, gymnastics, swimming and basketball were considered women's activities *par excellence*.

In the years that followed the Liberation, sport remained a man's affair in France. Of the 1.8 million people who were members of the federation in 1949, women only accounted for 4.3 per cent. In 1956, the French selection for the Olympic Games in Melbourne had only 18 women in a total of 140, i.e. less than 15 per cent of the delegation. In the press and on the radio, the only champions whose exploits were praised were men. The most media-focused championships such as the Tour de France, the five-nations tournament in rugby and the World Cup in football highlighted the values of masculinity. [40] However, the best athlete of the moment was arguably a woman, Micheline Ostermeyer, a triple medallist at the Olympic Games in London in 1948. [41] During the 1950s, masculinity remained defined by the expression and the control of power and physical strength (being individual or collective), success, family hierarchy, a desire for openness and large spaces, heterosexuality and the rejection of women from the areas where men dominated the scene. [42] As for sporting femininity, it demanded moral duty, modesty, awareness of the women's 'natural' weaknesses (menstruation, physical strength, psychological fragility) and fulfilment of her expected social functions: maternity and marriage.

War Context as Opportunity

Alice Milliat's and Marie-Thérèse Eyquem's achievements are of considerable and even astonishing importance given that they had to fight so hard against the patriarchal and conservative French society and its sport institutions. Fortunately, both female sport leaders were clever and to some extent lucky enough to use the opportunities presented by the particular context of the immediate post-war period. Indeed, one cannot fail but be surprised by the successful ways in which both women were able to impose themselves on the national scene and by the rapidity with which they gained sufficient power to develop their policies. In a way, everything was played out within only four years – between 1918 and 1922 for Alice Milliat and between 1940 and 1944 for Marie-Thérèse Eyquem, i.e. precisely in the aftermath of the two world wars which tore the twentieth century apart and affected French soil deeply and dramatically.

There is no coincidence in this statement. The Great War created the possibility of an increased freedom, for women in France were able to demonstrate that they could run the factories while their fathers and husbands were at the Front. [43] But what was possible in the context of war and demobilization was no longer acceptable once the nation returned to 'working order'. By 1920, French society had reverted to its conservative values [44] and multiplied the signs of a return to the traditional gender order and male domination. [45] The country developed, for instance, an ambitious policy to support a rising birth rate and enforced the laws against abortion. The scandalous book *La Garçonne* (The Flapper), of which one million copies were sold in 1922, caused its author, Victor Margueritte, to be removed from the Légion d'Honneur for having praised female homosexuality. [46]

The war, however, profoundly impacted the representations of the 'other'. Spectacles of violence and atrocities, the pain of injuries, exposure to death, demographic decline, the unbearable spectacle of the handicapped, disabled and other *gueules cassées* (broken faces), [47] but also the separation of couples and the guilty frustration of sexual desires, all led the *poilus* to redefine what a man was. [48] The context of war caused an intense sense of vulnerability among the French population and its soldiers. After 1920, moreover, the memory of the trenches stimulated the need to live more intensely in the present and resulted in new habits and behaviours reflected by the so-called 'roaring twenties'. Thus Alice Milliat was able to use the destabilization of pre-war certitudes to her advantage. The temporary modification of the gender order left her more space for action, at least with enough time to engage a set of institutional actions that otherwise would not have been so easily initiated.

Similarly, Marie-Thérèse Eyquem took from the war context an ability to reach an institutional position which gave her the opportunity to implement her ideas. Here again, the defeat of 1940 had immediate consequences for the definition of both masculinities and femininities, [49] together with an increasing sense of vulnerability that was reinforced by the presence of the Nazi troops and the Gestapo, the threat of the deportation, ration coupons and more generally by the extremely precarious living conditions of the civilian population. The effectiveness and the favourable perception of Marie-Thérèse Eyquem's actions after 1940 could be partly explained by the fact that she provided institutional responses and positive perspectives for women, while not contributing (only apparently, however) to the ideology of the *Révolution Nationale* of Marshal Pétain. After 1945, her further actions benefited from the euphoria of the Liberation in a context where women enjoyed social and political progress for a brief time, the most significant of which was the right to vote.

Thus the context of war created particular opportunities for both Alice Milliat and Marie-Thérèse Eyquem through which they were able to develop various strategies in order to achieve their goals.

Strategies: International Legitimacy

The use of international legitimacy to strengthen a national position is a classic strategy in the institutional history of sport. At the beginning of the twentieth century, for instance, the French federations were among the most active in the creation of international federations for that particular reason. Their wish was not the dissemination of principles of universalism but rather a way to impose their power in France, as has been demonstrated in the case of swimming, football, fencing and skiing. [50] Alice Milliat and Marie-Thérèse Eyquem adopted the same strategy in different contexts. Their position in France was fragile because of the low status of women's sport but was indirectly enhanced by their access to international leadership.

Indeed, the hostility Alice Milliat and the FSFSF (formerly known as FFSF) had to face in France led her to rapidly look for a strategic rapprochement with international sporting bodies to ensure that women were accepted at this level. For her, undoubtedly, the fact that the international federations would be open to women would have put strong pressure on the French federations. However, Alice Milliat's approaches to the international federations, including the most prestigious ones such as the International Association of Athletics Federations (IAAF) in 1921, received more or less polite rebuffs. [51] As for the IOC, the position of Pierre de Coubertin towards women athletes was well known: 'We believe that the Olympics should be reserved for men.' [52] For him, despite some exceptions in golf, tennis, archery and swimming, the Olympic Games should remain closed to women. Until his very last Olympics as IOC president in Paris in 1924, Pierre de Coubertin clung to his conservative principles, [53] despite the fact that Alice Milliat would have liked the French capital to welcome athletes of both sexes equally. [54]

Finding absolutely no support from the governing sport bodies which all agreed to maintain male hegemony, Milliat took the initiative of organizing the First International Meeting for women in athletics and physical education in Monte Carlo in April 1921, which was described by the press as the 'Women's Olympics'. Two other sports meetings were held in subsequent years. At the end of one held in Paris in October 1921, several months after the success of Monte Carlo, Alice Milliat proposed the creation of a Federation Sportive Féminine Internationale. With the support of the delegations of England, the United States, France, Italy and Czechoslovakia, the FSFI was born on 31 October 1921. The FSFI did not immediately elect a president, but Alice Milliat was strongly acclaimed to this position the following year. [55] With this new legitimacy, she defended the idea that women should take part in the Olympic Games with the same programme as the men's, though de Coubertin remained deaf to her wishes.

As a consequence, Alice Milliat organized the first 'Women's Olympic Games' in the Pershing Stadium in Paris in August 1922, with 300 female participants from five countries. The IOC reacted soon after and obliged her to rename the event 'First World Women's Games'. A second meeting followed in Goteborg (Sweden) in 1926 with eight nations, and then a third in Prague in 1930 with 16 nations. The last one was held in London in 1934. [56]

The strategy of Alice Milliat was relatively successful, but women lost their institutional autonomy during the process. The withdrawal of Pierre de Coubertin from the IOC's presidency in 1925 and his replacement by Comte Henri de Baillet-Latour paved the way for the integration of women in the forthcoming Olympic Games in Amsterdam in 1928. [57] Alice Milliat even succeeded in approaching the IOC as a member of the arbitration committee at these games. In spite of the 'incident' in the 800 metres athletic event during which one of the female runners collapsed, creating a huge debate within the IOC and subsequent discussions within the IAAF until the mid-1930s, the trend towards the integration of women into mainstream sport structures had become inevitable. The process, however, was also a sign of the end of specific female sport federations, without any guarantee of a representation of women in the male-dominated institutions. Still, in 1934 Alice Milliat sent a warning message to the world of sport:

> The FSFI will accept to give up the Women's World Games if a full program of women's athletics is included in the Olympic Games and under the condition that women are represented within the IOC. The FSFI also notes that the IOC is less and less willing to open the Olympic Games to women in all sports. For now, it is preferable to keep the Women's World Games which accept all female sports. [58]

Nevertheless, following the example of the Olympic Games in 1928, several major international federations decided to integrate women from 1936 on, causing the collapse of the FSFI. [59] A similar process occurred in France. Alice Milliat's FSFSF soon lost football thanks to the lack of players, then basketball in March 1936 with the withdrawal of the mandate previously given by the French Federation of Basketball, [60] followed by athletics when a French Federation of Women's Athletics was created within the French Federation of Athletics in May 1936. The death-blow was dealt by the French government itself, when it decided to put an end to the subsidies previously granted to the women's federation, which was finally disbanded in May 1936. [61]

Although it was successful for only a limited time, the strategy of using international legitimacy for national purposes was obvious. It was a strategy also used, although less strongly, by Marie-Thérèse Eyquem after the Second |World War. Moreover, the French sport leader constituted, together with American Dorothy Ainsworth and German Liselott Diem, an international network of militants aimed at promoting female physical education and sport. [62] As an Inspector of Youth and Sports, Marie-Thérèse Eyquem had less opportunity than Alice Milliat to travel abroad, but her position enabled her to meet the former president of the National Association of Physical Education for College Women (NAPECW), Dorothy Ainsworth, during her stay in Paris in 1947. According to Ann Hall and Gertrud Pfister, both women had a great deal of correspondence during these years. [63] When, in 1949, Dorothy Ainsworth organized the founding congress of the International Association of Physical Education and Sports for Girls and Women (IAPESGW) in Copenhagen, Marie-Thérèse Eyquem was one of the 200 delegates. She successfully organized the second congress of the association in Paris in 1953. On this occasion, she became vice president of the executive committee and Dorothy Ainsworth remained the chairperson. She kept this position during two successive terms until 1961, when she took over the presidency for four years. At a time when France was undergoing political instability and colonial troubles, leading to the decline of the Fourth Republic and the advent of the Fifth under the presidency of Charles de Gaulle (1959), Marie-Thérèse Eyquem multiplied international initiatives. In 1958, she contributed, for instance, to the establishment of the International Council for Health, Physical Education, Recreation, Sport and Dance (ICHPER) and served on its executive committee from 1961 on. She also became president of the Women's Commission of the Federation Internationale Catholique d'Education Physique (FICEP) [64] when this commission was created in 1947. She contributed to the creation of the International Council of Sport and Physical Education (ICSPE, later ICSSPE) in 1960 and immediately became a member of its executive board. [65] According to Ann Hall and Gertrud Pfister, her deepest wish was to become an IOC member – the first female one ever – but she was 'only' able to became the president of the French Pierre de Coubertin Committee in 1956. [66]

As president of the IAPESGW, the achievements of Marie-Thérèse Eyquem were relatively modest. However, unlike Alice Milliat's FSFI, all the institutions whose creation she contributed to survived and still retain influence. Moreover one can consider all her international initiatives as a strategy of international self-legitimization. Just as with Alice Milliat, the opportunities to influence decisions in France supported an increase in her symbolic weight at the international level.

Two Similar Conceptions of Physical Activity for Women?

Alice Milliat and Marie-Thérèse Eyquem campaigned for the development of women's participation in sport through their institutional initiatives, but also through the many texts they published in the feminist, sport and general press. These actions and discourses provide a relatively good idea of the conceptions and ideas that they promoted.

In contrast to Marie-Thérèse Eyquem, Alice Milliat did not synthesize her ideas into a book. One must be thankful to Nathalie Rosol for having collected most of her articles in her thesis. [67] This young sport historian has argued effectively that Alice Milliat had a double-edged discourse, alternating, challenging and disturbing proposals for the male community while supporting the gender order in other aspects. On the one hand, for instance, she wanted women to practise the same sports as men, including competitive sports. She also refused to allow men to become executives within the SFSFS in order to let the women have all the power: 'No males! No males!' proclaimed one of its members, Jeanne May, in 1920. [68] On the other hand, the president of the women's federation did not hesitate to promote discourses in favour of a rising birth rate. Sport, it was said in the bulletin of the FSFSF, gives 'an abdominal vigour, a heart force, a nervous resistance, to better address the role of women: motherhood'. [69] In the *Miroir des Sports*, whose readers were mostly male, Alice Milliat gave the same pledge of submission to the gender order: 'We need strong women able to give France healthy, strong and numerous children. ... Our goal is not to change women into phenomena who are capable of breaking records, trying to match male performance.' [70] The ability of sport not to take from women their beauty or even to make them more beautiful was also an argument often repeated: 'Our young female athletes were able to convince the public that the practice of athletic sports by women is necessary and could only develop grace, flexibility and health.' [71] The fact that the FSFSF used physiological tests to assess its members shows that it did not totally reject medical norms. [72] Finally, Alice Milliat was not opposed to a more educational and moderate approach to physical activity. The most controversial competitions such as the Olympics in Monte Carlo were accompanied by demonstrations of physical education and dance performed by Irène Popard and her students.

This mix of tradition and modernity could also be found throughout the career of Marie-Thérèse Eyquem. [73] She prepared, for instance, two biographies within a couple of years magnifying for one Pierre de Coubertin, for the other Irene Popard, reflecting the ambiguity of her conceptions. [74] But it is in *La Femme et le sport*, published in 1944, that she summed up best her approach towards women's sport. [75] Although written under the censorship imposed by the Vichy government, the book conformed fully to the conservative ideals of the time and to the traditional definitions of women's sport. The most suitable activities for women remained gymnastics, moderate athletics, swimming, basketball and outdoor sports. Physical education was presented as a necessary complement to sport. Competition was considered unsafe if it was not sufficiently regulated and controlled. [76] For the woman, the aim of physical activity was health, aesthetic values and motherhood: it allowed her to 'keep the muscle flexible, to increase her tone, to have easy maternity, to stay young longer'. [77] Eyquem's purpose was even more explicit after the Liberation, when she indicated in the *Encyclopédie générale des sports* in 1946 that the woman 'has the duty to educate her children well and to make her home comfortable, but also that she has the right, like every active human nature, to enjoy distraction before the labour to go back to work with greater courage afterwards'. [78]

Despite their militancy in favour of women's sport, Alice Milliat and Marie-Thérèse Eyquem did not break radically with the dominant models of their time. Their institutional initiatives reflected a conception that was more respectful of the gender order than might be supposed at first glance. Or was it only a strategy aimed at seducing the conservatism of the sport federations to better develop their ideas, as argued by French historian Nathalie Rosol? In the case of Marie-Thérèse Eyquem, it is possible to reach the same conclusion when considering the turn she took in the mid-1960s. Indeed, she accepted the presidency of an explicitly feminist and non-communist left movement, the Mouvement démocratique féminin (MDF), in 1965. The MDF was one of the most militant movements of the time, advocating free contraception, a reform of the matrimonial laws and support for the promotion of women in work. Through its journal, *La femme du XXème siècle*, it updated the positions of Simone de Beauvoir, but was finally overtaken by an even more radical trend after the revolution of May 1968: the Mouvement de Libération de la Femme (MLF). [79] On 13 October 1965, Marie-Thérèse Eyquem used her new position in the MDF to make the decision during a general assembly that the MDF would support the candidacy of François Mitterrand for the future presidential elections against Charles de Gaulle. She then became a member of the Fédération de la Gauche Démocrate et Socialiste then later of the Socialist Party and a few months later joined the counter-government of François Mitterrand. [80] Within 20 years, Marie-Thérèse Eyquem moved from a structure headed by the collaborationist right-wing government of Vichy to the Socialist Party. Some might see here pure opportunism; others may see more the evidence of a lucid strategy for the development of women's sport.

Conclusion

Despite the similarity of so many of their efforts, the roads of Alice Milliat and Marie-Thérèse Eyquem do not seem to have crossed. Alice Milliat, once removed from the sporting life after 1936, no longer commented on sport matters and never wrote about the actions of the one who, at least symbolically, succeeded her. Marie-Thérèse Eyquem, for her part, delivered in *La Femme et le sport* a few remarks about the former president of the FSFSF. In a couple of pages, she painted a flattering portrait of Alice Milliat, though her tribute was, to some extent, associated with a degree of moderation:

> I do not personally know Ms Milliat. I've heard both many good and many bad things about her, from which I deduced that she might have had a strong personality. Every superior being has enemies. Those who have approached her have kept as much admiration as esteem for her. Those who were ousted by her hold a grudge against her. What's more natural! She made mistakes. Who does not, if one excludes the amorphous? She was determined. It is a wonderful quality. ... For us who are judging fairly on the facts ... we find that she was the most significant figure of the French female sport between the two wars. ... She has left more than a name, a work; this needed to be said. [81]

Perhaps one could read within these lines a few criticisms addressed to someone who did not always know how to deal with male sporting power. In this great game of strategy, Marie-Thérèse Eyquem was obviously more artful than her predecessor. Beyond their differences and their similarities, the two sport leaders were nevertheless representatives of two forms of feminism, more strictly militant for the first one, more political for the second. In this sense, their work reflects the diversity of the initiatives that women had to take in France as elsewhere to challenge the gender order and prise open the doors of the stadium for women. [82]

Notes

[1] The name of Alice Milliat is deeply associated with the FSFI and is systematically mentioned in the works on the history of international women's sport. The name of Marie-Thérèse Eyquem appears especially in the works on de Coubertin, thanks to her book which glorifies the founder of the modern Olympic Games, Pierre de Coubertin, *l'Épopée Olympique*. It is also frequently associated with the history of women's sport in France in the 1940s and 1950s, thanks to another of her important books, *La Femme et le sport*.

[2] Leigh and Bonin, 'The Pioneering Role', 72–83.

[3] Both were published under my supervision. A large part of this paper is based on their work: Prudhomme-Poncet, 'Ces Dames du Ballon Rond'; Prudhomme-Poncet, *Histoire du Football*; Rosol, 'L'Athlétisme Français'. See also Rosol, 'Pour une Participation'; Rosol, 'Le Sport Vers le Féminisme'; Rosol, '"Faites vos Jeux!"'

[4] Drevon, *Alice Milliat*. A movie has been made by the author (*Alice Milliat, La Conquête du Sport Féminin*, 50 minutes, 2003). One must also highlight the chapter 'Les Batailles d'Alice Milliat' in Hubscher *et al.*, *L'histoire en Mouvement*.

[5] Munoz, 'Marie-Thérèse Eyquem'.

[6] Hall and Pfister, *Honoring the Legacy*.

[7] For a synthesis in English on the petite-bourgeoisie 'of the Belle-Epoque, see especially Crossik and Haupt, *The Petite-bourgeoisie*.

[8] For some hints on the history of this sports club, which was the largest female one in France in the 1920s, see Rosol, 'L'Athlétisme Français'.

[9] Geneviève Eyquem, interviewed by Laurence Munoz, 13 Jan. 2000, quoted in Munoz, 'Marie-Thérèse Eyquem'.

[10] A gendered history of the RCF is provided by Munoz, 'Le Rayon Sportif'.

[11] She published only three short papers in *La Femme du XXème Siècle*, which was the journal of the Mouvement Démocratique Féminin (Terret and Ottogalli-Mazzacavallo, 'Body, Sport and Feminist Movements').

[12] For an analysis of women's sport in France before the Great War, see Terret, 'Femmes, Sport, Identité'.

[13] Terret, *Sport et Genre*, vol. 4, 355–76. At this time, gymnastics and sport reflected two totally opposing conceptions of physical activity and were supported by radically different organizations. See Arnaud, *La Naissance*.

[14] En-Avant was first created as an association of gymnastics in 1912 before moving to sport during the war. Fémina-Sport and Académia were respectively created in 1912 and 1915. All three were located in Paris.

[15] *La Femme Sportive* 1 (1 May 1921); *La Française*, 14 Jan. 1922.

[16] Defrance, 'Histoire de Vie', 77–88.

[17] On the actions of Chéron, see Spivak, 'Education, Sport'.

[18] See for instance the newspaper *Le Miroir des Sports*, 16 Aug. 1923.

[19] See Hubscher, *L'Histoire en Mouvement*; Defrance, 'Le Sport Fançais', 79–106.

[20] Munoz, *Histoire du Sport Catholique*.

[21] See Munoz, 'Marie-Thérèse Eyquem'.

[22] Drigny, 'Le Triomphe', 1.

[23] Gay-Lescot, *Sport et Éducation*.

[24] Eyquem, 'Sportives Françaises', 1.

[25] Amar et Gay-Lescot, 'Sport dans la Tourmente', 377–94.

[26] Goubin *et al.*, *Le Siècle des Féminismes*.

[27] See for instance Bard, *Un Siècle d'Antiféminisme*. For an extensive view on women's sport in France, see Arnaud and Terret, *Histoire du Sport Féminine*; Terret, *Sport et Genre*. For a synthesis of this period, see Terret, 'Femmes, Sport'.

[28] Boigey, Manuel Scientifique, 200–203.

[29] Ministère de la Guerre, *Règlement Général d'Éducation Physique*; Simonet, *L'INSEP*.

[30] Boigey, *Manuel Scientifique*.

[31] Bard, *Les Garçonnes*.

[32] For an analysis of these representations, see Terret, 'Sports and Erotica'.

[33] Pociello, *Le Rugby*.

[34] *L'Auto*, 2 March 1922.

[35] De Villepion, *Nageons!*

[36] On the representation of Suzanne Lenglen, see Veray, 'Entre Héroïsation et Féminisme', 39–61. And more generally on this issue see Davisse and Louveau, *Sport, Ecole, Société*.

[37] Terret, 'LLes Femmes et le Sport', 287–307.

[38] Chevallier, *L'Ordre Viril*, 41. See on this issue Lascaud and Dutheil, 'Pratiques Physiques'; Delaplace, 'La Méthode Naturelle'. For a synthesis, see Pecout, *Les Chantiers*.

[39] Eck, 'Les Françaises Sous Vichy', 288.

[40] On the relationships between these sport events and the construction of masculinity, see for instance Terret, 'Le Tour', 211–38; Dine, *French Rugby*.

[41] For a biography, see Bloit, *Micheline Ostermeyer*. A more comprehensive approach was recently published by Erard, 'Micheline Ostermeyer'.

[42] See especially here Terret, 'Sport et Genre dans la Presse Sportive', 263–97.

[43] Thébaud, *La Femme au Temps*; Thébaud, 'La Grande Guerre', 31–74.

[44] Sohn, 'Chronologie et Dialectique'.

[45] Rauch, *L'Identité Masculine*.

[46] Bard, *Les Garçonnes*.
[47] Prost, *Les Anciens Combattants*.
[48] Capdevila, 'L'Identité Masculine'; Capdevila *et al.*, *Hommes et Femmes*.
[49] Duchen, 'Une Femme Nouvelle'.
[50] On the role of the French Federation of Swimming in the creation of the FINA, see Terret, *Histoire et Développement*. On the role of the French institutions on the creation of the FIFA in football, see Eisenberg *et al.*, *Cent Ans de Football*. On the action of the French sport leaders in the creation of the International Federation of Fencing and of the International Ski Federation, see Ottogalli-Mazzacavallo and Terret, 'The Foundation of the International Federation''; see also Arnaud and Terret, *Le Rêve Blanc*.
[51] Boulogne and Lennartz, *Un Siècle du CIO*, 225.
[52] Pierre de Coubertin quoted in *Revue Olympique*, July 1912.
[53] Auger, 'Une Histoire Politique'.
[54] Rosol, Rosol, '"Faites vos Jeux!"'
[55] Registre de la FSFI, Musée National du Sport, quoted by Drevon, *Alice Milliat*, 55.
[56] See especially Drevon, *Alice Milliat* for a detailed description of these events.
[57] Carpentier, *Le Comité International*.
[58] Minutes of the 12th congress of the IAAF, Stockholm, 28–29 Aug. 1934, 82–4 (IAAF Archives, Monaco).
[59] Minutes of the 13th congress of the IAAF, Berlin, July 1936, 19–21.
[60] *L'Auto*, 25 March 1936.
[61] *L'Auto*, 28 May 1936.
[62] Hall and Pfister, *Honoring the Legacy*.
[63] Ibid., 6.
[64] On the FICEP, see especially Groeninger, *Sport, Religion et Nation*.
[65] Bailey, *Science in the Service*, 44.
[66] Hall and Pfister, *Honoring the Legacy*, 55.
[67] Rosol, 'L'Athlétisme Français'.
[68] Jeanne May, 'Pas de Mâles! Pas de Mâles', *La Vie au Grand Air*, March–April 1920, 59.
[69] *La Femme Sportive* 1 (1 May 1921), 1.
[70] Alice Milliat, quoted in *Le Miroir des Sports*, July 1920, 34.
[71] *Bulletin Officiel du Racing Club de France*, 15 July 1920, 2.
[72] Milliat, 'Les Sports Féminins'.
[73] The same idea is also argued by Munoz, 'Marie-Thérèse Eyquem'.
[74] Eyquem, *Pierre de Coubertin*; Eyquem, *Irène Popard*.
[75] Eyquem, *La Femme et le Sport*, 290–1. She wrote also many editorials in the *Bulletin du Rayon Sportif Féminin* and published extensively in *Les Jeunes*, the journal of the FGSPF and in *Tous les Sports*, the journal of the Comité National des Sport under the Vichy régime.
[76] Eyquem, 'Connaissez-vous', 1; Eyquem, 'Comment est Organisé', 1.
[77] Eyquem, *La Femme et le Sport*, 290–1.
[78] Eyquem, 'Le Sport Féminin'.
[79] Chaperon, *Les Années Beauvoir*, 337; Picq, *Libération des Femmes*; Zancarini-Fournel, 'Genre et Politique'.
[80] Three years before her death in 1975 she was appointed national secretary of the Socialist Party in charge of the relationships with the associations. Together with Edith Cresson she was at this time the only woman to have reached this level of responsibility within the Socialist Party.
[81] Eyquem, *La Femme et le Sport*, 51–2.
[82] This paper is written with the support of the programme 'PRAS-GEVU: Violence, genre et pratique sportive' (ANR-08-VULN-001/PRAS-GEVU) of the National Agency for Research.

References

Amar M. and J.L. Gay-Lescot. 'Le Sport Dans la Tourmente, de Vichy à la Libération'. In *Histoire du Sport en France*, edited by P. Tétart. Paris: Vuibert, 2007.

Arnaud, P. *La Naissance du Mouvement Sportif Associatif en France*. Lyon: Presses Universitaires de Lyon, 1985.

Arnaud, P. and T. Terret. *Le Rêve Blanc, Olympisme et Sport d'Hiver*. Bordeaux: Presses Universitaires de Bordeaux, 1993.

Arnaud, P. and T. Terret, eds. *Histoire du Sport Féminine*. Paris: L'Harmattan, 1996.

Auger, F. 'Une Histoire Politique du Mouvement Olympique: l'Exemple de l'Entre-deux-guerres'. PhD diss., University Paris X-Nanterre, 1998.

Bailey. S. *Science in the Service of Physical Education and Sport*. Chichester: John Wiley, 1996.

Bard, C. *Les Garçonnes: Modes et Fantasmes des Années Folles*. Paris: Flammarion, 1998.

Bard, C., ed. *Un Siècle d'Antiféminisme*. Paris: Fayard, 1999.

Bloit, M. *Micheline Ostermeyer ou la Vie Partagée*. Paris: L'Harmattan, 1996.

Boigey, Maurice. *Manuel Scientifique d'Éducation Physique*. Paris: Masson, 1922.

Boulogne, Y.P. and K. Lennartz. *Un Siècle du CIO*, vol. 1: *1894–1942*. Lausanne: CIO, 1994.

Capdevila, L. 'L'Identité Masculine et les Fatigues de la Guerre (1914–1945)'. *Vingtième Siècle: Revue d'Histoire* 75 (2002): 97–108.

Capdevila, L., F. Rouquet, F. Virgili and D. Voldman, eds. *Hommes et Femmes dans la France en Guerre (1914–1945)*. Paris: Payot, 2003.

Carpentier, F. *Le Comité International Olympique en Crises: La Présidence de Henri de Baillet-Latour, 1925–1940*. Paris: L'Harmattan, 2004.

Chaperon, S. *Les Années Beauvoir, 1945–1975*. Paris: Fayard, 2000.

Chevallier. *L'Ordre Viril et L'Efficacité De L'Action, le Chef et Ses Jeunes*. No. 7, Série la Communauté Nationale, Uriage, éditions de l'Ecole nationale des cadres, 1941.

Crossik, G. and H.G. Haupt. *The Petite-bourgeoisie in Europe, 1870–1914: Enterprise, Family and Independence*. London: Routledge, 1997.

Davisse, A. and C. Louveau. *Sport, Ecole, Société: La différence des Sexes*. Paris: L'Harmattan, 1998.

Defrance, J. 'Histoire de Vie et Socio-Histoire du Champ Sportif: La Trajectoire Sportive et Politique d'Henry Paté'. In *Le Sportif, l'Entraîneur, Le Dirigeant*, edited by J.M. Delaplace. Paris: L'Harmattan, 1999.

Defrance, J. 'Le Sport Français Dans "l'entre-deux-guerres"'. In *Histoire du Sport en France*, edited by P. Tétart. Paris: Vuibert, 2007.

Delaplace, J.M. 'La Méthode Naturelle Dans les Chantiers de la Jeunesse (1940–1944)'. In *Le Sport et les Français Pendant l'Occupation*, edited by P. Arnaud, T. Terret, P. Gros and J. Saint-Martin. Paris: L'Harmattan, 2002.

De Villepion, G. *Nageons!*. Paris: Grasset, 1929.

Dine, P. *French Rugby Football: A Cultural History*. Oxford and New York: Berg, 2001.

Drevon, A. *Alice Milliat: La Pasionaria du Sport Féminin*. Paris: Vuibert, 2005.

Drigny, E.G. 'Le Triomphe de la Sportive'. *Tous les Sports* 53 (11 July 1942): 1.

Duchen, C. 'Une Femme Nouvelle Pour une France Nouvelle?' *Clio. Femmes, Histoire, Société* 1: *Résistances et Libérations. France 1940–1945*, no. 1 (1995).

Eck, H. 'Les Françaises Sous Vichy'. In *Histoire des Femmes en Occident*, vol. 5: *Le Vingtième Siècle*, edited by F. Thébaud. Paris: Plon, 1992.

Eisenberg, C., P. Lanfranchi, T. Mason and A. Wahl. *Cent Ans de Fotball Dans le Monde: Histoire de la FIFA (1904–2004)*. Paris: Le Cherche Midi, 2004.

Erard, C. 'Micheline Ostermeyer: l'exception normale d'une 'dissonance culturelle'. *STAPS* 76, no. 2 (2007): 67–78.

Eyquem, M.T. 'Connaissez-vous le Rayon Sportif Féminin'. *Les Jeunes* 3 (15 Jan. 1939): 1.

Eyquem, M.T. 'Sportives Françaises, Restez Toujours Unies'. *Tous les Sports* 20 (15 Nov. 1941): 1.

Eyquem, M.T. 'Comment est Organisé le Sport Féminin'. *Tous les Sports* 28 (1 Jan, 1942, deuxième année): 1.

Eyquem, M.T. *La Femme et le Sport*. Paris: Ed. J. Susse, 1944.

Eyquem, M.T. 'Le Sport Féminin'. In *Encyclopédie Générale des Sports* Paris: impr. de Montligeon, 1946.

Eyquem, M.T. *Irène Popard ou la Danse du Feu*. Paris: Les Éditions du Temps, 1959.

Eyquem, M.T. *Pierre de Coubertin, l'Épopée Olympique*. Paris: Calmann-Lévy, 1966.

Gay-Lescot, J.L. *Sport et Éducation Sous Vichy*. Lyon: Presses Universitaires de Lyon, 1991.

Goubin, E., C. Jacques, F. Rochefort, B. Studer, F. Thébaud and M. Zancarini-Fournel (eds) *Le Siècle des Féminismes*. Paris: Editions de l'Atelier, 2004.

Groeninger, F. *Sport, Religion et Nation*. Paris: L'Harmattan, 2004.

Hall, A. and G. Pfister. *Honoring the Legacy: Fifty Years of the International Association of Physical Education and Sport for Girls and Women*. Nanaimo: IAPESGW, 1999.

Hubscher, R., B. Jeu and J. Durry. *L'Histoire en Mouvement*. Paris: Armand Colin, 1992.

Lascaud, M. and F. Dutheil. 'Pratiques Physiques et Sportives, "Formation Virile et Morale" Dans les Chantiers de la Jeunesse, 1940–1944'. In *Le Sport et les Français Pendant l'Occupation. 1940–1944*, edited by P. Arnaud, T. Terret, P. Gros and J. Saint-Martin. Paris: L'Harmattan, 2002: 97–111.

Leigh, M.H. and T.M. Bonin. 'The Pioneering Role of Madame Alice Milliat and the FSFI'. *Journal of Sport History* 4, no. 1 (1977): 72–83.

Milliat, Alice. 'Les Sports Féminins'. *Almanach du Miroir des Sports*. Paris: Miroir des Sports, 1923.

Ministère de la Guerre. *Règlement Général d'Éducation Physique. Méthode Française*. Paris: Charles-Lavauzelle, 1927–1930.

Munoz, L. 'Marie-Thérèse Eyquem (1913–1978) Au Moment de l'Occupation'. In *Le Sport et les Français Pendant l'Occupation. 1940–1944*, edited by P. Arnaud, T. Terret, P. Gros and J. Saint-Martin. Paris: L'Harmattan, 2002: 65–72.

Munoz, L. *Histoire du Sport Catholique: La Fédération Sportive et Catholique de France (1898–2000)*. Paris: L'Harmattan, 2003.

Munoz, L. 'Le Rayon Sportif Féminin, De l'Éducation Physique aux Sports (1937–1967)'. In *Sport et Genre*, vol. 3: *Apprentissage du genre et institutions éducatives*, edited by J. Saint-Martin and T. Terret. Paris: L'Harmattan, 2005: 151–74.

Ottogalli-Mazzacavallo, C. and T. Terret. 'The Foundation of the International Federation of Fencing, Xith'. Paper presented at the ISHPES Congress, Stirling, Scotland, 14–18 July 2009.

Pecout, C., *Les Chantiers de la Jeunesse et la Revitalisation Physique et Morale de la Jeunesse Française (1940–1944)*. Paris: L'Harmattan, 2007.

Picq, F. *Libération des Femmes: Les Années Mouvements*. Paris: Seuil, 1993.

Pociello, C. *Le Rugby ou la Guerre des Styles*. Paris: Métailié, 1995.

Prost, A. *Les Anciens Combattants et la Société Française*. Paris: Presses de la Fondation Nationale des Sciences Politiques, 1977.

Prudhomme-Poncet, L. 'Ces Dames du Ballon Rond: Histoire du Football Féminin au XXème Siècle'. PhD diss., Université Lyon 1, 2002.

Prudhomme-Poncet, L. *Histoire du Football Féminin au XXe Siècle*. Paris: L'Harmattan, 2003.

Rauch, A. *L'Identité Masculine à l'Ombre des Femmes: De la Grande Guerre à la Gay Pride*. Paris: Hachette, 2004.

Rosol, N. 'Pour une Participation des Françaises aux Jeux olympiques (1900–1928): Un Combat Mené par Alice Milliat. In *Histoire du Sport Dans L'Entre-deux-guerres: Regards Croisés sur les Influences Étrangères*, edited by J.P. Saint-Martin and T. Terret. Paris: L'Harmattan, 2000.

Rosol, N. '"Le Sport Vers le Féminisme". L'Engagement du Milieu Athlétique Féminin Français au Temps de la FSFSF (1917–1936)'. *STAPS* 67 (Dec. 2004): 63–77.

Rosol, N. 'L'Athlétisme Français au Féminin (1912–Fin des Années 1970): Des Athlètes en Quête d'identité'. PhD diss., University Lyon 1, 2005.

Rosol, N. '"Faites vos Jeux!" Un Olympisme Féminin à Part?' In *Les Paris des Jeux Olympiques de 1924*, vol. 1: *Les Paris de la Candidature et de l'Organisation*, edited by T. Terret. Biarritz: Atlantica, 2008.

Simonet, P. *L'INSEP: De la Gymnastique Joinvillaise aux Sports Contemporains*. Paris: G. Klopp, 1998.

Sohn, A.M. 'Chronologie et Dialectique Entre Féminin et Masculin'. In *Le Genre Face aux Mutations*, edited by L. Capdevila. Rennes: Presses Universitaires de Rennes, 2004.

Spivak, M. 'Education, Sport et Nationalisme en France du Second Empire au Front Populaire: Un Aspect Original de la Défense Nationale'. State thesis, University of Paris 1 Sorbonne, 1983.

Terret, T. *Histoire et Développement de la Natation Sportive*. Paris: L'Harmattan, 1994.

Terret, T. 'Femmes, Sport, Identité et Acculturation: Eléments d'Historiographie Française'. *Stadion* XXVI, no. 1 (2000): 41–53.

Terret, T. 'Sports and Erotica: Erotic Postcards of Sportswomen during France's *Années Folles*'. *Journal of Sport History* 29, no. 2 (Summer 2002): 271–87.

Terret, T. 'Le Tour, les Hommes et les Femmes: Essai Sur la Visibilité Masculine et l'Invisibilité Féminine'. In *Maillot Jaune: Regards Croisés sur le Centenaire du Tour de France*, edited by P. Porte and D. Vila D. Biarritz: Atlantica, 2003.

Terret, T., ed. *Sport et Genre*, vol. 4: *'Objets, arts et médias'*. Paris: L'Harmattan, 2005.

Terret, T. 'Sport et Genre dans la Presse Sportive des Années Cinquante: L'Exemple de *Sport & Vie*'. In *Sport et Genre*, vol. 2: *'Excellence Féminine et Masculinité Hégémonique'*, edited by P. Liotard and T. Terret. Paris: L'Harmattan, 2005.

Terret, T. 'Les Femmes et le Sport de 1945 à Nos Jours'. In *Histoire du Sport en France*, vol. 2: *'De la Libération à Nos Jours'*, edited by P. Tétart. Paris: Vuibert, 2007.

Terret, T. 'Sport et Genre (1870–1945)'. In *Histoire du Sport en France:. Du Second Empire au Régime de Vichy*, edited by T. Tétart. Paris: Vuibert, 2007.

Terret, T. and C. Ottogalli-Mazzacavallo. 'Body, Sport and Feminist Movements in the Pre- and Post-Cultural Revolution of 1968 France'. Paper presented at the 4th meeting of the Transnational Scholars for the Study of Gender and Sport, Ludwigsburg, 28–30 Nov. 2008.

Thébaud, F. *La Femme au Temps de la Guerre de 14*. Paris: Stock, 1986.

Thébaud, F. 'La Grande Guerre: Le Triomphe de la Division Sexuelle'. In *Histoire des Femmes en Occident*, vol. 5: *Le Vingtième Siècle*, edited by F. Thébaud. Paris: Plon, 1992.

Veray, L. 'Entre Héroïsation et Féminisme: l'Image de Suzanne Lenglen de 1920 à 1926'. In *Images de la Femme Sportive*, edited by L. Guido and G. Haver. Geneva: Georg éditeur, 2003.

Zancarini-Fournel, M. 'Genre et Politique: Les Années 1968'. *Vingtième Siècle* 75 (July–Sept. 2002): 133–43.

Eliza Maria Mosher: Pioneering Woman Physician and Advocate for Physical Education

Alison M. Wrynn

Through her work as a prison physician, prison superintendent, college physician, college professor and university dean, Eliza Mosher touched in a substantive manner nearly every health-related career that women entered in the late nineteenth and early twentieth centuries. Mosher's benchmark work in the profession of physical education was of particular importance at a time when the field was just emerging. In a profession that accepted women on nearly equal terms with men from the outset, it was of importance that women of substantial academic and professional merit participated in the formative years of the field's chief professional body, the American Association for the Advancement of Physical Education. Mosher was such a woman.

Introduction

On the anniversary of the 50th year of her medical school graduation, Eliza Maria Mosher was asked by a reporter for the *New York Times* why she had never married. Mosher replied that she had spent her life married to her profession. [1] Mosher, who said that she believed that the highest achievement a woman could attain was that of motherhood, sought to come as close to motherhood as possible through her commitment to her profession. She had dedicated her life to her vocation of helping others.

As historians of women physicians and scientists have shown, late-nineteenth-century female medical doctors sought to establish close relationships within the accepted norms of the Victorian period. Some single women adopted children and others specialized in gynaecology and obstetrics. [2] Eliza Mosher was no different. As superintendent of the Massachusetts State Reformatory Prison for Women and as dean of women at the University of Michigan, she acted as the mother to hundreds of young women. Through her private medical practice Mosher could be 'mother' to thousands – or 'Auntie', as she encouraged all of her young patients to call her.

Through her work as a prison physician, prison superintendent, college physician, college professor and university dean, Eliza Mosher touched in a substantive manner nearly every health-related career that women entered in the late nineteenth and early twentieth centuries. Mosher's benchmark work in the profession of physical education was of particular importance at a time when the field was just emerging. In a profession that accepted women on nearly equal terms with men from the outset, it was of importance that women of substantial academic and professional merit participate in the formative years of the field's chief professional body, the American Association for the Advancement of Physical Education. Mosher was such a woman.

Unfortunately Mosher has not been remembered in the history of physical education. She is only briefly mentioned in Van Dalen, Mitchell and Bennett's 1953 text *A World History of Physical Education: Cultural, Philosophical and Comparative* and Mabel Lee's 1983 text *A History of Physical Education and Sport in the USA*. [3] Earlier, however, she had been considered a significant enough figure to be listed among the 'Pioneer Women in Physical Education' series published in a supplement to the *Research Quarterly* in 1941. Profiles were provided on 13 'pioneers' including: Delphine Hanna, Clelia Mosher, Ethel Perrin, Amy Morris Homans, Senda Berenson and others. [4] Mosher's decision to focus on her private practice throughout her lifetime, rather than a career in higher education, has made her a 'forgotten woman' in the history of American physical education.

Early Life, Education and Medical Training

Eliza Maria Mosher was born in 1846 in the Finger Lakes region of rural upstate New York. Her family were Quakers and she grew up imbued with a strong sense of the tenets of that religion. [5] Mosher demonstrated an early interest in medicine and as a child she regularly was allowed to assist her mother in treating family illnesses and injuries. Her mother gave permission for her to study nursing, although it was her own wish to be a doctor. [6]

According to historian Thomas Neville Bonner, American women who sought to enter the medical profession at the turn of the century were generally not supported in this decision by their parents. [7] Augustus and Maria Mosher, however, did support their daughter's wish to become a physician in several ways. Mosher's father encouraged Eliza to attain her goals. Although her father died when she was young, she remembered his lessons throughout her life. Initially Mosher's mother did not support her decision to be a doctor. As Mosher often told interviewers, her mother's opinion on medical education for women was that 'I would just as soon think of paying to have you shut up in a lunatic asylum'. [8] Her mother was persuaded when Eliza, in her persistent manner, took her mother to hear a lecture on anatomy and physiology delivered by a physician. Her mother relented and allowed Eliza to begin her studies at the New England Hospital for Women and Children in Boston, Massachusetts. [9]

However, Mosher was not immediately able to begin the study of medicine. An event that she would later claim profoundly affected her life occurred in 1867. She received word that her brother, who was living in Florida, was gravely ill with tuberculosis. Mosher, who at the time was teaching at the Friends School in Union Springs, immediately began the long journey to join her brother. While on a steamer from New York City to Savannah, Mosher met two elderly ladies whose appearance struck her. They wore 'hats brimmed with wide blue ribbons ... and one wore a pretty little cloth "chesterfield" jacket over a pretty white front in which were studs made of tan and gold', which, according to Mosher, was not the style of the time for older women. She learned they were suffragists from Massachusetts, and later managed to spend some time with them on board ship. [10] Later in life Mosher would become active in the suffrage movement as a member of the Kings County Women's Political Equality League in Brooklyn, New York. [11]

In 1869 Mosher went home to care for her mother, who was gravely ill; she returned to the New England Hospital following her mother's death. [12] In January of 1870, the board of regents at the University of Michigan decided to allow women to attend the university. The previously all-male school also decided to allow women into its medical school. [13] When she and five of her fellow students learned that the University of Michigan was accepting women students, they decided to apply to the programme together. [14] Before leaving for Michigan, Mosher spent the summer in Boston studying and preparing for medical school with Lucy Sewall. She was introduced during this time to other women physicians who were in professional positions in hospitals, prisons and asylums. [15]

In her extensive correspondence with her family, Mosher provides a picture of her experiences at the University of Michigan Medical School. The atmosphere at the medical school, Mosher wrote to her family in 1872, 'was not always welcoming'. [16] The medical faculty had firmly opposed the admission of women to the programme, with one medical school faculty member claiming that women were 'semi-invalids a large fraction of the month'. [17]

When Mosher entered medical school in 1871 only two six-month terms were required; and instruction was provided almost entirely by lecture, except for the anatomy course. When efforts were made to improve the medical curriculum at Michigan, in the second half of the 1870s, the primary force behind reform measures came from James B. Angell, president of the university, and Victor Vaughn, a biochemist and future dean of the medical school. [18] During her second year of medical school, Mosher worked as anatomy demonstrator and was required to 'quiz students' as well as take examinations herself. While quizzing students on the anatomy of the brain, Mosher was studying for her own examinations in physiology. [19] Her third year of medical school was spent at the Women's Medical College of the New York Infirmary. [20]

The Beginnings of a Medical Career

Upon completion of the medical degree in 1875, Eliza Mosher moved to Poughkeepsie, New York and set up private practice with a former University of Michigan classmate, Dr Elizabeth Gerow. The two were the first female doctors in Poughkeepsie, the site of Vassar College, where a potential female clientele seemed assured. [21] According to Mosher, the degree from the University of Michigan gave them extra standing in the medical community. [22] Mosher was unanimously elected a member of the local medical society – the Medical Society of Dutchess County – in June 1875. [23]

Mosher enjoyed private practice immensely, and in spite of the obstacles that then confronted female physicians she remained undeterred in her dedication to her new profession. [24] When Mosher had first established her practice in Poughkeepsie, she found that male physicians were cordial and offered little opposition. Nonetheless, she believed that the male medical establishment was reticent about recognizing women physicians as 'regulars'. As Mosher often told those who asked her, even some women were sceptical about female physicians. For example, when Elizabeth Blackwell's New York Infirmary for Women and Children had conducted a fund-raising drive in 1856, Fanny Kemble, whom Mosher characterized as one of the great actresses of her time, refused to contribute; her reply was 'Women doctors, never!' [25]

Mosher thought that women physicians were thwarted in the practice of medicine for paradoxical reasons. Some male physicians claimed that women physicians were not competent. They then proceeded to contradict themselves by claiming that women physicians would expropriate the profitable practice of obstetrics, in a day when general practitioners delivered babies. According to the *Boston Medical and Surgical Journal*, doctors felt that

> It is not a matter to be laughed down as readily as was at first anticipated. The serious inroads made by female physicians in obstetrical business, one of the essential branches of income to a majority of well-established practitioners, make it natural enough to inquire what course it is best to pursue. [26]

Historian Carroll Smith-Rosenberg maintains that male obstetricians who specialized were concerned both about the inferior position that they held within the medical community and the competition that new women physicians presented. [27] Moreover, Eliza Mosher claimed that women doctors were discouraged from practising by many of the substantially all-male medical societies. [28]

Mosher's burgeoning private practice was interrupted in 1877 when the governor of Massachusetts persuaded her to become the physician for the hospital at the State Reformatory Prison for Women which was located in Sherborn, Massachusetts. As historian Estelle Freedman has shown, many late-nineteenth-century women reformers worked as chaplains, physicians and superintendents to improve the conditions in women's prisons. [29] As a result of her Quaker upbringing, Mosher felt it was a 'calling' to go to the reformatory prison as physician.[30] Her assistant physician was Dr Lucy Hall, another University of Michigan Medical School graduate, with whom Mosher would later set up a private practice. In her work at the State Reformatory Prison for Women, Mosher was responsible for the health of the other staff as well as the prisoners. Her labour was increased when the chaplain, Miss Sarah Pierce, contracted typhoid fever and Mosher felt compelled to continue Pierce's religious efforts as well as the medical work. [31]

Within a short time, however, a serious disagreement arose between the superintendent of the prison and Dr Mosher. The dispute centred on what Mosher considered the superintendent's interference with her medical work. [32] This was a major factor in Mosher's decision to resign her post in 1879. Mosher's work was held in high esteem by the governor of Massachusetts, Thomas Talbot, and the commissioners of the prison when they reluctantly accepted her resignation. [33]

Having decided to leave her prison work, temporarily at least, Mosher made plans for additional medical study. She believed, and her medical friends concurred, that it was important for her to spend time studying medical practices in Europe. [34] Women who had been her teachers at the New England Hospital for Women and Children, with whom she had continued to keep in contact, encouraged her to seek opportunities similar to those that they themselves had while studying on the Continent or in Great Britain. [35] Mosher and her physician colleague Amanda Sanford visited the Great Ormond Street Children's Hospital and the clinic of Sir Morell Mackenzie at the London Throat Hospital while in England. In addition they attended rounds and visited clinics at the Hospital Laennec and the Hotel Dieu in Paris. [36]

Shortly after her return to the United States, Mosher was asked by the governor of Massachusetts to return to the Reformatory Prison for Women at Sherborn as superintendent. Although reluctant to take the position, Mosher finally accepted. [37] When installed as superintendent, she began to introduce reforms that for their time were innovative. These included such radical changes as cumulative punishments and a period of probation for newcomers – during which they would come under the beneficial influence of the superintendent and chaplain before being placed in the general prison population. [38]

It was while she was superintendent of the prison in Sherborn that Mosher began her association with Wellesley College, only six miles away. This was an association that would be strengthened in 1882 after she resigned as prison superintendent. Mosher made the most of the proximity and indulged herself in Wellesley campus life, noting in a letter to her niece that 'I have so many friends at Wellesley that I feel as if I have gotten back into my old boarding school life again, when I go there'. Students from Wellesley would come to the prison to visit the inmates and put on shows and skits at the holidays. [39]

Following her resignation as prison superintendent, Mosher spent two semesters lecturing at Wellesley. According to the *Wellesley Courant* of 26 May 1884, 'Dr Eliza M. Mosher, late Superintendent of Mass. Reformatory Prison for Women is giving a course of useful and interesting lecture[s] to the students on anatomy and physiology'. [40] She was listed as an instructor in physiology in 1883/4 in the Wellesley catalogue. Mosher had befriended Alice Freeman – then president of Wellesley – while the two were students at the University of Michigan. She was profoundly influenced by her experiences at Wellesley. [41] She delighted in giving lectures and was overjoyed at the kindness that the students showed her. Mosher was modest in her characterizations of how her lectures were proceeding, telling her family that her lectures were progressing 'not brilliantly of course. That would not be *me*, but *decently* well.' [42] Her interest in the welfare of students was shown in various ways. One of these was when Mosher, Marie Zakrzewska, Emily Blackwell, Mary Putnam Jacobi and a group of other women physicians offered Harvard University $50,000 if it would accept the gift as a fund to be used for the education of women physicians. The gift was refused. [43]

The position at Wellesley was a temporary one that had been arranged, in part, to accommodate Mosher while she recovered from a serious knee injury. Following corrective surgery to her knee, Mosher went to Brooklyn, New York to open a private practice. Her partner in the practice in Brooklyn was Dr Lucy Hall, who had been her assistant physician at the Massachusetts State Reformatory Prison for Women. [44]

Entering the World of Physical Education

After establishing her private practice in Brooklyn, Mosher was asked in 1884 to come to Vassar College as resident physician. She agreed on the condition that she and Lucy Hall could split the appointment so that they could continue their private practice. [45] Vassar College had established a department of physical education, and hired a resident physician, Alida C. Avery, in 1865. The College also employed Delia Woods as an instructor in physical training. Over the years, Vassar would hire other physicians and instructors to care for the health and physical training of students. The year before Mosher and Hall began their work at Vassar, Helen Putnam was hired as the teacher of physical education. Putnam had studied for two years at the Harvard Summer School of Physical Training with Dudley Allen Sargent. She would later become a physician. [46]

At Vassar, the Sargent System of gymnastic exercise was utilized and the college purchased a great deal of the equipment that had been devised by Sargent. While at Vassar, Mosher and Hall endeavoured to improve and regularize the physical examinations given to each young woman. According to the 1884–5 'Annual Report of the Resident Physician', the purpose of the examination was to keep a better record of the condition and improvement of the students. [47] The Vassar College Catalogue described the examinations as follows: 'Her physical development is ascertained, strength tested, heart and lungs examined, and information is solicited concerning her health habits and general health.' [48] Mosher's greatest contribution while at Vassar was systematizing these types of physical examinations, which were the first in the nation for women, and which served to establish early standards for physical examination norms that other physical educators could use in their research. She also advocated appropriate dress for gymnastic exercise and emphasized posture training, two areas to which she devoted considerable attention in her writings. [49]

In 1887 Mosher decided it was time to give up her work at Vassar and return to private practice full-time in Brooklyn. Part of her decision may have been that Lucy Hall also decided to leave Vassar. Hall attended the fourth international conference of the Red Cross in Geneva that year with Clara Barton, founder of the American Red Cross, and subsequently received a commission as surgeon on the staff of the Red Cross Hall at the National Drill and Encampment held in Washington. [50]

Even as Mosher was terminating her position at Vassar College, her interest in the field of teaching continued. She developed a Medical Training Department for the Union Missionary Training Institute in which she taught anatomy, physiology and hygiene. [51] In 1889, Mosher was asked by William G. Anderson, MD – who four years earlier had been the organizing force behind the first meeting of the Association for the Advancement of Physical Education – to assist with the opening of the Chautauqua, New York, summer school in physical education. Mosher served as a member of the board of directors of the Chautauqua for 20 years, and was the physical examiner of women students and lecturer on anatomy and hygiene. [52] As board vice-president, she influenced the direction and content of the programme. [53]

At the Chautauqua Summer School of Physical Education, Mosher also began her lifelong involvement with research on posture when she initiated a concentrated study on the relation of posture to health, subsequently becoming an acknowledged expert on the subject. [54] Her research on posture was presented before respected medical societies and published in such educational and medical journals as *The Educational Review* and the *Brooklyn Medical Journal*. [55]

Anderson was enthusiastic about Mosher's study of posture and, following one of her presentations, he expressed his belief that trained physicians such as Mosher were indispensable to the newly emerging field of physical education. [56] It was in part due to Anderson's influence that Mosher became involved with early organizational efforts to form a professional association of physical educators. Although Mosher was not present when the Association for the Advancement of Physical Education was founded in 1885 by Anderson and others, she became a member two years later. Helen G. Putnam, instructor of physical training at Vassar College, however, was present at the original meeting. [57] It is likely that Putnam had returned to Vassar following the meetings and encouraged then resident physicians Mosher and Hall to join the fledgling association.

In 1891 Mosher was elected a vice president of the American Association for the Advancement of Physical Education and in 1892 she was named first vice president. The respect that other members had for Mosher was evident when Mosher requested that she step down as first vice president in favour of Edward Hitchcock, Sr. A vote was taken and she was asked by the members to retain her position. Members of the American Association for the Advancement of Physical Education also greeted her research with great enthusiasm. In her presentation before the seventh annual meeting of the group in 1892, Mosher's work on posture and the symmetry of the body elicited the following comment from Edward Hitchcock: 'I conceive [this] to be one of the most important things brought before this Association for a long time.' [58]

In 1894 Mosher presented at the afternoon session of the ninth annual meeting of the American Association for the Advancement of Physical Education. Also presenting on Mosher's panel were G. Stanley Hall and George W. Fitz, the Director of the BS programme in anatomy, physiology and physical training at Harvard. [59] She also knew Jessie Hubbel Bancroft, another early leader of American physical education. Bancroft was director of physical training in the public schools of Brooklyn, where Mosher had her private practice. Bancroft then became the assistant director of physical training in the public schools of New York City. Together the two founded the American Posture League. After her relocation to Ann Arbor, Mosher continued her association with physical education, serving as president of the Michigan District Association of the American Association for the Advancement of Physical Education in 1897. [60] She continued as an active member of the American Association for the Advancement of Physical Education until 1909.

Although the demands of her Brooklyn practice kept her very busy, Mosher also served as a physician for charitable associations such as the Wayward Home and the Young Women's Christian Association. She believed in using her medical knowledge and skills to assist others and claimed:

> It may seem strange that all through my decision to study medicine and my long preparatory course the thought of it as a way of making money never once occurred to me. There was no special need of my earning, it was pure love born in me – a part of my very nature growing with my growth. [61]

Physical Education for Women at the University of Michigan

In 1896 Mosher was asked by President James B. Angell to become the first dean of women at the University of Michigan and to establish a systematic programme in physical education for women. Angell began as Michigan's president in 1871, the year after the University of Michigan became co-educational. He was a staunch defender of higher education for women. In response to Edward H. Clarke's vituperative writings against women in higher education, Angell replied in 1879:

> the solicitude concerning the health of the women has not proved well-founded. On the contrary, I am convinced that a young woman, coming here in fair health … is quite as likely to be in good health at the time of her graduation as she would have been if she remained at home. [62]

In 1895, the year before Mosher arrived, 250 women took part in gymnasium work. That number was reduced just before Mosher's arrival to 100 due to the fact that women were permitted to use the gymnasium only in the early morning hours. [63]

President Angell contended that Mosher was the best woman to run the gymnasium programme for women at the University of Michigan. [64] He had talked with Alice Freeman Palmer, the president of Wellesley College, about the programme he hoped to develop and the possibility of Mosher running it. Mosher initially expressed hesitation at the thought of leaving her thriving practice and her friends in Brooklyn. One of her initial objections was that no arrangement had been made for her to receive the title of professor. Angell engaged her attention by sending her the plans for the new gymnasium for women that had been planned and asking Mosher for her suggestions. [65] He also began to broach the subject of what she would teach, and what her title and salary would be. Mosher was not satisfied with Angell's initial offers and in late November 1895 wrote that she wished to have her name withdrawn from consideration for the position. [66] Angell responded quickly and asked her to reconsider, informing her that 'We have no thought of any other but your [own], and are determined of doing everything to meet your wishes'. [67] In the end, the president convinced Mosher to visit Ann Arbor, and by the third week of December she had decided to accept a full professorship and the title of women's dean. [68] She was also named professor of hygiene in the Department of Literature, Science and Arts.

Although the salary of $2500 was substantially less than she was earning through private practice, Mosher agreed to return to her alma mater, with the stipulation that she could leave as soon as she had the physical education programme sufficiently organized. [69] She was grateful that friends and colleagues supported her decision to return to Michigan. Although she modestly expressed the belief that she could succeed in the position, she confided to her good friend, Lucy Salmon that 'I do not feel well equipped for the work however, and I fear I shall do some parts of it quite imperfectly, but I shall do my best and that is all anyone can do'. [70] Prior to leaving New York for her new post, Mosher sailed to Europe to visit various women's colleges in order to prepare for her new position, stopping at Girton, Newnham, Somerville, Lady Margaret Hall and St Hugh's. [71] There, according to historian Kathleen McCrone, young women were engaging in sports such as lawn tennis, field hockey and other games. [72]

By 1896, Mosher had been a physician for 21 years, resident physician at Vassar College for six years, and had worked with students at Wellesley College. Like President Angell, she did not believe that college life had a deleterious effect on a girl's health. In her mind only those girls who had unhealthy eating habits or who worried too much over their studies suffered from the college experience. Mosher disputed those physicians who claimed that college life was too rigorous for all women by concluding that physicians who made such claims had not made as systematic a study of the health of college women as she had. Mosher maintained that the best physical work for a college girl was a course of general exercises in the gymnasium. It was imperative that the student receive a thorough physical examination upon entering college and before taking up such work. The examination should be made by a physician who had experience with student health. [73] It was on the basis of such examinations that the physician and the physical director would decide together on the best kind of work for the student.

Mosher was eclectic in her choice of gymnastic exercise for the students. She was a strong believer in the Swedish system of exercise, which was widely used in educational institutions – especially for females. However, she was of the opinion that it was important to take the best from each system (Swedish, German, Sargent's etc.), and create an individual system of exercises at Michigan. Mosher also supported athletic games for girls, provided they were sufficiently prepared for the demands of the activity. According to Mosher, all students of physical training should be given instruction in hygiene and physiology. If the student had a firm understanding of the underlying processes of the body, or the 'human machinery', in Mosher's words, then she would be more interested in her health. With a fundamental knowledge of botany, biology, zoology, human anatomy, human physiology, hygiene, physical culture and physiological psychology, the student would better understand the 'fundamental laws of life'. [74]

When she arrived at Michigan, Mosher began a system of physical examinations for all incoming women students much as she had instituted at Vassar years earlier. The examination enabled her to advise students on the gymnasium work they would need and introduced her to the students. During Mosher's first year at Michigan, 153 women were enrolled for gymnasium work. [75] She kept careful records on each student in gymnasium work each year and was able to observe any changes over the course of the year. Initially, female students were not required to undertake gymnasium work; thus Mosher worked towards ensuring that physical training would become a required subject for students. In 1898 gymnasium attendance was made mandatory for all freshmen, men and women. Mosher hired a director of the gymnasium, Alice Snyder, to oversee the programme that included callisthenics, marching, apparatus work, basketball and track. [76] Snyder continued as the director of the gymnasium and enrolled in the Medical School of the University of Michigan in 1898. Upon Mosher's resignation in 1902, Dr Snyder was named director of Barbour Gymnasium in her place. [77] Her Michigan students recalled that Mosher was always available to them. She was devoted to her work and spent many long hours trying to solve problems that the university had not been prepared to address before she became dean of women. She gave special attention to women students in the medical school and was always ready to discuss their work with them.

During her years at the University of Michigan, Mosher was able to carry on a limited private practice. She also went into the public schools and continued her quest for school desks and chairs for children that would improve their posture. During the academic year she took courses at the medical school in histology, microscopical pathology, tumours, the pelvic organs and electricity and its application in disease. [78] While on the faculty, she also spent another year in Europe in an effort to keep up with the latest medical developments. Upon her return in 1902, she resigned her post at the University of Michigan. Her work at Ann Arbor was applauded by many people. Professors with whom she had worked sent letters of recommendation on her behalf. [79] Elizabeth Blackwell wrote from England saying she had heard 'of the admirable work which you have accomplished during your connection with the University of Michigan. I can well believe this and I hope that you will be able, later, to send us equally encouraging accounts of your work in Brooklyn.' [80]

Later Career

Mosher returned to Brooklyn and entered practice with her cousin Dr Burr Burton Mosher. [81] Following her return to private practice, she found more time for writing and other activities. She worked on civic projects including the Milk Committee of the Medical Society of the County of Kings (the only woman MD on the committee); and she became chairman of the Cleaner Brooklyn Commission of the Brooklyn Chamber of Commerce. [82] In 1907, she was appointed a delegate to a nationwide meeting of milk commissioners. [83] She resumed her lecturing at Adelphi College, the Union Missionary Training School, the YWCA and Chautauqua; she also organized and gave lectures on hygiene at the meetings of the Public Health Education Committee of the American Medical Association. [84]

In 1910, Mosher became senior editor of *The Woman's Medical Journal* and president of the Women's Medical Society of New York. *The Woman's Medical Journal* began publication in 1893 and continued on until 1919 when it was renamed *The Medical Woman's Journal*. It was the official publication of the Medical Woman's National Association. [85] She published articles in *The Woman's Medical Journal* on a variety of topics including sterility in women and its treatment through 'instrumental impregnation'. In an article on pelvic disorders in women, Mosher commented favourably on Mary Putnam Jacobi's essay 'The Question of Rest for Women'. [86] Jacobi's Boylston Prize-winning essay, published in response to the vituperative remarks about women written by Dr Edward Clarke, was an important publication for women physicians in the 1870s. Mosher also extended her clinical research over the decade to include detailed clinical study of the abdomen. [87] She also was involved in research on cancer. [88] Her work in this area was supported by her good friend and noted New York physician William Seaman Bainbridge. Her interest in cancer may have been stimulated in part by the fact that she had personal experience with the disease. Mosher's biographer, Florence Hazzard, has claimed that Mosher twice had surgery to remove cancerous growths. [89]

For the remainder of her career, Mosher continued to be involved in professional medical associations. She was a member of the American Medical Association and, in 1914, she spoke at a banquet held for women physicians attending the American Medical Association's meetings that year. Also present at the event were other physicians who were associated in a variety of ways with physical education. These included Stanford University physician and professor of personal hygiene Clelia Duel Mosher, Goucher College professor of physiology and hygiene Lilian Welsh and physician Kate Campbell Mead, who established the Baltimore Evening Dispensary for Working Women and Girls. [90]

In 1925, on the occasion of the 50th anniversary of her medical school graduation, a large testimonial dinner was held in her honour. Of the hundreds who attended the dinner many were influential physicians and physical educators. Sharing a table were James Huff McCurdy, MD, director of physical training at Springfield College, R. Tait McKenzie, MD, director of the gymnasium at the University of Pennsylvania, William G. Anderson, MD, of Yale University and Watson L. Savage, MD. These men were all important connections to the profession of physical education's legacy and strong alliance with the field of medicine; an association Mosher shared. Also present were Clark Hetherington and Ethel Perrin, who were a part of the 'new guard' of leadership in American physical education – one that was much more closely connected to education than to medicine. [91]

Following her 50th anniversary dinner, she travelled across the country to the Canadian Rockies and California. She met with women physicians at the medical women's clubs of San Diego, Los Angeles and Hollywood. She returned to New York with the intention of establishing a similar group of local medical women. [92] Mosher's views were of interest to many people, and during an interview in 1925 she expressed her opinions on current fads and fashions which effected health. Although Mosher was glad that the corsets of the late nineteenth century had been cast aside, she believed that contemporary fashion was equally injurious to women's health. Rubber girdles, tight bodices, hip-binding corsets and all the other accoutrements worn in search of the 'boyish form' were an aberrant constraint of the body and perilous to its reproductive function. Even after 50 years of practising medicine Mosher continued to see patients every day. She continued to give lectures and remained involved in civic organizations. [93]

The next year she went to Ann Arbor to attend the dedication for the new women's building named in her honour Mosher-Jordan Hall, and she began to plan a trip abroad for 1928 with a group of friends, to visit Palestine and Egypt, and was 'hoping to see some hospital work while abroad'. She confided to a former student that she was worried that the recent publicity about her age and lengthy practice might adversely affect her private practice. [94] Eliza Mosher passed away in 1928 during her convalescence from a fractured leg, injured while she was leaving her church. [95]

Conclusion

Mosher's personal life was, in many ways, fully dedicated to her profession. Like many late-nineteenth and early-twentieth-century women physicians, she never married. Her closest personal relationship was with Lucy Hall Brown, who worked with her at Sherborn Prison and shared her medical practice in Brooklyn for many years as well as the position of resident physician at Vassar College from 1884 to 1887. In *To Believe in Women: What Lesbians Have Done for America – a History*,

Lillian Faderman claimed that Mosher and Hall 'lived in [an] intimate relationship ... and were partners in both medicine and life'. [96] Medical historian Regina Morantz-Sanchez – while agreeing with Faderman that some medical women in the late nineteenth century lived in close, intimate relationships that may have been lesbian in nature – contended that Mosher and Hall's relationship was 'less intense and might best be characterized as one of mentor and novitiate'. [97] Whatever her relationship to Hall Brown might have been, Mosher spent the majority of her life dedicated to her patients, students, friends and colleagues. [98]

Mosher's legacy to the field of physical education derives from the early role she played as a vice president of the American Association for the Advancement of Physical Education, the strong programme that she established at the University of Michigan and the curiosity and research ethic that imbued her life's work. Mosher entered the field of physical education in its formative years. She established the programme at the University of Michigan for women and left while it was still in its infancy to return to her first love, private practice. Mosher's history illustrates for us that there were a number of women in the formative years of the physical education profession who were viewed as valuable contributors to the field. At a time when other professions were organizing and excluding women, physical education was different. Women were included from the earliest years as members, conference speakers and officers of the organization. Eliza Mosher was one step away from the presidency of the AAAPE in 1892, more than 38 years before the organization would elect its first female president, Mabel Lee in 1930. [99]

As Regina Morantz-Sanchez has contended, Mosher, and most other women physicians of her generation, 'crafted a version of female professionalism that utilized the language of fellow-feeling and sympathy'. [100] Mosher may have imbued her practice and career with such emotions, but whether giving physical examinations, studying posture or gynaecological matters, Mosher attacked each problem with tenacity and dedication. She did not train a cadre of students to follow in her footsteps. However, through her dedicated service and in her private practice she influenced thousands of young women by her example.

Notes

[1] 'Oldest Woman Doctor Diagnoses Life', *New York Times*, 29 March 1925, 5.
[2] Abir-Am and Outram, *Uneasy Careers*, 47.
[3] Wrynn, 'Contesting the Canon'.
[4] The complete list of biographies provided in the supplement includes: Abby Shaw Mayhew, Anne Barr Clapp, Delphine Hanna, Clelia Duel Mosher, Eliza Maria Mosher, Ethel Perrin, Harriet Isabel Ballintine, Amy Morris Homans, Lillian Curtis Drew, Jesse H. Bancroft, Senda Berenson and Marien Foye Carter.
[5] 'Memorial', 13.
[6] Hazzard, 'Pioneer Women'.
[7] Bonner, *To the Ends of the Earth*.
[8] 'Oldest Woman Doctor', 5.

[9] Opened in 1862 by Dr. Marie Zakrzewska, the New England Hospital had as its goal to 'provide for women medical aid by competent physicians of their own sex, to assist educated women in the practical study of medicine and to train nurses for the care of the sick'. Mosher considered herself a part of the 'third generation' of women doctors in the United States, and greatly respected those who had preceded her. Both British and American women physicians forged a strong alliance around the New England Hospital. These pioneer women physicians included Elizabeth and Emily Blackwell, Marie Zakrzewska, Susan Dimock, Mary Putnam Jacobi, Sophia Jex-Blake and others who knew and supported one another. The Blackwells and Zakrzewska were among the pioneers. The women they trained included several of Mosher's teachers at the New England Hospital for Women and Children. Dr Elizabeth Blackwell, who Mosher would later meet and visit while on a trip to England in 1880, was the first woman to earn a medical degree from an American medical school when she was awarded the MD from the Geneva (New York) Medical College in 1849.

[10] Mosher Diary, 1908, Box 3, Eliza M. Mosher Papers (hereafter cited as Mosher MSS), Bentley Historical Library, University of Michigan, Ann Arbor, MI, USA. A few years later, while studying at the New England Hospital for Women and Children with Dr Lucy Sewall, Mosher discovered that Dr Sewall was related to the two women she had met on the steamer. While at the New England Hospital for Women and Children, she spent a great deal of time with the Sewall family and became Lucy Sewall's private student. As was typical of many late-nineteenth-century upper-middle-class Bostonians, the Sewall family was interested in a number of progressive reform ideas. Through them Mosher was introduced to John Greenleaf Whittier, William Lloyd Garrison, Wendall Phillips and Lucy Larcom, a cousin of Louisa May Alcott, and herself a well-known writer.

[11] 'Women Suffragists Active', *Brooklyn Daily Eagle*, 11 April 1894, 12.

[12] 'Memorial', 9.

[13] Donnelly, *The University of Michigan*, 1784–5; Monetta L. Harr, 'Invading the All-Male School (125 years ago)', *Jackson Citizen-Patriot*, 10 Sept. 1995, B4.

[14] Biographical Sketch by Florence Hazzard, 1, Box 3, Mosher MSS (hereafter 'Biographical Sketch').

[15] Eliza M. Mosher to family, 15 June 1871, Box 1, Mosher MSS.

[16] Eliza M. Mosher to family, 14 Feb. 1872, Box 1, Mosher MSS.

[17] Davenport, *Fifty Years of Medicine at the University of Michigan*, 20.

[18] Ludmerer, 'The University of Michigan Medical School'.

[19] Eliza M. Mosher to family, June 1873, Box 1, Mosher MSS.

[20] Biographical Sketch.

[21] Cornelia M. Raymond, to Florence W. Hazzard, 20 Nov. 1942, Biographical File, Vassar College Libraries, Special Collections.

[22] 'A Woman Doctor Who "Stuck It Out"', *The Literary Digest*, 4 April 1925.

[23] Membership Certificate, 9 June 1875, Box 1, Mosher MSS.

[24] Biographical Sketch.

[25] 'Oldest Woman Doctor', 5.

[26] 'Editorial', *Boston Medical and Surgical Journal*, 16 Feb. 1853.

[27] Smith-Rosenberg, 'The Abortion Movement and the AMA', 231–2.

[28] 'A Woman Doctor Who "Stuck It Out"'.

[29] Freedman, *Their Sister's Keepers*.

[30] Biographical Sketch.

[31] Mosher to Satie, 6 April 1879, Box 1, Mosher MSS.

[32] Mosher to Satie, 4 Aug. 1879, Box 1, Mosher MSS.

[33] Thomas Talbot to Eliza M. Mosher, 9 Sept. 1879, Box 1, Mosher MSS.

[34] Mosher to Satie, 29 June 1879, Box 1, Mosher MSS.

[35] Bonner, *To the Ends of the Earth*, 141.
[36] Mosher, 'Eliza Maria Mosher, MD', 629; Mosher to family, 14 May 1880, Box 1, Mosher MSS.
[37] Barrows, 'The Massachusetts Reformatory Prison for Women'. Mosher was followed as superintendent of the Sherborn Prison by Clara Barton – more well known for her Red Cross work. Mosher's future medical partner in Brooklyn and at Vassar College, Lucy Hall-Brown, worked as the Sherborn prison physician for many years as well.
[38] Biographical Sketch.
[39] Florence W. Hazzard, Notes from Mosher's letters to family, 'Eliza Mosher at Wellesley', 29 Jan. 1882 and 3 Dec. 1882, Biographical Files, Wellesley College Archives (hereafter 'Hazzard')
[40] Florence W. Hazzard to the Registrar, 5 Nov. 1942, Biographical Files, Wellesley College Archives.
[41] Biographical Sketch.
[42] Hazzard, 21 April 1884 and 21 May 1883.
[43] 'A Woman Doctor Who "Stuck It Out"'; 'Annual Reports of the President and Treasurer of Harvard College, 1881–1882', Pusey Library, Harvard University Archives.
[44] 'Of Pride to All Women', *New York Times*, 3 May 1896, 27.
[45] Biographical Sketch.
[46] Henry Noble MacCracken to Florence W. Hazzard, 10 Nov. 1942, Biographical File, Vassar College Libraries, Special Collections.
[47] 'Annual Report of the Resident Physician, 1884–1885', Lucy M. Hall and Eliza M. Mosher to President Caldwell, 10 May 1885, Archives File, Vassar College Libraries, Special Collections.
[48] *Twenty-third Annual Catalogue*, 16.
[49] Rice *et al.*, *A Brief History*, 276.
[50] 'Notes, 1884–1887', untitled, undated, Biographical File, Vassar College Libraries, Special Collections.
[51] Biographical Sketch.
[52] 'Memorial', 9–11.
[53] Biographical Sketch.
[54] Mosher, 'Eliza Maria Mosher, MD', 629.
[55] Mosher, 'Habitual Postures of School Children', and 'Flat Chest; Produced by Habits of Posture'.
[56] Mosher, 'The Influence of Habitual Posture'.
[57] 'List of Members'.
[58] *Proceedings*, 1891, 1892.
[59] *Proceedings*, 1894, 4.
[60] 'Report of Local Societies', 42.
[61] 'Of Pride to All Women', 27.
[62] Bonner, *To the Ends of the Earth*.
[63] 'Department of Physical Education History', Box 5, Margaret Bell Papers, Bentley Historical Library, University of Michigan.
[64] Materka, *Kinesiology*.
[65] James B. Angell to Eliza M. Mosher, 1 Aug. 1895 and 30 Oct. 1895, Box 1, Mosher MSS.
[66] Eliza M. Mosher to James B. Angell, Brooklyn, 28 Nov. 1895, Box 1, Mosher MSS.
[67] James B. Angell to Eliza M. Mosher, 4 Dec. 1895, Box 1, Mosher MSS.
[68] Mosher to Katherine Cowan, Brooklyn, 23 Dec. 1895, Box 1, Mosher MSS.
[69] Biographical Sketch.
[70] Mosher to Professor Salmon, 30 Jan. 1896, Autograph File, Vassar College Libraries, Special Collections.
[71] 'Of Pride to All Women', 27.

[72] McCrone, *Playing the Game*, 24–30.
[73] 'Gymnastics for Women', *New York Times*, 25 Jan. 1896, 3.
[74] Lecture Outlines, Box 3, Mosher MSS.
[75] 'Department of Physical Education History'.
[76] Shaw, *The University of Michigan*.
[77] 'Department of Physical Education History'.
[78] 'Memorial', 8 and 9.
[79] Francis W. Kelsey to Lucy Hall Brown, 21 May 1902, Box 1, Mosher MSS.
[80] Elizabeth Blackwell to Eliza M. Mosher, June 1902, Box 1, Mosher MSS.
[81] 'Dr. Mosher Resigns', clipping from the *Michigan Ann Arbor News* (1902), Box 1, Mosher MSS.
[82] 'The Golden Jubilee of an Eminent Physician', The Editor's Page, *Medical Review of Reviews*, Box 3, Mosher MSS.
[83] Mosher to Satie, 3 May 1907, Box 1, Mosher MSS.
[84] Mosher Diary, 1908 and Mosher to Satie, 10 May 1908, Box 1, Mosher MSS.
[85] Lemons, *The Woman Citizen*, 252.
[86] Mosher, 'Instrumental Impregnation'; Mosher, 'The Aetiology, Prophylaxis', 87.
[87] Mosher, 'Eliza Maria Mosher, MD', 629.
[88] Mosher, 'Benign Neoplasms of the Breast in Women', 151.
[89] Florence W. Hazzard to Miss Weed, 26 Feb. 1943, Biographical Files, Wellesley College Archives.
[90] 'Annual Banquet of Women Physicians', 147–148.
[91] 'Program-Dinner to Doctor Eliza M. Mosher', 25 March 1925, Biographical File, Vassar College Libraries, Special Collections.
[92] 'Urges Association', 6.
[93] 'Oldest Woman Doctor', 5.
[94] 'Memorial', 9.
[95] Biographical Sketch.
[96] Faderman, *To Believe in Women*.
[97] Morantz-Sanchez, 'The Many Faces of Intimacy'.
[98] Ogilvie and Harvey, 'Lucy Hall Brown'. Lucy Hall married R.G. Brown in 1891 at the age of 48, but according to one source continued to practice in Brooklyn with Mosher until moving to Los Angeles with her husband in 1904 for her health. She died in 1907 from heart problems. Mosher was absent from the Brooklyn practice from 1896 to 1902 due to her work at the University of Michigan.
[99] Wrynn, 'Contesting the Canon'.
[100] Morantz-Sanchez, 'Entering Male Professional Terrain'.

References

Abir-Am, Pnina G. and Dorinda Outram, eds. *Uneasy Careers and Intimate Lives, Women in Science, 1789–1979*. New Brunswick, NJ: Rutgers University Press, 1987.
'Annual Banquet of Women Physicians Attending Meeting of American Medical Association'. *The Woman's Medical Journal* 24 (July 1914): 147–148.
Barrows, Isabel C. 'The Massachusetts Reformatory Prison for Women'. In *The Reformatory System in the United States: Reports Prepared for the International Prison Commission*, edited by S.J. Barrows, 56th Congress, Document No. 459. Washington, DC: Government Printing Office, 1900.

Bonner, Thomas Neville. *To the Ends of the Earth: Women's Search for Medical Education.* Cambridge, MA: Harvard University Press, 1992.

Davenport, Horace W. *Fifty Years of Medicine at the University of Michigan, 1891–1941.* Ann Arbor, MI: The University of Michigan Medical School, 1986.

Donnelly, Walter A., ed. *The University of Michigan: An Encyclopedic Survey.* Ann Arbor, MI: University of Michigan Press, 1958.

Faderman, Lillian. *To Believe in Women: What Lesbians Have Done for America – A History.* New York: Houghton-Mifflin, Co., 1999.

Freedman, Estelle B. *Their Sister's Keepers: Women's Prison Reform in America, 1830–1930.* Ann Arbor, MI: The University of Michigan Press, 1980.

Hazzard, Florence W. 'Pioneer Women in Medicine: Spread to the States Prior to 1900'. *Medical Women's Journal* 55, no. 2 (1948): 38–43, 68.

Lemons, J. Stanley. *The Woman Citizen: Social Feminism in the 1920s.* Urbana, IL: University of Illinois Press, 1973.

'List of Members'. *Proceedings of the American Association for the Advancement of Physical Education,* 1887.

Ludmerer, Kenneth M. 'The University of Michigan Medical School: A Tradition of Leadership'. In *Medical Lives and Scientific Medicine at Michigan, 1891–1969,* edited by Joel D. Howell. Ann Arbor, MI: The University of Michigan Press, 1993.

Materka, Pat, ed. *Kinesiology: A Michigan Tradition.* Ann Arbor, MI: The University of Michigan, 1994.

McCrone, Kathleen. *Playing the Game: Sport and the Physical Emancipation of English Women, 1870–1914.* Lexington, KY: The University Press of Kentucky, 1988.

'Memorial'. *Bulletin of the Medical Women's National Association,* Jan. 1929: 13.

Morantz-Sanchez, Regina. 'The Many Faces of Intimacy: Professional Options and Personal Choices among 19th and Early 20th century Women Physicians'. In *Uneasy Careers and Intimate Lives, Women in Science, 1789–1979,* edited by Pnina G. Abir-Am and Dorinda Outram. New Brunswick, NJ: Rutgers University Press, 1987.

Morantz-Sanchez, Regina. 'Entering Male Professional Terrain: Dr. Mary Dixon Jones and the Emergence of Gynecological Surgery in the Nineteenth-Century United States'. *Gender & History* 7, no. 2 (1995): 201–221.

Mosher, Eliza M. 'Habitual Postures of School Children'. *Educational Review,* Nov. 1892 (in Box 3, Mosher MSS).

Mosher, Eliza M. 'The Influence of Habitual Posture on the Symmetry and Health of the Body'. *Brooklyn Medical Journal,* July 1892 (in Box 3, Mosher MSS).

Mosher, Eliza M. 'Flat Chest; Produced by Habits of Posture. Its Prevention and Correction'. *Brooklyn Medical Journal,* June 1896 (in Box 3, Mosher MSS).

Mosher, Eliza M. 'The Aetiology, Prophylaxis and Early Treatment of Pelvic Disorders in Girls and Young Women'. *The Woman's Medical Journal* 19 (May 1909): 87.

Mosher, Eliza M. 'Instrumental Impregnation'. *The Woman's Medical Journal,* Oct. 1912 (in Box 3, Mosher MSS).

Mosher, Eliza M. 'Benign Neoplasms of the Breast in Women'. *The Woman's Medical Journal* 25 (July 1915): 151.

Mosher, Eliza M. 'Eliza Maria Mosher, MD: Pioneers in Physical Education'. *Research Quarterly* 12 (supplement 1941): 629.

Ogilvie, Marilyn Bailey and Joy Dorothy Harvey. 'Lucy Hall-Brown'. In *The Biographical Dictionary of Women in Science: Pioneering Lives from Ancient Times to the Mid-20th Century.* London: Taylor & Francis, 2000.

Proceedings of the American Association for the Advancement of Physical Education. New York: AAAPE, 1891, 1892, 1894.

'Report of Local Societies'. *American Physical Education Review* 2 (1897): 42.

Rice, Emmet A., John L. Hutchins and Mabel Lee. *A Brief History of Physical Education*. 4th edn. New York: The Ronald Press, Co., 1958.

Shaw, Wilfred B., ed. *The University of Michigan: An Encyclopedic Survey*. Ann Arbor, MI: University of Michigan Press, 1942.

Smith-Rosenberg, Carroll. 'The Abortion Movement and the AMA, 1850–1880'. In *Disorderly Conduct: Visions of Gender in Victorian America*. New York and Oxford: Oxford University Press, 1985.

Twenty-third Annual Catalogue of the Officers and Students of Vassar College, Poughkeepsie, New York, 1887–1888. Poughkeepsie, NY: Haight and Dudley Printers, 1888 (in Vassar College Libraries, Special Collections).

'Urges Association'. *Bulletin of the Medical Women's National Association* 14 (Oct. 1926): 6.

Wrynn, Alison M. 'Contesting the Canon: Understanding the History of the Evolving Discipline of Kinesiology'. *Quest* 55, no. 3 (2003): 244–56.

Recreation and Racial Politics in the Young Women's Christian Association of the United States, 1920s–1950s

Martha H. Verbrugge

Founded in the early twentieth century, the Young Women's Christian Association of the United States of America was one of the country's largest independent organizations for women. Unusually cross-class and multi-racial, the group's members, professional staff and volunteer officers frequently debated the YWCA's principles and programmes before mid-century, especially in relation to its segregated black centres. The most contested sites of discrimination were the gymnasium, swimming pool, and summer camp. This essay examines the arguments of advocates and opponents of interracial recreation between the 1920s and 1950s as well as their practical struggles over local policies and reforms. Based on the archival records of the YWCA National Board and nine representative city associations (white and black), the essay demonstrates the important role of voluntary groups and non-professional women in female recreation. More broadly, it explores the volatile politics of race relations, social justice and active bodies.

Introduction

> And where does the pulse [of inclusion] beat the faintest? ... It is where we have facilities, such as gymnasiums, pools, camps and residences, that one part of the Association tends most frequently and most persistently to set up barriers against another. [1]

Founded in the early twentieth century, the Young Women's Christian Association of the United States of America sought 'to advance the physical, social, intellectual, moral, and spiritual interests of young women'. [2] The group's symbol – a triangle – signified its concern for each member's body, mind and soul. Services ranged from vocational training, temporary housing, and meals to Bible study, social programmes, and recreation. [3] The 'YW' soon became one of the largest independent women's groups in the country. By mid-century, it 'claimed to represent three million women and girls', including members (who signed a religious pledge) and participants (who joined classes and activities). [4]

The YW was unusually diverse. Wealthy and middle-class white volunteers served on the national board, raised funds, and directed local associations. Women of colour ran affiliate centres in urban neighbourhoods and black schools. College-educated professionals oversaw daily operations and special departments. Countless females – school-aged and adult, single and married, immigrant and native-born, employed and leisured – enrolled in YW programmes. Inclusiveness, though, strained the bonds of Christian sisterhood. Working girls resisted middle-class regimens at YW boarding houses. [5] 'Conservative Protestants struggled with those influenced by the social gospel over programs, policies, and theology.' [6] When the Industrial Department became increasingly pro-labour after the First World War, some leaders feared that worker education had become too radical. [7] Black-white relations were especially volatile. 'In all of [the YW's] work with, and for, women,' historian Adrienne Lash Jones observes, 'the most overwhelming obstacle to social progress continued to be relations between the races'. [8] Discrimination was particularly entrenched in recreation. Long after local associations integrated various committees and clubs, the interracial use of gymnasiums, swimming pools and summer camps remained controversial. As one city reported in the early 1930s, health education and physical activity is 'a place where we must go more slowly [on integration] and sometimes seem to be standing still, and what is worse, sometimes [are] going backward'. [9]

This essay examines the racial politics of recreation in the YWCA between the 1920s and 1950s. After summarizing physical education and race relations in the organization, I analyse black and white leaders' arguments for and against interracial recreation and their clashes over policy. My vantage point is ground-level; although the National Board articulated a general direction for the YWCA, community groups determined local rules and practices. My sample comprises representative associations, white and black, in nine major cities in the Northeast, Midwest and Far West. [10] These case studies demonstrate the important role of voluntary organizations and non-professional women in female recreation. The history of the YWCA also illuminates the centrality of active bodies in disputes over racial justice.

Recreation and Health Education

Initially, physical activity in the YWCA consisted of exercise classes. [11] The earliest known example is callisthenics at the YW boarding house in Boston during the late 1870s. In 1906, two-thirds of city associations offered physical education; about one-half had gymnasiums; virtually none had a swimming pool. [12] Recreation programmes grew rapidly after national consolidation of the YWCA. In 1908, the organization served more than 21,000 girls and women in nearly a hundred gymnasiums around the country; by 1916, gym classes handled about 65,000 participants and more than 32,000 enrolled in swimming classes. [13] By 1920, local centres offered callisthenics, games and sports, medical examinations and instruction in hygiene and personal growth. Members could learn to play golf and tennis, ride a bicycle with new friends, join a sports club or get advice about clothes, posture and grooming. [14] Outreach programmes also became common. During the First World War, the YWCA sponsored recreation for industrial workers and military families, and its crusade for sex education and social morality reached thousands of Americans. After the war, the YW collaborated with other voluntary and professional groups in educating doctors, recreation leaders, and the general public about 'positive health'. Calling these diverse initiatives 'health education', the YW urged each young woman to lead a 'dynamic' and 'more abundant life' while serving her faith, family, and community. [15]

Programmes continued to diversify between the 1920s and 1950s. [16] Health instruction included medical check-ups, hygiene lectures, nutrition counselling, sex education, and tips about clothing, cosmetics, relaxation and 'weight normalizing'. Physical activities ranged from informal exercise, games, dance and 'splash parties' at the swimming pool to hiking, camping, horseback riding and other outdoor recreation. Following the lead of many collegiate physical educators, national officers frowned on elite competition and endorsed moderate play days. [17] Nevertheless, many community associations sponsored high-level athletic tournaments and meets. Finally, YWs organized family events and co-ed entertainment, thereby becoming vital social centres in their communities.

Girls and women took advantage of these programmes in large numbers. In 1930 some 340,458 individuals across the country enrolled in physical activities and more than 232,000 medical examinations were conducted at local YWCAs. [18] In 1947, more than 392,000 members and non-members participated in health education programmes. [19] In 1929, a total of 208 YW camps were operated by 168 cities, with more than 82,000 attendees; in 1954, more than 300 associations and branches ran summer camps. [20] Inclusiveness, though, did not mean interaction; black and white girls rarely swam or played with one another during the YW's first half-century.

Race Relations in the YWCA, 1906–1946

To understand the racial politics of recreation, one must review the general course of black-white relations in the YWCA. [21] During the late 1800s, many women's groups – white and black, secular and religious – engaged in community service. In 1906, two predominantly white organizations – one conservative and evangelical, the other more reform-minded – combined to form the Young Women's Christian Associations of the United States of America. Rather than assimilate extant Christian groups among black women, the all-white National Board left them intact, thereby institutionalizing segregation in the new organization. In 1915, the board designated each local black YW as a 'branch' of the 'central' (that is, white) association in its community; in the absence of a branch, the white group was responsible for services among African Americans. Although black women exercised authority in each branch through all-black administrative bodies, their independence was constrained by white central associations and their Committees on Colored Work.

During and after the First World War, the black presence in the YW grew significantly. Between 1915 and 1920, the number of branches tripled, and black volunteers and paid staff became more common at the local and national levels. [22] Although some operations during the 1920s and 1930s were interracial, most community programmes remained segregated. [23] As one black staff member later observed, '"Separate" meant inferior, despised, and unequal'. [24] Many black personnel shared Anna Arnold Hedgeman's resentment over meagre budgets, second-rate facilities, inferior salaries, limited power and entrenched prejudice. By the early 1920s, 'the battle lines were drawn', notes historian Adrienne Lash Jones. 'For the remainder of the century, the [YWCA] would continue to be an arena in the struggle for black and white Christian women to find common ground.' [25]

The YW embarked on this journey during a critical time in American race relations. The inter-war decades saw vigorous campaigns for equality as well as setbacks. Many African Americans lost their jobs during demobilization; violence against minority groups intensified after the First World War; legal manoeuvres restricted black voting rights. During the Great Migration of the 1920s, many black men and women left the South 'for northern cities and midwestern communities in search of a brighter future'. As historians Darlene Clark Hine and Kathleen Thompson continue, however, the Great Depression 'embroiled [blacks] in a fierce struggle for jobs, housing, education, and first-class citizenship. As their economic status worsened, they also increasingly faced brutal violence, race riots, and blatant racial discrimination and segregation.' [26] Federal projects brought relief for many Americans, but few New Deal programmes targeted black communities and some even harmed them. [27]

During the 1940s, the drive for racial justice became more militant. Black business associations, churches, women's clubs and student groups protested against discrimination; membership in the NAACP and Urban League surged; African American magazines and newspapers publicized the movement's activities and ideas. [28] For blacks and whites alike, the Second World War raised difficult questions. Why were illiteracy and ill-health so prevalent among black soldiers? How could the United States ask young African Americans to die for freedom overseas (in segregated units), but deny them equality back home? In the public sector, civil rights gained momentum with President Roosevelt's Executive Order 8802 on employment in 1941 and the Supreme Court's landmark 1954 ruling on school desegregation in *Brown v. Board of Education of Topeka*. [29] Developments in the private domain were mixed; the Congress of Industrial Organizations supported black labourers, but some voluntary women's organizations failed to address racial issues. [30] Although some African Americans were confident at mid-century that integration was within reach, large obstacles remained. Racism was widespread, black political power was constricted, and new repression loomed under the banner of anti-communism. [31]

The YWCA traversed this landscape with conviction and foreboding. Prodded by an interracial coalition, observes historian Nancy Robertson, white leaders moved from 'justifying policies and practices of racial segregation in the South and the North as compatible with democracy, Christianity, and sisterhood to a policy, if not a practice, of questioning segregation'. [32] Although the branch system continued, many community centres addressed racial disparities in staff appointments, committee membership, club activities, dining services, residences and policy-making bodies. In 1936, for instance, 42 of the 65 communities with black branches had interracial city-wide boards. [33] Important changes also occurred at the national level. During the 1930s, the YWCA supported federal anti-lynching legislation and various initiatives of the NAACP and National Council for Negro Women. [34] These affirmations of social justice set the YWCA apart from many white women's groups that were more prominent, but less courageous. The YW also began taking a hard look at itself. In 1931, Susan Lynn writes, 'the National Board abolished the separate National Council for Colored Work and decided that all professional staff would serve the entire membership, rather than a racially designated portion of it'. In 1936, Lynn continues, the national convention adopted a 'somewhat vague but nevertheless significant statement of interracial intent' that committed the YWCA 'to build a fellowship "in which barriers of race, nationality, education, and social status are broken down in the pursuit of a common objective of a better life for all"'. [35]

In 1944, a special commission issued its report on interracial policies and practices in community associations. Co-directed by Juliet O. Bell, a white woman, and Helen J. Wilkins, a black woman, the study demonstrated that most local activities were segregated and black members and staff faced myriad barriers. Its conclusions were blunt: segregation violated the YWCA's pledge to build a democratic, Christian fellowship; the only remedy was full integration. [36] Against this backdrop, the 1946 national convention adopted its landmark Interracial Charter:

> Wherever there is injustice on the basis of race, whether in the community, the nation or the world, our protest must be clear and our labor for its removal, vigorous and steady. And what we urge on others we are constrained to practice ourselves. We shall be alert to opportunities to demonstrate the richness of life inherent in an organization unhampered by artificial barriers, in which all members have full status and all persons equal honor and respect as the children of one Father. [37]

After considerable debate, a majority of delegates directed the national board and local associations, as Adrienne Lash Jones summarizes, to 'actively integrate Black women into programs, facilities, and governing bodies', at least where 'no legal restrictions' existed. 'Eventually [this] meant dismantling all segregated branches.' [38] Implementing the charter proved difficult. Black leaders educated the YWCA about racism and steered it towards integration. National officers wrote practical handbooks on race relations and advised countless local associations. [39] As insiders acknowledged, community centres were 'morally rather than legally bound' to abide by the charter; each group would 'work out its salvation on the strength of its own conviction'. Local decisions, rather than a national pledge, determined the character and pace of integration in the YWCA. [40]

Justice was especially hard-won in recreation. Initially, most white associations prohibited African Americans from using central gyms, swimming pools and camps. [41] In the 1930s, Boston and Chicago had non-discrimination policies throughout their main facilities, with the exception of pools and camps. In the early 1940s, almost no health education classes for non-members were interracial, including none in the South. [42] Among local centres in the Midwest and Northeast equipped with pools in 1941, one-half excluded blacks, while another third allowed only restricted access; only 16 per cent did not discriminate. [43] By the mid-1940s, nearly 40 per cent of more than 170 local associations 'permitted Negroes to use the gymnasium with white people'; integrated swimming pools and camps were relatively scarce (27 and 23 per cent, respectively). [44] By 1947, equitable policies for recreation facilities were more common outside the South. [45]

Local Opposition

Passionate arguments arose whenever local associations considered interracial recreation. Opponents typically were white members of governance boards and professional staffs. Their position rested on three claims: black women are different, diseased and disruptive. First, anti-integrationists believed that all blacks were lower-class, uneducated and crude. [46] A young day camper in Chicago 'stated that she did not like negro girls' because 'they were rough'. [47] Casual interaction between people whose intellect and refinement differed so sharply was unthinkable; as a white worker in the Orange, New Jersey YWCA observed, 'It would not look well for a wealthy woman to meet her maid swimming in the same pool.' [48]

Moreover, African Americans supposedly had little enthusiasm or aptitude for certain physical activities. As one association reported, 'Negro girls [had] never shown any noticeable interest' in organized swimming meets. [49] Perhaps their apathy indicated inability? White personnel of a 'Stay-at-Home' camp in Chicago concluded that girls were separated by race during integrated swim periods because most whites were 'advanced swimmers and the colored girls [were] beginners'. [50] Both nature and nurture seemed pertinent; lack of skill compounded black girls' habit of clustering together. As a homogeneous group, conservatives explained, blacks preferred to congregate in 'self-sustaining' communities. [51] This tendency rendered integration unnecessary; as a white trustee of Cleveland's YWCA reasoned, 'swarms of colored girls' will not appear if we open the central pool 'because they already have splendid facilities' in their neighbourhoods 'which they do not use to any great extent'. [52] By this logic, segregation was not an instrument of bigotry, but an expression of racial difference.

Among all presumed differences, disease seemed the most dangerous. Many white women in the YWCA viewed African Americans as reservoirs of filth and contagion.

Recreation posed special hazards. In the gymnasium, girls handled the same equipment and their bodies could touch; at summer camp, they might share canoes, badminton racquets and sleeping quarters; swimming raised urgent 'questions of cleanliness and fear of social diseases' – whether the two races used a particular pool together or separately. [53]

White personnel typically viewed pool sanitation in racial terms. If swimmers were white, safety was a simple administrative matter. When Cincinnati's central association opened its new pool (for whites only) in 1929, the managers scheduled regular pool cleaning, required medical examinations of all girls and took measures to control ringworm, especially athlete's foot. [54] By contrast, black swimmers posed a more sinister problem. If 'dirtiness' was intrinsic to black bodies (not simply a function of poor hygiene), could any YW safely integrate its pool? When this question arose in Wichita, Kansas, during the early 1930s, association leaders sought scientific advice; much to their surprise, the municipal parks department reported that the 'water in the pool used by the negroes tested very favorably in comparison with other neighborhood pools used by white people'. [55]

Even empirical data, however, could not overturn deep-rooted prejudice. Racist assumptions about black 'contamination' – as a literal and figurative threat – had a long history in Western culture. During the early twentieth century, the new germ theory implicated poor hygiene and faulty sanitation in many ailments; public health reports suggested that tuberculosis, syphilis and other infectious diseases were prevalent among black Americans; war-time jingoism and an influx of foreigners heightened white suspicions about 'others'. [56] As fear of intimate contact intensified, many white-dominated communities tried to protect their public beaches and pools from black 'pollution'. [57]

Disputes over interracial swimming were as much about sexuality as race. As historian Jeffrey Wiltse argues, the popularity of co-ed recreation in the early twentieth century attached more ominous meanings to integration. Drawing on old stereotypes of black men as immoral and hypersexual, segregationists forecast disaster if swimming pools – a site where bodies were so visible and close – became both mixed-gender and interracial. [58] This sexually charged fear resonated through the YW during the inter-war years, when local associations introduced more co-ed events and considered interracial programmes for females. White leaders' minds raced to other possibilities. Uneasy about the inclusion of black girls at Chicago's summer camps, a counsellor wondered 'what such "Intermingling of the Races" … might lead to'. [59] The answer, according to a board member in Cleveland, was 'social dancing and inter-marriage'. [60] If black bodies and souls were unclean, conservatives believed, white ladies could not remain pure when exercising with black women, much less black men. Moreover, if white members felt unsafe, they might desert the organization.

Behind this solicitude over people's feelings was a practical matter: White flight meant lost revenue. As did other units, Health Education served dues-paying members; recreation programmes were a popular benefit for established clubs and interest groups. Even more critical for the ledger was the department's role in generating extra income; non-members paid a fee for recreation activities, as did outside groups that rented the gymnasium or pool. To balance the budget, association leaders monitored the Health Education's bottom line closely, often favouring fees and activities that attracted customers to the gym and pool. [61] This revenue (along with money from residences and food services) could make or break a local association.

Would 'interracial fellowship' jeopardize financial security by driving white participants away? [62] This concern was 'almost overwhelmingly apparent' when Juliet Bell and Helen Wilkins surveyed local associations in the early 1940s. One association reported 'that its greatest interracial lags come at the point of health education and camp. "The Health Education Department is an income department," it explains, "and since the community follows the pattern of segregation, we are afraid we cannot keep it open at all if Negroes are admitted to its facilities."' [63] Similarly, white leaders of Chicago's central YW worried that the presence of African Americans might damage its image; there was 'economic pressure', they noted, to 'maintain the value of our property in the eyes of the community'. [64] In sum, conservative whites argued that black participants jeopardized the cohesiveness, cleanliness, solvency and good name of local associations – all the more so in the casual intimacy of the gymnasium and pool. For segregationists, the menacing black was not an abstraction, but a real person.

Local Support

The chief advocates of integrated recreation were black leaders, professional staff and club members. Various white allies joined the cause, including national personnel, local volunteers and progressive members of the Girl Reserves, Industrial and Business clubs, and collegiate groups. They challenged segregationists' three assertions of black difference, disease, and disruption. First, integrationists argued, blacks' apparent lack of participation and ability was not a racial trait. Perhaps, they countered, white prejudice made blacks feel unwelcome in the gymnasium and pool; maybe African Americans were tired of discrimination and false friendliness; maybe programmes were inconvenient or too expensive. [65] Simply put, blacks' supposed shortcomings were the *result* of segregation, not a justification for it. Reformers insisted that central associations become interracial, so that 'Branch constituents feel at home there'. [66] We also should move beyond notions of difference, a staff member in Chicago urged, by recognizing the similarities, even identity between black and white Americans. [67]

Second, science and experience had refuted the allegation that blacks were exceptionally germ-ridden. 'Generally', one black leader observed, 'the health standards of the Negroes using the pool are on the same level as the white people using the pool.' If hygiene is the chief concern, Cordella Winn continued, why not certify all swimmers, irrespective of race? The YWCA 'should require uniform health examinations by our own physicians and eliminate any unhealthy person regardless of nationality or race. The color of the skin, whether white or black, should not be a requirement for the use of the pool.' [68] A national staff member from 1918 to 1938, Winn understood that accusations of black contamination were driven by racism, not sanitation, and that pool regulations enforced discrimination, not hygiene. As another critic shrewdly noted, 'Those who object to using the same pool with Negroes do not usually object to using a pool with uncultured white people.' [69]

Checking for disease, however, was easier than eliminating bias. In the early 1940s, the Health Committee of one local YWCA demanded that a group of black girls undergo 'an extra-rigorous health examination not required of white constituents. Although this examination revealed conclusively that the "health hazard" was wholly in the committee's mind, the pool is still not open to Negroes in that Association on the same basis as to other constituents.' [70] Even health clearances, one worker in Wichita concluded, would not 'dispose of irrational fear which may be an unrecognized cloak for race prejudices.' [71]

Finally, while acknowledging that integration presented social and financial hurdles, reformers insisted that prejudice should not be allowed to delay justice. A staff member in Warren, Ohio, reported that her association had organized swimming classes for grade-school girls, black and white, who had passed a medical inspection. In protest, several women on the association's Health and Recreation Committee resigned and three parents withdrew their daughters from the activity. The director was unfazed; the volunteers, she observed, 'were not good committee members to begin with,' and she saw no reason to placate narrow-minded parents. [72]

Activists also dismissed the charge that blacks were pursuing a radical agenda at a reckless pace. African Americans 'wanted no gifts, no charity, but merely their rights', Anna Hedgeman declared. [73] The perfect time would never come, another leader observed, when all constituencies were equally ready for integration; local associations must not sanction 'hesitancy and fear' simply because the 'educational process' had to be slow and careful. [74] If gradualism ensured racial justice, it seemed appropriate; if caution merely reduced white discomfort, it was unprincipled.

Although tangible costs also loomed, many local centres reported that interracial recreation did not hurt registrations or revenue. [75] Others regarded their losses as 'temporary' and 'insignificant'. [76] Moreover, if solvency was the prime concern, what could be more 'uneconomic' than operating both a central association and a branch, 'merely because of color prejudice'? [77] For black and white reformers, qualms over the emotional and financial cost of integration were a flimsy cover for discrimination and inaction. Simply put, associations should be willing to sacrifice income and members if that was 'the price of ... integrity.' [78]

The appeal to integrity was compelling. Between the 1920s and 1940s, many activists in the United States decried the contradiction between racial discrimination and the country's principles of democracy and fairness. How could a just nation tolerate race riots, lynching and economic deprivation at home, along with bigotry in military forces fighting oppression overseas? As a YW staff member in Denver observed, 'It is easy to be interested in people in other countries but when it comes to living democratically in Denver, that is different isn't it?' [79] If inequality was an affront to American ideals, it also belied the YW's philosophy of Christian sisterhood; we have pledged, reformers pointed out, to grant to 'all persons equal honor and respect as the children of one Father.' [80]

Many constituencies challenged their local associations to be honourable. According to young white participants in Chicago, 'segregation and race hatred are not compatible' with the core principles of the YWCA. Practising what they preached, the girls refused to swim at the association's West Side pool in 1935 when the facility banned the group's black members. [81] In 1938, the black leader of Cincinnati's West End branch scolded the organization's board of directors for neglecting health activities at her centre. Appealing to their conscience and pride, Virginia K. Jones reminded the group that 'we are one Association with a common purpose for all'; therefore, 'sub-standard' programmes at the branch reflected poorly on the entire organization. [82] Jones had allies on Cincinnati's Girl Reserve Committee, a group of board members and staff that oversaw programs for teenagers. In 1938, the committee recommended that all clubs for girls

> be organized on an open membership basis, inclusive of all nationalities and races. ... We believe that organization on the basis of race sets up wrong ideals of living for the girl herself, retards her individual development, is contrary to the best interests of our democratic method of government and life as well as contrary to the spirit of Christianity. [83]

In sum, black women in the YWCA and their white supporters contested racial myths as untrue and segregation as unjust. In the process, reformers replaced demeaning stereotypes of black females with affirmative images that aligned them with mainstream values while honouring their unique history and identity as African Americans. [84]

Local Negotiations

Racial politics boiled over whenever local associations debated which operations, if any, would be integrated and by what means. Conservatives rationalized the status quo or grudgingly accepted small changes. Integrationists pushed their organizations forward by gentle and sometimes forceful methods. Case studies of various cities demonstrate the tactics and resolve of both sides as well as the unique weight of interracial recreation.

Blacks' exclusion from central YWCAs forced them to rely on branch facilities for physical activities. Most black centres, however, lacked the space and equipment needed for even token exercise. Occasionally, central associations allowed branches to rent space at a black school, church or YMCA. Whether a site was owned or rented, separate always meant unequal. During the 1920s, for example, Chicago's YWCA operated a central white association (known as the Loop), a predominantly white branch, and a black branch. [85] Originating as a neighbourhood centre on Indiana Avenue, the black association was renamed the South Parkway Branch in 1927, following the purchase of a three-storey building that featured a residence hall, but lacked a gymnasium. [86] When the basement was converted into a gym 25 years later, branch leaders reported that this 'very cold room' was 'unsafe for any type of activity' due to its two centre posts, poor ventilation and cracked cement floor. [87] Because South Parkway also had no pool, the city-wide Health Education Department arranged in 1929 for branch members to swim at a local black school. [88] White administrators probably were relieved that Chicago's central YW also lacked a pool because, as one black officer wryly observed, this precluded any fight over integrating the Loop. [89]

Many central associations, though, had no such cover. If a main YW had first-rate resources, then a separate property for blacks looked more like deliberate discrimination than a goodwill gesture. During the 1920s and early 1930s, Cincinnati's West End branch frequently appealed to the city's central association for better equipment and facilities. [90] In 1928, the white YW and white YMCA agreed to let the branch rent the gymnasium and pool at the city's black YMCA; there, West End girls enjoyed basketball and bowling, practised international folk dances, studied hygiene during National Negro Health Week and earned life-saving certificates at the pool. [91] Just one year later, the white YW opened a new building and swimming pool, exclusively for whites. [92]

In October 1935, the West End branch requested access to the central YWCA. Denying the proposal as 'unadvisable,' the Health Education Committee promised that 'every effort [would] be made to help them find desireable [sic] equipment.' [93] The city-wide Executive Committee and Board of Directors concurred, arguing that equipment at the central YW was already 'used to the fullest degree' and that 'colored girls using the pool would cause many of our members to withdraw.' [94] A month later, representatives from the central association visited two of the buildings where branch girls played and swam. The inspectors declared that the West End YMCA was 'despicably filthy' and the Stowe School was 'in an even dirtier condition'. Branch girls, they concluded, would be better off conducting a 'purely recreational program' in their own building, and the City-Wide Health Education Committee concurred. [95] Thus black members were literally right back where they started, in a facility without a gym or pool.

In protest, the West End's Committee on Management expressed its desire to 'continue their regular physical education program at [the] YMCA'. [96] Citing the 'real meaning of the words "participation" and "association"', the branch's chief officer urged white leaders to share responsibility for the health and development of Cincinnati's black girls and women. 'The West End Branch is yours,' she pointed out, and it 'will make progress only as the whole association moves along with it.' [97]

The black director's call to conscience fell on deaf ears. Despite some progress, West End staff reported that health education at the branch remained seriously handicapped during the 1930s and 1940s. [98]

In other cities, white associations took the opposite tack by ensuring that facilities for African Americans were comparable to those of the central YWCA. The Indianapolis YWCA is a case in point. [99] Founded in 1895, the organization settled into new quarters in 1909. Its buildings housed a 10ft x 40ft indoor pool (the first such facility in the state) and a gymnasium (at the time, the third largest women's gym in the United States). A second pool measuring 22ft x 60ft was added in 1914. The association established a branch in 1923. Following a city-wide fund-raising campaign, the branch moved in 1929 to a new building featuring a 40ft x 100ft gym and a 20ft x 72ft pool. A camp for black girls opened in 1937 (12 years after a camp for whites had started). Few black branches in northern cities had such diverse options for recreation; fewer still had facilities that seemed comparable to those of their central association.

Good fortune, though, did not connote equity; the intent was to control and marginalize the branch, rather than enhance black programmes and autonomy. White leaders of the Indianapolis YWCA regarded the city's small black population as a potentially disruptive force. The 'talking points' for the branch building campaign in the 1920s emphasized that the city's 25,000 black females 'were capable of becoming either an asset or a liability'. [100] Donors were assured that a well-endowed but segregated branch would be a 'constructive' force of culture, recreation and character development, thereby reducing the economic and moral burden that black girls posed to mainstream society. This mindset drove racial policies in the Indianapolis YW for decades. It was one of the last northern associations to integrate; many of its committees, programmes and facilities, including the main pool, remained segregated until 1959, more than a decade after the YWCA's Interracial Charter.

Many whites approved dual facilities because the arrangement symbolized equality while maintaining segregation. The high expense of double operations, though, led some YWCAs to explore other means to the same end. Such was the case in Denver. [101] Founded in 1887, the Denver Women's Christian Association was a charter member of the national YWCA. A similar group for black women, established by African Americans in 1916, became an official branch in 1920. Located in the Five Point district, the branch was a vital community centre for African Americans; in 1923, it housed 310 women, helped more than 300 find jobs, served over 300 members through interest clubs and programmes, and marshalled some 60 volunteers. The branch had its own tennis court, but rented the swimming pool of a local school. [102] In 1927, the central association's spacious new building included a restaurant, auditorium, swimming pool and gymnasium. Since these first-rate facilities were closed to them, branch members were forced to continue renting the gym and pool of a black YMCA. [103] This costly arrangement ended in the late 1930s when the Health Education Committee permitted blacks to use the central association's gym and pool, with two restrictions. Black swimmers were required to pass a special 'health examination', supposedly mandated by the city's health code; second, blacks were allowed to swim only when whites were not in the pool – a practice known as biracialism. [104]

Granting access to a facility at different times according to race became a common practice; one example is the Boston YWCA. [105] Instead of establishing a branch, the Boston YW allowed some African Americans to join the association's regular clubs and departments. In 1928, the YWCA prepared to open a new building on Clarendon Street, close to the centre of the city's black community. Access was non-discriminatory, except the pool:

1. A club or group of colored girls may have the exclusive use of the pool as does any other club or group.
2. In the pool there will be definite periods of class instruction and plunges for colored girls.
3. Where colored girls are members of a club or group they may swim that period with the group if the club or group agrees. [106]

Codifying biracialism in the first two rules, Boston assigned the best pool times to large revenue-generating white groups within and outside the YW, leaving only inconvenient slots for black girls. Except for an occasional member of the Industrial club or Girl Reserves (third rule), few African Americans could use the pool. [107] By favouring whites and representing blacks as dangerous, unworthy 'others', biracialism was discrimination by another name.

Despite biracialism's appeal, conservative whites feared that it might lead to integration. During the early 1930s, the white YW in Wichita, Kansas, permitted branch girls to use its gymnasium once a week and its camp for one or two sessions each summer. These concessions inspired a local black university to request that female undergraduates and teachers be allowed to swim at the central pool. White leaders imagined all sorts of disturbing scenarios: If we open our pool to an outside group of blacks, will our branch make a similar request? 'Having decided that a class could be offered [to a branch group] at a given hour and day, was it not probable that sooner or later other colored girls who could not come at that hour would apply for enrollment' as individuals? What if they want to swim when white patrons typically use the pool? Although Wichita's YW envisioned a slippery slope to desegregation, it clung to biracialism. [108]

Elsewhere, black and white activists pressed for genuine integration. Invariably, the process was contested and progress was incremental. Consider the evolution of camping programmes in Cincinnati. [109] After operating summer sessions in Ohio and Kentucky for several decades, the YWCA opened Camp Lenmary in 1927 on donated property near New Trenton, Indiana. Welcoming white girls aged 8–18, Camp Lenmary was self-supporting within just six years. Meanwhile, Cincinnati's West End branch had access to camps run by black churches and the black YMCA;

such arrangements, though, were ad hoc and branch leaders regarded the facilities as 'entirely unsatisfactory'. [110]

During the 1940s, Cincinnati's Girl Reserves and other groups condemned the whites-only policy at Camp Lenmary as backward and unfair. Over the next ten years, they helped change practices in health education and other programmes from total segregation to biracial activities at limited sites, then from general biracialism to limited interracial activities and, finally, to general integration. In November 1942, the City-Wide Girl Reserve Committee recommended that Camp Lenmary 'be made available for the use of the younger girls' camping program of the West End Branch YWCA', with implicit endorsement of interracial sessions. [111] After learning of successful biracial and interracial camps in other associations, Cincinnati's Program Committee endorsed biracialism, reasoning that 'it might be best to start by setting aside a period at Lenmary for the use of Negro girls'. [112] The Board of Directors approved separate sessions for white and black youngsters at the camp beginning in 1943. [113]

In 1944, the YW's new Inter-Racial Practices Committee summarized for the board the association's biracial and integrated activities. To build 'an inclusive program', one member urged, 'we can only go ahead step by step and side by side'. [114] Heeding this advice, Cincinnati's YWCA began liberalizing its policies, incrementally. In 1945, it instituted biracial use of the central association's pool by children and, several months later, by adults (a change that drew 'some reaction'). [115] A year later, the Board of Directors agreed that any pre-existing interracial groups of the YWCA 'be granted the use of the pool upon special arrangement with the Health Education Department'. [116] In 1948, the board adopted the national Interracial Charter 'as a goal to which we work'. [117] Towards the end of 1950, the Health Education Committee recommended that all classes in the department be interracial. Such a sweeping policy seemed too radical for the city-wide Executive Committee; by including the gymnasium, pool and co-ed dancing, it raised the spectre of interaction between women and men of both races. Therefore, the Executive Committee and Board of Directors approved women-only interracial gym classes and swimming at the central building. [118] In January 1951, the Electors' Assembly of the Cincinnati YWCA adopted the national Interracial Charter, making it an association-wide commitment. [119] During the 1950s, the organization continued integrating various activities and facilities. [120]

Proponents, though, could never rest easy. As negotiations in Chicago, Cleveland and Denver illustrate, incremental change rarely guaranteed full justice and interracial activities did not automatically eradicate discrimination. Initially, Chicago's West Side branch served mainly white clients. The neighbourhood's increasing diversity, however, forced leaders to reconsider the centre's relationship to blacks and other local groups. [121] Between the 1920s and 1940s, activities at the West Side changed from outright exclusion of minorities to occasional interracial programmes for select groups and, finally, to a policy, if not practice, of full access regardless of race. [122] In 1927, following the dismissal of a Hindu girl from the

West Side pool, Chicago's Metropolitan Board of Directors assumed authority over the interracial use of facilities. [123] Responding to 'a group of Filipinos' in 1929, the board ruled that the West Side gym could not be rented for dancing on Sunday evenings. [124] In 1930, the West Side Committee of Management codified the board's implicit standard by declaring that 'groups meeting regularly at the West Side Branch be limited to white people'. [125] After rescinding this policy in 1933 following protests from the Girl Reserves, leaders permitted pre-existing interracial groups to use the building, except for the pool. [126] This rule quickly came under fire because, as interracial groups objected, it ignored the recreational needs of West Side blacks and violated YW objectives. [127] Following a recommendation by the West Side Health Education Committee and Committee of Management, the Metropolitan Board of Directors allowed the centre 'to experiment with inter-racial policies with the existing groups', as of January 1937. Proponents reassured uneasy colleagues that the trial applied exclusively to the West Side and involved 'only girls who would naturally come to the branch activities'. [128]

Despite progress in the early 1940s, some leaders and members remained unsatisfied. The health education committees at the central Loop, the South Side centre and the West Side centre went on record supporting more liberal policies. [129] In 1942, the Metropolitan Board of Directors eliminated 'all restrictions on the use of facilities in the Health Education Department at the West Side Center'. [130] Nevertheless, most recreation and health programmes in the early 1940s remained sharply divided by race. [131] Although the McCormick boarding house accepted black girls as transient guests and diners, its pool was closed to groups with black members and to individual 'girls who look colored'. [132] In 1944, progressive leaders secured the Metropolitan Board's approval of a city-wide non-discrimination policy: The 'activities and facilities of the Chicago YWCA [shall] be available to all young women and girls on the basis of their interest and need alone'. [133] Prompted by the national office, the Chicago YWCA also established an Interracial Practices Committee. [134] During the late 1940s and 1950s, scarce resources and staff still hampered recreation programmes, and racial separation persisted under the guise of decentralized neighbourhood centres. Still, over a 20-year period, teenage members, young white working-class women and progressive leaders had changed Chicago's official position from prohibiting interracial activities to endorsing, if not always facilitating, equity.

The final steps towards justice were often the most difficult. Although inclusiveness might be an attractive principle, practising it tested one's integrity. In Cleveland, the first moment of truth occurred during the early 1900s. [135] As Dorothy Salem notes, a surge in black population challenged the city's tradition of 'relatively liberal race relations'. Shifting course, white civic leaders, male and female, advocated racial segregation and separate organizations, such as the Phyllis Wheatley Association (PWA). By embedding themselves in PWA governance and finances, 'white YWCA leaders could maintain control over the local programs and leadership, while avoiding the conflicts of black participation in local, regional, and national YWCA conferences and conventions'. [136] During the 1930s, only a few groups, including Health Education and the Younger Girls, experimented with interracial programmes.

In the early 1940s, local and national developments forced Cleveland's YW to address its racial practices. Young members pointed to the exclusion of black girls from the association's swimming pool as blatant discrimination. [137] Although some white leaders took this indictment to heart, most resisted even the appearance of self-examination and reform. Participants in the association's self-study decided to keep their deliberations private and asked that the group's name be changed from 'Interracial Practices Committee' to 'Race Relations Committee', lest its work be 'misinterpreted'. [138] Other white leaders simply denied that major reforms were necessary, maintaining that the association was 'not behind in practice but simply in policy'. [139] The real crisis in Cleveland, explained the Board of Trustees in 1941, is the general plight of the city's minorities, not their participation in the YWCA; instead of democratizing the association, the board wholeheartedly protested against the housing industry's 'exploitation of Negroes through high rentals'. [140] In 1942, the Cleveland YWCA adopted a comprehensive interracial policy. Some trustees nervously asked 'exactly where this [rule] would apply', and if it would entail 'a concerted drive for Negro members' or the addition of blacks to the board. [141] Although delays continued through the 1940s, many units within Cleveland's YWCA, including Health Education, gradually opened their programmes to minorities. [142]

In Denver, city-wide developments during the 1930s and 1940s improved the climate for racial progress. In 1931, the city created an Interracial Commission with representatives from schools, churches, labour organizations and voluntary associations. With a seat on the Executive Committee, the YWCA got a fuller picture of black-white relations in the city, especially discriminatory education, employment and recreation. In the 1940s, the influx of Japanese Americans and Spanish-speaking Americans prompted the city and the YWCA to think about social problems in more inclusive terms. [143] Following visits from national YWCA officers between 1938 and 1949, the central association and branch established committees that engineered key reforms. [144]

At the forefront were black and white women well-schooled in Denver politics and activism. [145] They asked blunt questions: Why should the plans for a new branch building include residence quarters when 'one all-association residence', namely, the ample accommodations at the central building, 'could meet the housing needs of Negro girls and women arriving in Denver'? Why does Denver hold two annual meetings, segregated by race, when the YW is a single organization for all women? [146] Recognizing that 'wholesale' transformation was impractical, activists proposed small, 'careful' steps toward integration. [147] In 1945, the board considered a motion from the Health Education Committee that would allow a lone 'Negro woman applicant' to use the swimming pool 'on an individual basis for a trial period'; after lengthy discussion of 'some of the problems', the board consented, because an 'experiment in the field of race relations' was 'not unusual' for the YWCA. [148]

White denial proved the biggest roadblock. Trying to evade responsibility for discrimination, conservatives argued that racial separation was a natural and effective division of resources, that African Americans created the very problems they complained about, and that blacks were 'too emotional' to look at race relations in an 'objective' way and must accept 'other people's point of view'. [149] Racial injustice, activists countered, was real and pernicious and solutions required a collective commitment. Whatever the project, one leader concluded, whites and blacks should have 'real conviction' about becoming an interracial group and then 'be ready to sell ideas' to their constituencies. [150] The arguments and experiments worked; during the 1940s, Denver's Board of Directors gradually opened the association's main pool, exercise classes and summer camp to African American, Japanese and Hispanic girls.

At mid-century, many pockets of inequity remained in local associations around the country, from administration and personnel to services and facilities. Nevertheless, historian Susan Lynn concludes, 'community YWCAs had achieved a significant degree of racial integration by the mid-1950s'. [151] A 1955 survey reported that 40 per cent of local groups were integrated relative to volunteers, staff, 'special activities such as camping and conferences, institutional facilities (residences, food service, swimming pool), and regular program groups', while 'another 30 percent were integrated in four of these [five] areas'. [152] By 1957, nearly three-quarters of swimming pools were interracial. [153] During the next two decades, several decisions underscored the organization's resolve. In 1967, the national YWCA finally severed ties with local associations that failed to comply with the Interracial Charter, then two decades old. [154] In 1970, the national convention passed the 'One Imperative' that committed the YWCA to 'thrust our collective power to eliminate racism wherever it exists and by any means necessary'. [155] Setbacks notwithstanding, the YWCA's racial progress set it apart from many predominantly white women's organizations in the United States that neglected such issues both before and after mid-century. [156]

History and Politics of Active Bodies

Given the popularity of recreation at the YWCA, some scholars have dismissed the organization – and its male counterpart, the YMCA – 'as no more than "a gym and swim club for the middle class"'. [157] The YWCA, however, holds three important lessons about the history of female physical activity. First, experts and non-experts alike have influenced American ideas and practices of women's recreation. The YWCA employed white and black women with backgrounds in medicine, public health, social work and physical education. Women without professional training, though, also played a significant role in determining which girls and women exercised, how, where and with whom. Second, the YW alerts us to the diverse contexts in which physical activity is regulated. Historians have examined school-based physical education, competitive athletics and scientific research about exercise.

Notably, some scholars have begun studying less familiar, but equally critical, sites where active bodies are constructed, both materially and ideologically. These include workplaces, community centres, social service agencies and voluntary organizations.

Finally, the YWCA illuminates the powerful relationship between active bodies and social justice. Of all the settings in which integrationists and their adversaries contested racial issues in the YW before mid-century, health programmes and recreation were the most divisive and intractable. Racial politics converged on the gym and pool because of the literal and symbolic meanings of active bodies. For many white Americans in the early twentieth century, black bodies, more than black minds or souls, came to signify multiple forms of difference and corruption – physical, sexual, moral and social. Encountering 'otherness' in the flesh seemed profoundly unsettling. As leaders of one local YW acknowledged, interracial recreation scared white women 'because of the close physical contacts involved'. [158] In the gymnasium, camp and pool, physical separation could instantly disappear: blacks and whites learned, exercised and swam together; bodies became tangible, active and exposed; interaction was intimate and unscripted.

Interracial recreation took the true measure of white prejudice. Blacks do not want to integrate the association's pools due to some unusual desire to swim, Cordella Winn remarked in 1938, but because 'this is a test of white people's sincerity'. [159] For Winn and other progressives, health programmes marked the final station in resistance and justice. In the gymnasium and pool, black girls and women were physically present, active, skilled and 'clean'. Recreation opened a critical path to re-creation, allowing black self-definition and agency to be embodied.

Similar struggles over physical space and bodies occurred between the 1920s and 1950s at municipal parks and pools, the playing fields of high schools and colleges, and America's commercial arenas and stadiums. Conflicts over who would exercise, where and with whom were especially intense in urban areas. 'In overcrowded residential areas,' observes Elisabeth Lasch-Quinn, 'recreational facilities held great significance, as symbols of territorial boundaries, possession, power, and freedom.' [160] Confrontations were particularly significant when black girls and women were involved. 'More than any other body,' two scholars argue, the black female body 'politically belies the American declaration of democracy, equality, and freedom. ... No other body in the United States has been so materially and discursively hobbled.' [161] In the gymnasiums and pools of the YWCA, dominant assumptions about black women's physicality could be enforced *and* uprooted, and physical and social equity was thwarted *and* advanced.

Acknowledgement

This essay is dedicated to my mother, Helen R. Verbrugge (1918–2002), who participated in the YWCA Girl Reserves of Grand Rapids, Michigan, during the 1930s, and Henrietta Roelofs (1878–1942), her half-sister, who held key positions with the national YWCA from 1906 to 1939.

Notes

[1] Bell and Wilkins, *Interracial Practices in Community YWCAs*, 57.

[2] Report of the First Biennial Convention (New York, 1906), 13, quoted in Robertson, *Christian Sisterhood*, 18.

[3] Overviews include Mjagkij and Spratt, *Men and Women Adrift*, 1–21; Robertson with Norris, '"Without Documents"', 271–97.

[4] Lynn, *Progressive Women*, 56.

[5] Heath, 'Negotiating White Womanhood', 86–110.

[6] Robertson with Norris, '"Without Documents"', 275.

[7] Frederickson, 'Citizens for Democracy', 75–106.

[8] Jones, 'Young Women's Christian Association', 1299; also Jones, 'Phyllis (Phillis) Wheatley Clubs and Homes', 920–3. Extended analyses include Jones, 'Struggle Among Saints', 160–87; Lynn, Progressive Women, 40–67; Robertson, *Christian Sisterhood*; and Robertson, '"Deeper Even Than Race?"'

[9] 'Practices', 1, *ca.* early 1930s, Folder: Materials for 1932 Convention Working Group: Furthering Interracial Relations, Record Group 6, Series IV, Subseries C: Interracial/Racial Justice, YWCA of the USA Records, Sophia Smith Collection, Smith College, Northampton, MA (hereafter cited as RG 6: IV-C, National Records).

[10] My sample includes Boston, Cambridge, Chicago, Cincinnati, Cleveland, Indianapolis, Minneapolis, Denver and Los Angeles. Southern associations did not consider interracial activities until the mid-twentieth century.

[11] General histories are Garden, 'The YWCA's First 100 Years', 16–17, 53, and Gates, *Health*, 172–201.

[12] Cory, 'The Physical Department'.

[13] Garden, 'The YWCA's First 100 Years', 17, and Gates, *Health*, 179.

[14] Anna L. Brown, *Department of Hygiene and Physical Education* (New York: National Board of the YWCA of the USA, 1915), Folder: Publications, Administration, in Record Group 6, Series V, Subseries B: Health and Recreation, National Records, and Gates, *Health*, 177–89.

[15] Gates, *Health*, 8–11, 13–16, 181–89; Gates, 'Living Up', 284–5; Gates, 'To Your Health!', 100–1, 123; and Meanes, *Handbook of Positive Health*.

[16] On the 1930s, see Gates, *Health*, 16–18, 24–145; 'Helping Each Girl',15, 30; and *A Symposium on Health and Recreation*. On the 1940s, see McWilliams, 'War Steps Up Health', 536, and Richards, 'Washington Wartime Woes', 190–1.

[17] Gates, *Health*, 199, and Gates, 'Trends in Athletics', 366–9.

[18] Gates, 'National Association', 62.

[19] 'The Nation-Wide Constituency', 17.

[20] Garden, 'The YWCA's First 100 Years', 16, and Gates, *Health*, 197.

[21] See note 8.

[22] Jones, 'Struggle Among Saints', 176–80; Jones, 'Young Women's Christian Association', 1300–2; Robertson, *Christian Sisterhood*, 25–70; and Salem, *To Better Our World*, 208–19.

[23] On early interracial work, see Baker, *Negro-White Adjustment*, 32–3, 185–8.

[24] Hedgeman, *The Trumpet Sounds*, 32, and 30–63, 72–79 in general. Hedgeman (1899–1990) worked in local YWs in Ohio, New Jersey, New York and Pennsylvania during the 1920s and 1930s. See entry by Nancy Marie Robertson in Ware, *Notable American Women*, 285–6.

[25] Jones, 'Struggle Among Saints', 184.

[26] Hine and Thompson, *A Shining Thread*, 241.

[27] Kirby, 'The Roosevelt Administration', 265–88.

[28] Sitkoff, *A New Deal for Blacks*, 298–302, 312–14.

[29] Ibid., 321–5.

[30] Lynn, *Progressive Women*, 2, 65, and Sitkoff, *A New Deal for Blacks*, 169–89.

[31] Giddings, *When and Where*, 238–41; Kirby, *Black Americans*, 218–35; and Sitkoff, *A New Deal for Blacks*, 298–300, 309–14, 324–5.

[32] Robertson, '"Deeper Even Than Race?"', 7.

[33] Ibid., 321, n.75, and 296–309. See also Cuthbert, 'The Negro Branch Executive', 190–1, and Lynn, *Progressive Women*, 42–6.

[34] Robertson, *Christian Sisterhood*, 138–47.

[35] Lynn, *Progressive Women*, 43.

[36] Bell and Wilkins, *Interracial Practices in Community YWCAs*. On recreation, see 48–9, 54–6, 57–8, 69–73.

[37] From 'The Interracial Charter', reprinted in Sabiston and Hiller, *Toward Better Race Relations*, 179–80.

[38] Jones, 'Young Women's Christian Association', 1302.

[39] Height, *Step By Step*; 'Dorothy Irene Height' in Hill, ed., *The Black Women Oral History Project*, vol. 5: 33–295; Lynn, *Progressive Women*, 49–60; and Sabiston and Hiller, *Toward Better Race Relations*.

[40] Quotation from Sabiston and Hiller, *Toward Better Race Relations*, 3. See also Lynn, *Progressive Women*, 49–60, and Robertson, *Christian Sisterhood*, 165–9, 175–7.

[41] See reports and letters in Folder: Materials for 1932 Convention Working Group, RG 6: IV-C, National Records.

[42] Bell and Wilkins, *Interracial Practices in Community YWCAs*, 58–60.

[43] Department of Data and Trends, 'Interracial Practices of the YWCA as Related to Swimming Pools [April 1941]', 2–3, Folder: Community Associations, Swimming Pools, Policies and Practices, 1932–41, RG 6: IV-C, National Records (hereafter cited as 'Interracial Practices', Folder: Pools, Policies and Practices).

[44] Department of Data and Trends, 'Interracial Commission Report, Key to Chart, Based on return to Questionnaire 1', 16 Oct. 1944, Folder: Interracial Study, Commission to Gather Interracial Experiences, 1941–45, RG 6: IV-C, National Records.

[45] 'Health Education Facilities', 3, in untitled document, Folder: Interracial Study, Follow-Up, General, RG 6: IV-C, National Records.

[46] For historical background, see hooks, *Ain't I A Woman*, 51–86, and Young, 'Racializing Femininity', 67–90.

[47] 'Summary of the Attempt Within the Girl Reserve Department to Bring About a Better Feeling Between the Races with the GR Dept.–West Side', 4, document 5, in 'Compilation of Available Records Showing Inter-Racial Policies and Practices of the Chicago YWCA, 1927–1937', comp. Elsabelle Goss, Box 33, Folder 17, Records of the Young Women's Christian Association of Metropolitan Chicago, Accession No. 74-013 (Suppl. I), Special Collections, The Richard J. Daley Library, University of Illinois at Chicago (hereafter cited as Chicago Records.)

[48] Quoted in Baker, *Negro-White Adjustment*, 142.

[49] 'Interracial Practices', 5, Folder: Pools, Policies and Practices, RG 6: IV-C, National Records.

[50] 'Summary of the Attempt', 5, document 5, in 'Compilation', comp. Goss, Box 33, Folder 17, Chicago Records. For historical context, see Miller, 'The Anatomy of Scientific Racism', and Vertinsky and Captain, 'More Myth than History'.

[51] 'Questionnaire About Interracial Practices in YWCA, Form B', 1941–42, 6, Box 33, Folder 17, Chicago Records.

[52] Minutes, Board of Trustees, 17 Sept. 1940, 3, Box 4, Volume: Jan. 1939–Dec. 1940, Records of the Young Women's Christian Association of Cleveland, Collection MSS. 3516, Library of the Western Reserve Historical Society, Cleveland, Ohio (hereafter cited as Cleveland Records).

[53] 'Interracial Practices', 5, Folder: Pools, Policies and Practices, RG 6: IV-C, National Records.

[54] 'Minutes of Health Education Committee, February '29', 1, Box 11, Folder 27; 'Report for September [1929]', 1, Box 11, Folder 27; 'Minutes of Health Education Department, February 1931', Box 12, Folder 7; 'Report of Health Education, October 1931', Box 12, Folder 7; and 'Health Education Department Annual Report, 1931', Box 12, Folder 7, Records of the Young Women's Christian Association of Cincinnati, Collection MSS. 619, Library of the Cincinnati Historical Society, Cincinnati, Ohio (hereafter cited as Cincinnati Records).

[55] Letter from Helen D. Beavers, General Secretary, Wichita YWCA, to Gretta Smith, Secretary, National Services Division, 21 March 1932, 1, Folder: Community Associations, Swimming Pools, Policies and Practices, RG 6: IV-C, National Records. See also 'Special Practices – From a New England city' [n.d.], Folder: Materials for 1932 Convention Working Group, RG 6: IV-C, National Records.

[56] See McBride, *From TB to AIDS*, 9–24, 33–9, 46–67, and Tomes, *The Gospel of Germs*. Prejudice extended to non-infectious diseases, such as sickle cell anemia; see Wailoo, *Drawing Blood*, 134–61.

[57] Wiltse, *Contested Waters*, 121–53.

[58] Ibid., 123–35. On discourse about black male sexuality, see D'Emilio and Freedman, *Intimate Matters*, 34–7, 103–7, 216–21, and Jordan, *White over Black*, 32–5, 150–4.

[59] 'Summary of the Attempt', 5, document 5, in 'Compilation', comp. Goss, Box 33, Folder 17, Chicago Records.

[60] Minutes, Board of Trustees, 17 Sept. 1940, 4, Box 4, Volume: Jan. 1939–Dec. 1940, Cleveland Records.

[61] 'November [1929] Pool Report', Box 11, Folder 27, Cincinnati Records.

[62] 'From a Western city' in 'Practices', 1, Folder: Materials for 1932 Convention Working Group, and 'Association D' in Appendix III of 'Interracial Practices', 9–10, Folder: Pools, Policies and Practices, RG 6: IV-C, National Records.

[63] Bell and Wilkins, *Interracial Practices in Community YWCAs*, 58; also 69.

[64] Ruth L. Packard, 'Inter-Racial Progress in the Chicago Y.W.C.A., 1930–36', 5, document 1, in 'Compilation', comp. Goss, Box 33, Folder 17, Chicago Records.

[65] 'Report of Cordella A. Winn, July 1938', 10, Folder: Reports, Secretaries', Winn, and 'Interracial Practices', 5, Folder: Pools, Policies and Practices, RG 6: IV-C, National Records; 'Interracial Practices Committee, January 19, 1945', 5, Box 40, Folder 10, and 'Interracial Practices of Girl Reserve Department, Y.W.C.A. of Chicago, Illinois', 4, in appended material of 'Interracial Policy of the YWCA' [*ca.* 1945], Box 40, Folder 10, Chicago Records; and Sabiston and Hiller, *Toward Better Race Relations*, 160–5.

[66] Minutes, Interracial Integration Committee, 8 November 1951, Box 22, Folder 535, Records of the YWCA of Metropolitan Denver, Stephen H. Hart Library, Colorado Historical Society, Denver, CO (hereafter cited as Denver Records).

[67] Packard, 'Inter-Racial Progress', 5, document 1, in 'Compilation', comp. Goss, Box 33, Folder 17, Chicago Records.

[68] 'Report of Cordella A. Winn, July 1938', 9, Folder: Reports, Secretaries', Winn, RG 6: IV–C, National Records.

[69] Baker, *Negro-White Adjustment*, 145.

[70] Bell and Wilkins, *Interracial Practices in Community YWCAs*, 70.

[71] Beavers to Smith, 21 March 1932, 2, Folder: Pools, Policies and Practices, RG 6: IV-C, National Records.

[72] 'From Work Books – Leadership Institutes, 1946', Folder: Interracial Study, Follow-Up, General, RG 6: IV-C, National Records.

[73] Hedgeman, *The Trumpet Sounds*, 34.

[74] 'Interracial Practices', 6, Folder: Pools, Policies and Practices, RG 6: IV-C, National Records.

[75] For example, 'Excerpts from Letters to Mrs. Henry A. Ingraham, President of the National Board, from Community Associations [Central Region], October 1, 1944 to March 1, 1945', 9 [Warren, Ohio], Folder: Interracial Study, Follow-Up, Community Comments, National Records.

[76] 'Annual Narrative Report for the Program Year 1950–1951, Health Education Department', 4, Box 7, Folder 15, Cincinnati Records.

[77] Hedgeman, *The Trumpet Sounds*, 32–3.

[78] 'Statement of Inter-Racial Policies of the Young Women's Christian Association of Chicago', [ca. 1943–44], 1, Box 41, Folder 7, Chicago Records. See also Bell and Wilkins, *Interracial Practices in Community YWCAs*, 73–5.

[79] 'Meeting of Representatives', 3, Box 17, Folder 442, Denver Records.

[80] 'The Interracial Charter', in Sabiston and Hiller, *Toward Better Race Relations*, 180.

[81] See 'Report of the Metropolitan Industrial Department for the Year Ending August 31, 1936', in 'The Industrial Department–Chicago YWCA and Race Relations', document 7, in 'Compilation', comp. Goss, Box 33, Folder 17, Chicago Records.

[82] 'Report of Progress of the West End Branch YWCA Given at Board Meeting December 4, 1935 by Virginia K. Jones, Branch General Secretary', 3, Box 37, Folder 2, Cincinnati Records.

[83] Quoted in 'Report of Junior Activities Department [West End Branch], March 1938', 1, Box 37, Folder 5, Cincinnati Records.

[84] For historical context, see Peterson, 'Foreword', ix–xvi.

[85] See Boynton, '"It Surely is Grand"', 184–5, 376 (Table 13); and Box 47, Folder 1: 1927, and Box 48, Folder 1: 1934, Chicago Records. On women's groups in Chicago, see Knupfer, *Toward a Tenderer Humanity* and Meyerowitz, *Women Adrift*.

[86] 'South Parkway YWCA Report to the Metropolitan Welfare Council, September '52–'53', 5–6, Box 5, Folder 10, Chicago Records.

[87] Dorothy T. Mills, 'Health Education Report', 3–4, Box 25, Folder 16, Chicago Records. See also 'South Parkway YWCA Report to the Metropolitan Welfare Council, September '52–'53', 5–6, Box 5, Folder 10, Chicago Records.

[88] 'President's Report,' 19 Jan. 1929, 1, Box 47, Folder 3: 1929, Chicago Records.

[89] Cordella A. Winn, 'Chicago – Interracial', 3, document 8, in 'Compilation', comp. Goss, Box 33, Folder 17, Chicago Records.

[90] For background, see Anderson, 'Home and Community'; Heath, 'Negotiating White Womanhood'; Hook, 'The YWCA in Cincinnati'; and Spratt, '"Women Adrift"'.

[91] The 1928 contract is found in Box 36, Folder 7: Reports, 1928, Cincinnati Records. On typical activities in the 1920s, see 'Annual Report of Branch Secretary, 1928', 4, Box 36, Folder 7; 'Annual Report of Health Education Department, 1929', Box 36, Folder 8; and 'Report of General Secretary, January, 1928', 4, Box 11, Folder 10, Cincinnati Records. On the 1930s, see 'Health and Recreation Department, 1935,' Box 37, Folder 2, and 'Annual Report, Health and Recreation Department, 1936', Box 37, Folder 3, Cincinnati Records.

[92] 'Report of General Secretary, January, 1929'; 'Report of General Secretary, September, 1929', 2; and 'Annual Report of General Secretary, 1929–30', 4, in Box 11, Folder 25, Cincinnati Records.

[93] 'Minutes of Health Education Committee, October 18, 1935', Box 14, Folder 4, Cincinnati Records.

[94] 'Minutes of Executive Committee, Monday, November 4, 1935', Box 2, Folder 13, and Minutes, Board of Directors, 6 November 1935, Box 4, Folder 13, Cincinnati Records.

[95] 'Report of Study of Health Education Facilities at West End', Box 14, Folder 18; 'Report of Health Education Dept. November, 1935', Box 14, Folder 4; and 'Minutes of

City-Wide Health Education Committee Meeting, Dec. 2, 1935', Box 14, Folder 4, Cincinnati Records.

[96] 'Minutes of City-Wide Health Education Committee Meeting, Dec. 2, 1935', Box 14, Folder 4, Cincinnati Records.

[97] 'Report of Progress of the West End Branch YWCA, Given at Board Meeting December 4, 1935 by Virginia K. Jones, Branch General Secretary', 2–3, Box 37, Folder 2, and Minutes, Board of Directors, 4 Dec. 1935, Box 4, Folder 13, Cincinnati Records.

[98] Minutes, Board of Directors, 4 Dec. 1935, Box 4, Folder 13; 1 March 1944, Box 5, Folder 4; and 7 Jan. 1948, Box 5, Folder 8, Cincinnati Records.

[99] Background information from Bell, 'A History of the Phyllis Wheatley Branch', 18, 37, 47–8, 57–8, 68, Box 8, Folder 7; 'History and Development of the Phyllis Wheatley Branch Y.W.C.A. of Indianapolis, Indiana', Box 9, Folder 1; 'Highlights of the History of Indianapolis YWCA', Box 9, Folder 1; and 'Young Women's Christian Association' (ca. 1957), Box 9, Folder 4, Records of the Young Women's Christian Association of Indianapolis, Collection M485, Library of the Indiana Historical Society, Indianapolis, Ind. (Hereafter cited Indianapolis Records.) See also Records of the Phyllis Wheatley Branch of the Young Women's Christian Association of Indianapolis (hereafter cited as Indianapolis Records), Collection M494.

[100] Quoted in Bell, 'A History of the Phyllis Wheatley Branch', 47.

[101] Histories include Goldstein, *An Inventory*, 5–11; Goldstein, 'Breaking Down Barriers'; and several archival documents: Folder 1046: 'Story of Denver Y.W.C.A. to March 1, 1934'; Folder 1055: Frances G. Elliott, 'Summary: The Committee of Management of the Phyllis Wheatley Branch, YWCA' (1949); and Folder 1056: Nelsine Howard Campbell, 'History: Phyllis Wheatley Branch, Young Women's Christian Association, Denver Colorado' (1935), in Box 43, Denver Records.

[102] Monthly reports of Health Education Department, 1921–1927, Box 9, Folder 195, Denver Records.

[103] Dorothy Guinn, 'Branch Among Colored Women', 1931, 2, in 'Annual Report to the National Board of the YWCA', Box 15, Folder 375, Denver Records.

[104] Typewritten chronology, n.d., Box 17, Folder 441; typewritten notes on Interracial Practices, 26 Oct. 1946, Box 17, Folder 441; and 'Notes of the Meeting of the Interracial Study Committee, November 3, 1944', Box 17, unnumbered folder, Denver Records; also Goldstein, 'Breaking Down Barriers', 49.

[105] Secondary studies include Cochrane, '"And the Pressure"', 259–69, and Cochrane, 'Compelled to Speak'.

[106] See Marjorie E. Monroe, 'Summary of Chronological History of Interracial Practices of the Boston YWCA, 1918–1944', 3–4, and Monroe, 'Chronological History of Interracial Practices, Boston YWCA, 1918–1944', 8–9, Box 31, Folder 447, Records of the Boston Young Women's Christian Association, Collection 89-M3, Arthur and Elizabeth Schlesinger Library on the History of Women in America, Radcliffe Institute, Harvard University, Cambridge, MA (hereafter cited as Boston Records).

[107] Monroe, 'Chronological History', 9, Box 31, Folder 447, Boston Records.

[108] Beavers to Smith, 21 March 1932, and Smith to Beavers, 11 April 1932, Folder: Pools, Policies and Practices, RG 6: IV-C, National Records.

[109] Hook, 'The YWCA in Cincinnati', 133–35.

[110] 'Report of Progress of the West End Branch YWCA Given at Board Meeting, December 4, 1935 by Virginia K. Jones, Branch General Secretary', 3, Box 37, Folder 2, Cincinnati Records.

[111] 'Memo – Recommendation to Program Committee on Use of Camp Lenmary by Negro Girls, 2/11/42', Box 15, Folder 16, Cincinnati Records.

[112] 'Minutes of Program Meeting, March 10, 1942', Box 15, Folder 17, Cincinnati Records.
[113] Minutes, Board of Directors, 1 April 1942, 6 May 1942, and 4 November 1942, Box 5, Folder 2, and 'West-End Committee, February 24, 1942', Box 15, Folder 16, Cincinnati Records.
[114] Minutes, Board of Directors, 6 Dec. 1944, 2–3, Box 5, Folder 4, Cincinnati Records.
[115] Minutes, Board of Directors, 3 Jan. 1945; 4 April 1945, 3; and 3 Oct. 1945, 2, Box 5, Folder 5, Cincinnati Records.
[116] Minutes, Board of Directors, 11 May 1946, 3, Box 5, Folder 6, Cincinnati Records.
[117] Minutes, Board of Directors, 6 Oct. 1948, 5, Box 5, Folder 8, Cincinnati Records.
[118] See 'Annual Narrative Report for the Program Year 1950–1951', 2, Box 7, Folder 15; 'Annual Narrative Report for the Program Year 1950–1951, Health Education Department', 3–4 (30–31 in previous report), Box 7, Folder 15; Minutes, Executive Committee, 2 Oct. 1950, 2, and 30 Oct. 1950, Box 2, Folder 18; and Minutes, Board of Directors, 4 Oct. 1950, 4; 1 Nov. 1950; and 6 Dec. 1950, 2, Box 5, Folder 10, Cincinnati Records.
[119] Meeting of Electors' Assembly, 30 January 1951, Box 5, Folder 11, Cincinnati Records.
[120] Hook, 'The YWCA in Cincinnati', 135, n.27.
[121] Boynton, '"It Surely is Grand"', 185.
[122] 'History of Interracial Policies in Health Education Department', appended to 'Interracial Policy of the YWCA', Box 40, Folder 10, and Cordella A. Winn, 'Chicago – Interracial', document 8, in 'Compilation', comp. Goss, Box 33, Folder 17, Chicago Records. See also Boynton, '"It Surely is Grand"', 185–91.
[123] Minutes, Metropolitan Board of Directors, 14 July 1927, 1–2, Box 47, Folder 1, Chicago Records.
[124] Minutes, Metropolitan Board of Directors, 14 Nov. 1929, Box 47, Folder 3, Chicago Records.
[125] Quoted in 'Record of Actions From the West Side Committee of Management of the Y.W.C.A. in Regard to Participation of Negro Girls in West Side Branch Activities', document 4, in 'Compilation', comp. Goss, Box 33, Folder 17, Chicago Records.
[126] Letter from the Committee of Management of the West Side Branch of the YWCA to the Metropolitan Board of the YWCA of Chicago, 19 Jan. 1937, document 3, in 'Compilation', comp. Goss, Box 33, Folder 17, Chicago Records.
[127] Letter, document 3; 'Record of Actions', document 4; 'Summary of the Attempt Within the Girl Reserve Department to Bring About a Better Feeling Between the Races Within the G.R. Department', document 5; and 'The Industrial Department-Chicago YWCA and Race Relations', document 7, in 'Compilation', comp. Goss, Box 33, Folder 17, Chicago Records.
[128] Minutes, Metropolitan Board of Directors, 22 Jan. 1937, 4–5, Box 48, Folder 4, and 'Record of Actions', document 4, in 'Compilation', comp. Goss, Box 33, Folder 17, Chicago Records.
[129] 'Annual Report 1942–1943, Health Education Department – The Y.W.C.A. of Chicago', 19–20, Box 34, Folder 4, and Minutes, Metropolitan Board of Directors, 22 May 1942, Box 49, Folder 3, Chicago Records.
[130] Minutes, Metropolitan Board of Directors, 22 May 1942, 4, Box 49, Folder 3, Chicago Records.
[131] 'Questionnaire About Interracial Practices in YWCA Form A', 1941–42, 11–13, Box 33, Folder 17, Chicago Records.
[132] 'Annual Report 1942–1943, Health Education Department – The YWCA of Chicago', 20, Box 34, Folder 4, and 'Race Relations in Y.W.C.A. [February 1938]', 2, document 2, in 'Compilation', comp. Goss, Box 33, Folder 17, Chicago Records.
[133] Minutes, Metropolitan Board of Directors, 22 Dec. 1944, 3, Box 49, Folder 5, Chicago Records.
[134] Minutes and interim reports are found in Box 40, Folder 10, Chicago Records. The committee's final report, 'Interracial Policy of the YWCA', is appended to 'Report of the Interracial Practices Committee, February 28, 1945', Box 40, Folder 10; see also Metropolitan Board of Directors, Box 49, Folder 6: 1945, Chicago Records.

[135] Histories include Boynton, '"It Surely is Grand"', and Spratt, 'To Be Separate or One'.

[136] Salem, *To Better Our World*, 134, 139.

[137] Letter from Virginia Esch to Mrs Judson L. Stewart, 26 June 1940, copy attached to Minutes, Board of Trustees, 17 Sept. 1940, Box 4, Volume: Jan. 1939–Dec. 1940, Cleveland Records.

[138] 'Progress Report of Interracial Committee given by Mrs Roudebush to Board of Trustees, Tuesday, October 15, 1940', copy attached to Minutes, Board of Trustees, 15 Oct. 1940, Box 4, Volume: Jan. 1939–Dec. 1940, and Minutes, Board of Trustees, 16 Dec. 1941, 1–2, Box 4,Volume: 1941–Jan. 1942, Cleveland Records.

[139] Minutes, Board of Trustees, 19 May 1942, 3, Box 5, Volume: Feb. 1942–Dec. 1945, Cleveland Records.

[140] Minutes, Board of Trustees, 16 Dec. 1941, 1, Box 4, Volume: 1941–Jan. 1942, Cleveland Records.

[141] Minutes, Board of Trustees, 16 June 1942, 6–7, and 22 Sept. 1942, 2–3, Box 5, Volume: Feb. 1942–Dec. 1945, Cleveland Records.

[142] On Health Education, see Minutes, Board of Trustees, 29 Feb. 1944, 4, and 28 March 1944, 2, Minutes, Board of Trustees, Box 5, Volume: Feb. 1942–Dec. 1945, Cleveland Records.

[143] On the Interracial Commission, see Box 15, Folder 369; on the YW and Japanese Americans, see Box 18, Folders 443–448, Denver Records.

[144] In 1938, Mildred H. Esgar led a comprehensive Program Study; see Box 15, Folder 388, Denver Records. Denver also was among nine cities included in Bell and Wilkins's landmark report in 1944.

[145] Goldstein, 'Breaking Down Barriers', 45–6.

[146] Minutes, Committee of Management, 4 May 1948, 1, Box 19, Folder 469; Report of Residence Committee, 13 Dec. 1944, Box 17, Folder 442; and minutes, Committee of Management, 8 Oct. 1945, 1–2, Box 19, Folder 467, Denver Records.

[147] Minutes, Committee on Interracial Integration, 5 Feb. 1948, Box 17, Folder 441, Denver Records.

[148] Minutes, Board of Directors, 9 April 1945, 2, and 8 May 1945, 1–2, Box 2, Folder 10, Denver Records.

[149] Quoted phrases from minutes, All-Association Leadership meeting, 14 April 1942, Box 1, Folder 9, and 'Notes of the Meeting of the Interracial Study Committee, November 3, 1944', 1, Box 17, unnumbered folder, Denver Records. Other examples from newspaper article, *ca.* 1931–1935, Box 15, Folder 369, and typed summary of progress, *ca.* 1949, Box 17, Folder 441, Denver Records.

[150] 'Meeting of Representatives', 28 Nov. 1944, 3, Box 17, Folder 442, Denver Records.

[151] Lynn, *Progressive Women*, 55.

[152] Ibid.

[153] Ibid., 190, n.28.

[154] Robertson, *Christian Sisterhood*, 177.

[155] Jones, 'Young Women's Christian Association', 1299, 1302–3.

[156] Lynn, *Progressive Women*, 2, 5, 41–42, 64–67.

[157] Quoted in Robertson, *Christian Sisterhood*, 3.

[158] 'Association D', in Appendix III of 'Interracial Practices', 10, Folder: Pools, Policies and Practices, National Records.

[159] 'Report of Cordella A. Winn, July 1938', 10, Folder: Reports, Secretaries', Winn, National Records.

[160] Lasch-Quinn, *Black Neighbors*, 157. Examples include Kirk, '"A Study in Second Class Citizenship"'; Rosenzweig, 'Middle-Class Parks'; and Wolcott, 'Recreation and Race'.

[161] Bennett and Dickerson, 'Introduction', in Bennett and Dickerson, *Recovering the Black Female Body*, 13.

References

Anderson, M. Christine. 'Home and Community for a Generation of Women: A Case Study of the Cincinnati YWCA Residence, 1920–1940'. *Queen City Heritage* 43 (1985): 34–41.

Baker, Paul E. *Negro-White Adjustment: An Investigation and Analysis of Methods in the Interracial Movement in the United States.* New York: Association Press, 1934.

Bell, Juliet O. and Helen J. Wilkins. *Interracial Practices in Community YWCAs: A Study Under the Auspices of the Commission to Gather Interracial Experience.* New York: National Board, Young Women's Christian Association, 1944.

Bell, Ruth Hamlin. 'A History of the Phyllis Wheatley Branch of the Indianapolis Young Women's Christian Association, 1923–1944'. MA thesis, Indiana University, 1948.

Bennett, Michael and Vanessa D. Dickerson, eds. *Recovering the Black Female Body: Self-Representations by African American Women.* New Brunswick, NJ: Rutgers University Press, 2000.

Boynton, Virginia Ruth. '"It Surely is Grand Living Your Own Life": The Search for Autonomy of Urban Midwestern Black and White Working Class Women, 1920–1950'. PhD diss., Ohio State University, 1995.

Cochrane, Sharlene Voogd. '"And the Pressure Never Let Up": Black Women, White Women, and the Boston YWCA, 1918–1948'. In *Women in the Civil Rights Movement: Trailblazers and Torchbearers, 1941–1965*, edited by Vicki L. Crawford, Jacqueline Anne Rouse and Barbara Woods. Brooklyn, NY: Carlson Publishing, 1990.

Cochrane, Sharlene Voogd. 'Compelled to Speak: Women Confronting Institutional Racism, 1910–1950'. *New England Journal of Public Policy* 7 (Fall/Winter 1991): 47–59.

Cory, Alberta J. 'The Physical Department of the Young Women's Christian Association in the United States'. *American Physical Education Review* 11 (1906): 95–103.

Cuthbert, Marion. 'The Negro Branch Executive'. *The Womans Press* 27 (April 1933): 190–1.

D'Emilio, John and Estelle B. Freedman. *Intimate Matters: A History of Sexuality in America.* New York: Harper & Row, 1988.

Frederickson, Mary. 'Citizens for Democracy: The Industrial Programs of the YWCA'. In *Sisterhood and Solidarity: Workers' Education for Women, 1914–1984*, edited by Joyce L. Kornbluh and Mary E. Frederickson. Philadelphia, PA: Temple University Press, 1984.

Garden, Mary-Stuart. 'The YWCA's First 100 Years'. *Journal of Health, Physical Education, and Recreation* 26 (Feb. 1955): 16–17, 53.

Gates, Edith M. 'Trends in Athletics for the Girls and Women in Employed Groups'. *American Physical Education Review* 34 (1929): 366–69.

Gates, Edith M. *Health Through Leisure-Time Recreation: The Health Education Program of the YWCA.* New York: The Womans Press, 1931.

Gates, Edith M. 'Living Up to "Health Education"'. *The Womans Press* 25 (May 1931): 284–5.

Gates, Edith M. 'To Your Health! What Is Your Y.W.C.A. Five-Year Plan for Health and Happiness?' *The Womans Press* 26 (Feb. 1932): 100–1, 123.

Gates, Edith M. 'National Association of Employed Officers of the YWCA – Part II'. *Journal of Health and Physical Education* 4 (Jan. 1933): 62.

Giddings, Paula. *When and Where I Enter: The Impact of Black Women on Race and Sex in America*, 2nd edn. New York: Quill of William Morris, 1996.

Goldstein, Marcia Tremmel. *An Inventory of the Papers of the YWCA of Metropolitan Denver.* Denver: Colorado Historical Society, 1991.

Goldstein, Marcia Tremmel. 'Breaking Down Barriers: The Denver YWCA and the Phyllis Wheatley Branch, 1940 to 1949'. *Historical Studies Journal [of the University of Colorado at Denver]* 12 (1995): 35–69.

Heath, Sarah. 'Negotiating White Womanhood: The Cincinnati YWCA and White Wage-Earning Women, 1918–1929'. In *Men and Women Adrift: The YMCA and the YWCA in the City*, edited by Nina Mjagkij and Margaret Spratt. New York: New York University Press, 1997.

Hedgeman, Anna Arnold. *The Trumpet Sounds: A Memoir of Negro Leadership*. New York: Holt, Rinehart and Winston, 1964.

Height, Dorothy I. *Step By Step with Interracial Groups*, 2d edn. New York: The Woman's Press, 1948.

'Helping Each Girl to Find Her Best Health'. *Sportswoman* 7 (Oct. 1930): 15, 30.

Hill, Ruth E., ed. *The Black Women Oral History Project*. Westport, CT: Meckler, 1990.

Hine, Darlene Clark and Kathleen Thompson. *A Shining Thread of Hope: The History of Black Women in America*. New York: Broadway Books, 1998.

Hook, Alice P. 'The YWCA in Cincinnati: A Century of Service, 1868–1968'. *Bulletin of the Cincinnati Historical Society* 26 (1968): 119–36.

hooks, bell. *Ain't I A Woman: Black Women and Feminism*. Boston, MA: South End Press, 1981.

Jones, Adrienne Lash. 'Phyllis (Phillis) Wheatley Clubs and Homes'. In *Black Women in America: An Historical Encyclopedia*, edited by Darlene Clark Hine, II. Brooklyn: Carlson Publishing, 1993.

Jones, Adrienne Lash. 'Young Women's Christian Association'. In *Black Women in America: An Historical Encyclopedia*, edited by Darlene Clark Hine, II. Brooklyn: Carlson Publishing, 1993.

Jones, Adrienne Lash. 'Struggle Among Saints: African American Women and the YWCA, 1870–1920'. In *Men and Women Adrift: The YMCA and the YWCA in the City*, edited by Nina Mjagkij and Margaret Spratt. New York: New York University Press, 1997.

Jordan, Winthrop D. *White over Black: American Attitudes Toward the Negro, 1550–1812*. Chapel Hill, NC: University of North Carolina Press, 1968.

Kirby, John B. 'The Roosevelt Administration and Blacks: An Ambivalent Legacy'. In *Twentieth-Century America: Recent Interpretations*, edited by Barton J. Bernstein and Allen J. Matusow, 2nd edn. New York: Harcourt Brace Jovanovich, 1972.

Kirby, John B. *Black Americans in the Roosevelt Era: Liberalism and Race*. Knoxville, TN: University of Tennessee Press, 1980.

Kirk, John A. '"A Study in Second Class Citizenship": Race, Urban Development, and Little Rock's Gillam Park, 1934–2004'. *Arkansas Historical Quarterly* 64 (2005): 262–86.

Knupfer, Anne Meis. *Toward a Tenderer Humanity and a Nobler Womanhood: African American Women's Clubs in Turn-of-the-Century Chicago*. New York: New York University Press, 1996.

Lasch-Quinn, Elisabeth. *Black Neighbors: Race and the Limits of Reform in the American Settlement House Movement, 1890–1945*. Chapel Hill, NC: University of North Carolina Press, 1993.

Lynn, Susan. *Progressive Women in Conservative Times: Racial Justice, Peace, and Feminism, 1945 to the 1960s*. New Brunswick, NJ: Rutgers University Press, 1992.

McBride, David. *From TB to AIDS: Epidemics among Urban Blacks since 1900*. Albany, NY: State University of New York Press, 1991.

McWilliams, Marion Lerrigo. 'War Steps Up Health and Recreation Programs'. *The Womans Press* 37 (Dec. 1943): 536.

Meanes, Lenna L. *Handbook of Positive Health*, rev. edn. New York: Women's Foundation for Health, 1928.

Meyerowitz, Joanne J. *Women Adrift: Independent Wage Earners in Chicago, 1880–1930*. Chicago: University of Chicago Press, 1988.

Miller, Patrick B. 'The Anatomy of Scientific Racism: Racialist Responses to Black Athletic Achievement'. *Journal of Sport History* 25 (1998): 119–51.

Mjagkij, Nina and Margaret Spratt, eds. *Men and Women Adrift: The YMCA and the YWCA in the City*. New York: New York University Press, 1997.

'The Nation-Wide Constituency of the YWCA's'. *The Woman's Press* 42 (Dec. 1948): 17.

Peterson, Carla L. 'Foreword'. In *Recovering the Black Female Body: Self-Representations by African American Women*, edited by Michael Bennett and Vanessa D. Dickerson. New Brunswick, NJ: Rutgers University Press, 2000.

Richards, Irene. 'Washington Wartime Woes of a Health Education Director'. *The Womans Press* 38 (April 1944): 190–1.

Robertson, Nancy Marie. '"Deeper Even Than Race"?: White Women and the Politics of Christian Sisterhood in the Young Women's Christian Association, 1906–1946'. PhD diss., New York University, 1997.

Robertson, Nancy Marie. *Christian Sisterhood, Race Relations, and the YWCA, 1906–46*. Urbana, IL: University of Illinois Press, 2007.

Robertson, Nancy with Elizabeth Norris. '"Without Documents No History": Sources and Strategies for Researching the YWCA'. In *Men and Women Adrift: The YMCA and the YWCA in the City*, edited by Nina Mjagkij and Margaret Spratt. New York: New York University Press, 1997.

Rosenzweig, Roy. 'Middle-Class Parks and Working-Class Play: The Struggle Over Recreational Space in Worcester, Massachusetts, 1870–1910'. *Radical History Review* 21 (Fall 1979): 31–46.

Sabiston, Dothory and Margaret Hiller. *Toward Better Race Relations*. New York: The Woman's Press, 1949.

Salem, Dorothy. *To Better Our World: Black Women in Organized Reform, 1890–1920 (Black Women in United States History*, vol. 14). Brooklyn: Carlson Publishing, 1990.

Sitkoff, Harvard. *A New Deal For Blacks: The Emergence of Civil Rights as a National Issue*. New York: Oxford University Press, 1978.

Spratt, Margaret Ann. 'To Be Separate or One: The Issue of Race in the History of Pittsburgh and Cleveland YWCAs, 1920–1946'. In *Men and Women Adrift: The YMCA and YWCA in the City*, edited by Nina Mjagkij and Margaret Spratt. New York: New York Univeristy Press, 1997.

A Symposium on Health and Recreation by Ten YWCA Leaders. New York: The Womans Press, 1936.

Tomes, Nancy. *The Gospel of Germs: Men, Women, and the Microbe in American Life*. Cambridge, MA: Harvard University Press, 1998.

Vertinsky, Patricia A. and Gwendolyn Captain. 'More Myth than History: American Culture and Representations of the Black Female's Athletic Ability'. *Journal of Sport History* 25 (1998): 532–61.

Wailoo, Keith. *Drawing Blood: Technology and Disease Identity in Twentieth-Century America*. Baltimore, MD: Johns Hopkins University Press, 1997.

Ware, Susan, ed. *Notable American Women: A Biographical Dictionary Completing the Twentieth Century*. Cambridge, MA: Belknap Press of Harvard University Press, 2004.

Wiltse, Jeff. *Contested Waters: A Social History of Swimming Pools in America*. Chapel Hill, NC: University of North Carolina Press, 2007.

Wolcott, Victoria W. 'Recreation and Race in the Postwar City: Buffalo's 1956 Crystal Beach Riot'. *Journal of American History* 93 (2006): 63–90.

Young, Lola. 'Racializing Femininity'. In *Women's Bodies: Discipline and Transgression*, edited by Jane Arthurs and Jean Grimshaw. London: Cassell, 1999.

Leading the Way in Science, Medicine and Physical Training: Female Physicians in Academia, 1890–1930

Susan G. Zieff

In the late nineteenth and early twentieth centuries, the profession of physical education was influenced by the ideas and research activities of physicians interested in understanding the role of physical training in health. Physicians Lilian Welsh and Clelia Mosher were among those physicians who contributed to both curricular developments in hygiene and physical education programmes in higher education and to scientific research that provided the basis for health claims from exercise, while employed by institutions of higher learning. In their decades of service to Goucher College (Welsh) and Stanford University (Mosher), these doctors also used science to diminish the claims of physiological inferiority of women thereby furthering the cause of higher education for women.

Introduction

A recent report published by the non-profit Center for Work-Life Policy investigated attitudes towards women and work in the fields of science, engineering and technology and found that the majority of women experienced harassment and dismissive attitudes by their male colleagues while on the job. [1] Underlying this culture of workplace sexism, suggest the authors of the report, is the perception that 'women are simply not as good in math and science as men are'. [2] Yet, 66 per cent of workers in the earliest stages of scientific and medical research are women, suggesting that factors within these occupational cultures, rather than qualifications, play a role in limiting women from advancing through the ranks.

In the last decades of the nineteenth-century, the question of women's intellectual capacity, intertwined with the basic premise that women's bodies were simply not strong enough to withstand the rigours of the intellectual work required in higher education, also limited access to the medical and scientific professions – at any level. This paper explores the career paths of two female physicians, Clelia Mosher (1863–1940) and Lilian Welsh (1858–1938), as exemplars of women who negotiated professional terrain within medicine and science while also making extensive and important contributions to the emerging field of physical training. [3] Mosher, Stanford University's iconoclastic physician and professor of physical training for 22 years, and Welsh, at Goucher College for 30 years, also studied the effects of education on their female students while instituting preventive measures based largely on physical activity. Through research and curricular developments these two physicians brought their personal experiences of gender bias to bear on the process of advancing the cause of physical and intellectual education for women.

Public debate of the 'Woman Question' in the last decades of the nineteenth century focused on the nature of women's role in society utilizing a discourse rooted in the new discipline of physiology. To differing degrees, many of the most vocal critics of higher education for women agreed with writer Grant Allen's declaration that 'almost all must become wives and mothers'. [4] Another prominent spokesman for this position was Edward Hammond Clarke, a Harvard Medical School professor, whose 1873 treatise *Sex in Education; or a Fair Chance for Girls* framed the argument for separate, different and unequal education for females. Clarke's main argument was that stress from intellectual work would cause damage, possibly permanent, to the developing reproductive organs of college women. [5] The perceived connection between mental activity and reproduction led other mainstream physicians and those who subscribed to the views that Clarke articulated, to claim that female students' femininity, defined in large part by reproductive capabilities, would be compromised by their engagement in intellectual work.

The professional lives of Mosher and Welsh came almost two decades after the publication of *Sex in Education; or a Fair Chance for Girls* (1873). Yet Clarke's treatise continued to raise alarm among educators and parents about the dangers to the developing reproductive systems of young women from too much 'brain-work', leaving a legacy reaching far wider than the halls of the women's colleges, many of which were founded during this period of anxiety about the female body. The numbers of female students increased dramatically during these years, perhaps adding to public concerns about female health. [6] At the same time, female educational institutions were forced to develop a variety of instructional strategies such as limiting the number of courses students could take to prevent the ill-health and physiological breakdown that was thought to result from excessive intellectual activity. In response to the growing concern over female students' health, colleges instituted programmes of medical surveillance and health monitoring. Among the most important and effective strategies were the establishment of hygiene and physical training programmes; the employment of a female physician to prescribe and oversee regimens of therapeutic exercise; the collection of health data emphasizing anthropometric and menstrual cycle record-keeping; and the supervision of students' daily lives, including workload and participation in physical activity. Complementary to these curricular components was the research conducted by the physician/physical directors of many of these institutions.

With a subject population at hand and a professional agenda aimed at advancing their occupational ambitions, Mosher and Welsh undertook the study of the female body in its physical and physiological dimensions. Paradoxically, the implementation of physical training programmes promising to improve their health allowed many young women to be more vigorously active than would have been possible outside the collegiate setting.

Mosher was more prolific in publishing her research than Welsh; during her time at Stanford that concluded in 1929, she published numerous research articles investigating the specific and special factors associated with physical training in women. Welsh, on the other hand, is noteworthy for her efforts to incorporate scientific physical training courses in the overall curriculum at Goucher at the same time constructing a major's programme of study that rivalled those at the most competitive institutions. Despite long, productive careers, Mosher achieved full professor status only the year before her retirement in 1929, as did Welsh in her last year at Goucher in 1924, suggestive of their personal experiences with professional bias.

Physiology and Physical Training: Mosher's Career and Curricular Contributions

Mosher's legacy of insistence on demonstrating equal physical capacity among males and females, her condemnation of various social conventions that limited women both physically and intellectually, and her commitment to rigorous scientific physiological research to provide evidence for her convictions mark her as a 'scientist' of the new study of the body that began in the last decades of the nineteenth century. As an undergraduate, Mosher attended Wellesley College, Cornell University and the University of Wisconsin before receiving her AB degree in zoology from Stanford in 1892. She was among the 20 per cent of women at Stanford who chose scientific majors. [7]

In 1893, Mosher became an instructor in the Department of Hygiene and Physical Training at the recently opened Stanford University beginning a more than 30-year tenure interrupted only twice, when she left for four years of medical school at Johns Hopkins and for a year of medical service in Paris during the First World War. Between 1893 and 1896, Mosher completed her master's degree work in physiology at Stanford and taught courses in gymnastic exercises and physical training to women; the latter course included medical gymnastics and athletic games. [8] Her instructional responsibilities increased during 1895, her second year in which she co-taught with Thomas Denizen Wood (professor and head of the department), a course in personal hygiene that incorporated first aid and emergency information, as well as a course in anthropometry for majors. As Frederick Burk, director of the San

Francisco Normal School, noted in a letter to Mosher: 'to do such work in hygiene and practical physiology as you wish to do, a medical course in the best school in the country [is] necessary'. [9] It was advice that Mosher adopted.

Mosher's choice of Johns Hopkins was carefully considered; at that time its medical school was considered among the finest in the country and she would have access to the institution's scholarly publications and most renowned professors and medical researchers. Indeed, Mosher published two articles in the *Johns Hopkins Hospital Bulletin* and formed a close relationship with Howard Kelly, then establishing a national reputation in gynaecological and obstetrical surgery. He supervised her study on gallstone frequency. [10] Upon graduation, Mosher applied for a fellowship with Dr William Howell, following a career path typical of medical school graduates, but was denied. She then took a position with Kelly as an extern in the Johns Hopkins Hospital Dispensary, but rejected his offer of a permanent position the following year because of his refusal to include with her duties an assistantship in gynaecological surgery. Kelly did not believe that any man would be willing to work under a woman. [11] In 1905, Mosher was still attempting to stabilize her income with research fellowships; for her application to the Carnegie Institution, then Stanford president David Starr Jordan wrote a letter of recommendation that suggested both knowledge of and support for her scientific work. [12] Eventually, and as was typical of other female medical scientists, her inability to find support within the male-dominated medical community necessitated a turn towards educational institutions for financial and collegial support.

On her return to California, Mosher continued teaching courses in physiological hygiene and physical culture, this time at the San Francisco State Normal School and the private Miss Harker's School in Palo Alto, California. Hoping to find a site in which to conduct her research and with an offer of higher compensation, she accepted the position of director of the women's gymnasium and professor of hygiene at Stanford University in 1910. Mosher's teaching repertoire included courses she taught previously, including physical training and hygiene, and a physical training methods component of a course in supervising children's play. The latter course combined instruction in the techniques and teaching of gymnastics and games and personal hygiene. [13] She also encouraged athletic activities for girls and women – including tennis, swimming, hiking, bicycling, horseback riding and basketball – that were still regarded as 'dangerous' for the female physique. [14]

Under assistant professor and gymnasium director Mosher, courses listed in the 1911 Stanford University *Register* noted that the Roble Gymnasium (for women) was a 'laboratory of personal hygiene' in which students could reach their 'highest physical efficiency'. [15] One year later, Encina Gymnasium (for men) indicated its function as a 'laboratory of personal hygiene'. [16] At that time, the focus of these programmes was to coordinate classes for students preparing to teach physical training, direct playground work or, in the case of the male students, to become proficient in the theory and technique of sports and gymnastics. Five years later, with text identical to that used in Mosher's personal communication, the goals of Roble Gymnasium were 'to improve the standard of physical health of the women and to increase their mental and physical efficiency'. [17] The physical training requirement for the first two years of undergraduate work was expanded to include all undergraduates during the 1917–18 school year in order to 'encourage the habit of exercise; and to stimulate a widespread interest in physical activity of all kinds, especially in those forms which will be available to the women after leaving college'. [18]

Few additional notable curricular changes were instituted until 1923 when Mosher corresponded with Stanford president Ray Lyman Wilbur about a proposed one-hour weekly course in personal hygiene to replace a quarterly course meeting three times per week:

> I am opposed to reducing the physical activity of women to two periods a week. There is not much over a half hour of exercises at each hour and already the stronger women are asking for enrollment in two or more courses to get sufficient exercise. On the other hand the women who wish to escape physical activity are aided with the already too small requirement. [19]

In the early decades of the twentieth century, and with scientific advances in the fields of applied physiology and preventive medicine, Mosher viewed the field of physical training as one of functionality rather than the acquisition of basic knowledge: 'This then is our object: to develop the individual to her highest capacity in health and beauty; and to render her physically, mentally, and ideally fit for normal life. This double purpose kept firmly in mind, physical training becomes laboratory work in personal hygiene.' [20]

The profession of physical education, based on various systems of gymnastics and physical training, was hindered by a lack of science and research, Mosher asserted. In 1925, she voiced these concerns in a confidential letter to Lou Henry Hoover (Mrs Herbert Hoover) in which she attempted to resign her membership from the Medical Committee of the National Amateur Athletic Federation (NAAF). At the present time, Mosher asserted, 'there is danger of [the work of the Committee] being only the usual physical training worker's so-called "research" which is usually of doubtful scientific value, as I have seen it'. [21] At NAAF meetings, she noted, 'there is not a single member of the Committee who has any conception of what research really means'. The following year, when asked by President Wilbur to inspect a potential laboratory space, Mosher noted:

> I could have spent the evening with the blood pressure paper and as I thought of the possibilities of having this quiet place all to myself to go on my research work on the blood – if it could be had entirely separate from the Physical training department – well it took away my breath. [22]

Mosher viewed physical training as 'applied physiology', no more than a branch of preventive medicine, the legitimate scientific goal of her work.

Measuring and Monitoring the Female Body: Mosher's Anthropometric Research

The health of women was of continuing interest to Mosher; her entire research output focused on investigating the impact of presumed sex differences on the lives and health of women. In her cumulative 37-year period of scientific productivity (extending back to her master's work), the topics that received her greatest attention included: the mechanisms of female respiration, normal and dysfunctional menstruation, and female growth patterns – including the development of strength. The period between 1910 and 1929 was especially productive; more than a dozen and a half scholarly articles, monographs and research notes were published during that time.

Her work began to bridge the gap between the form-based natural sciences of the mid-nineteenth century and the function-based physiological approaches gaining prominence by the early twentieth century, though some of her later studies were frankly anthropometric in nature. In the 1921 publication of 'Concerning the Size of Women, Preliminary Note', in which she charted the height of Stanford University women over 30 years, Mosher reported average gains of one to one and one-tenth inches. From this data, she concluded that '[t]he racial as well as economic importance of these changes, which point to a more fully developed and more perfectly functioning type of woman, can hardly be overestimated'. [23] Her correlation of a variable of outward form, in this case height, with internal function was aligned with the conclusions of anthropometric work conducted for several decades by other physical educators. [24]

Moving beyond a simple descriptive account of the students' growth patterns, Mosher addressed the question of 'causal factors' that might influence the height of students. Comparing the results of Stanford women with those of Vassar and Smith Colleges, she noted the changes in fashion and different levels of physical activity of the subjects. An associate professor at that point, she asserted that the increases in height of college women 'proved' the benefits of college life and its requirement of systematic physical education. Not only was college life not detrimental to young women, college exercise programmes aided in the development of a 'finer physical type of woman'. [25] Mosher was convinced that increased physical activity among women, whether college-going or not, improved their physical capacity, 'insuring better wives and mothers, and consequently a better race'. [26] External measures were used once again to demonstrate enhanced capacity of internal functions, in this case, reproduction.

A study published in 1918 on previously collected data [27] demonstrated her continued explorations of the relationship between biological and social causes of female physical incapacity. The study, 'The Muscular Strength of College Women', co-authored with Ernest Gale Martin, professor of physiology at Stanford, had been conducted on female Stanford students. The authors concluded that '[there] is no difference in the muscular strength of women and men which is due to sex as such'. [28] Her research outcomes did not dissuade her from reiterating the socially prominent message of motherhood as the primary role of women. The economic demands that might compel women to work 'must not divert the girl's attention too much from her racial obligations', Mosher declared. She then added: 'Since she in consequence may recognize too late the fact that no woman reaches her fullest development who is not a wife and mother.' [29]

Posture was another indicator of 'the perfect functioning of the body' according to Mosher, and with Stanford mechanical engineering professor E.P. Lesley, she devised an instrument known as a 'schematograph' to measure posture and the contours of the body by reflecting a silhouette onto graph paper. [30] The invention was patented and sold to university physical training departments nationwide. [31] Posture analyses, like anthropometry, were used in an effort to evaluate the inner workings of the body through external measures. Articles on posture were published into the 1920s and 1930s in journals such as *Hygeia*, the *American Physical Education Review* and *Research Quarterly for Exercise and Science*. Although efforts to improve posture among adults and children alike drew popular support for its presumed health benefits, posture analyses (as with anthropometry) were eventually discredited for lack of scientific evidence. [32]

Determining the Nature of Menstruation: Healthy Function or Pathology?

Four of Mosher's works of scholarship that emphasized physiological rather than anthropometric measures focused on menstruation. Contrary to the contemporary view that treated the reproductive cycle as incapacitating or as pathology, Mosher explored the social conditions and causes of conditions such as dysmenorrhoea (painful menstruation). Among the most significant factors she identified were those she termed 'psychical influences' including the pervasive and negative use of the phrase 'sick time' to refer to menstruation. Included among the causes of menstrual disorders were family causes, unsuitable clothing and its effect on respiration, the muscular consequences of physical inactivity, poor posture and inadequate digestive function. [33]

Although Mosher did not allow her female students to participate in 'active work in physical training or athletics during the menstrual period', they were required to don gymnasium dress and report to her where they received an 'informal talk on some hygienic subject' and filled out a card where data on menstruation was recorded. [34] Finally, the student was required to perform the 'Moshering' abdominal exercises she invented to strengthen weak abdominal muscles and alleviate the 'insufficient use of the diaphragm' that caused 'undue congestion of the uterus' and pain during menstruation. [35] In her 'Report on Exercise as a Factor in the Relief o Menstrual Disturbances', published in the 1917–1918 *Bulletin of the Mary Hemenway Alumnae Association of the Department of Hygiene at Wellesley College*, Elizabeth A. Wright noted that Mosher's exercises proved that 'intelligently directed exercise is a factor of considerable importance in the relief of various menstrual disturbances'. [36]

In addition to her hypotheses of the social causes of menstrual 'suffering', Mosher asserted that 'true dysmenorrhea' – a rare occurrence – was wrongly associated with the 'lessened sense of well being and diminished sense of efficiency, which may accompany the lowered general blood pressure occurring near or at the menstrual flow, to the function of menstruation'. [37] In three reports on normal and dysfunctional menstruation, she identified both physiological and psychological factors she believed exerted influence on this function. Data were collected on 2,000 cases extending over 12,000 menstrual periods and included subjective observations by her subjects. The duration of her study and the quantity of data collected were noted by Boston gynaecologist George Engelmann, a former president of the American Gynecological Society. [38] Although Mosher refused to release her data to Engelmann for his review, she later published her conclusions in *Health and the Woman Movement* (1916). This work was published in five revised editions between 1916 and 1927 as *Woman's Physical Freedom* and *Personal Hygiene for Women*. Hygiene for women, broadly defined, included attention to the feet, dress, eating and sleeping habits, as well as a positive attitude toward menstruation and menopause.

Mosher became a fellow of the American Medical Association (1906–36) and the American Association for the Advancement of Science (AAAS). The category of 'fellow' had been created by the AAAS in the 1870s as a way of separating ordinary members from fellows who were 'professionally engaged in science, or have by their labors aided in advancing science', suggesting a certain amount of recognition of Mosher among her peers. [39] An entry for her was also included in the fourth edition of *American Men of Science* (1927), James McKeen Cattell's biographical dictionary that recruited nominations from the rosters of scientific societies, institutions of higher education and from *Science, The Nation* and *Popular Science Monthly*. Mosher was not included in Howard Kelly's *American Medical Biographies* published in 1920, although she had been his student and extern at Johns Hopkins. Her exclusion was perhaps due in part to medical institution sexism, but likely also due to the limited role she played as a practising physician.

The route of employment ultimately taken by Mosher was one less of passion than expediency. The closure to her of most forms of medical employment for women cost her in terms of financial and professional success; what she gained from her tenure with Stanford was an environment that provided research opportunity and an available pool of subjects. Her inclusion as one of only three female full professors at Stanford before the Second World War places her in the ranks of that institution's most esteemed faculty members. [40] Although she implemented the measurement and exercise prescription components of a 'medicalized' programme, Mosher also worked to demonstrate that the ill-health of women was exacerbated by the social perception of female weakness; for both of these conditions, exercise was prevention and remedy.

Lilian Welsh: Preventing Ill Health through Physiology and Hygiene

In a career that spanned 30 years, Lilian Welsh, physician and public health advocate, encouraged her students at the all-female Goucher College near Baltimore, Maryland, to question the expectation of ill-health with which many of them entered college. Through classroom and gymnasium work, Goucher students were given the tools and responsibility for the development and preservation of their personal health, unlike the emphasis on physical activity and teacher training at Stanford. After 1894, Goucher no longer offered its teacher-training programme. However, many aspects of a medically-oriented hygiene and physical training programme, including physical evaluations and exercise prescription were incorporated into the curriculum at Goucher.

From the late 1880s until Welsh arrived in 1894, the curriculum at Goucher combined measurement and gymnastic work with coursework in hygiene and physiology under the influence of its first three directors, Alice Hall, Mary Mitchell and Lilian Welsh, all trained in medicine. Under the leadership of Hall, Mitchell and Welsh, the Department of Anatomy, Physiology and Hygiene at Goucher further developed a conceptual and course-based link with the college's preliminary medical curriculum and with the medical school at nearby Johns Hopkins University. Prescribed and elective forms of gymnasium and physical training work continued to be offered, providing a conceptual and behavioural link between performance in the gymnasium and classroom work in the biomedical sciences.

Like Mosher, Welsh did not apply her medical training in hospital or clinical work but through her influence on curricular developments at Goucher, and in the broader medical community of Baltimore [41] she integrated the fields of physiology, hygiene and preventive medicine. One goal of her hygiene course was, for example, to develop in her students a familiarity 'with the sources to which they might look in the future for authoritative information on hygienic subjects'. [42] Employed by the Department of Physiology and Hygiene, Welsh also taught in the Biology Department. Her course on animal physiology and histology was the only course available on campus offering instruction in histology, circulation, respiration, digestion and other physiological phenomena, making it a choice of candidates for medical school.

In the late 1890s, students taking the elective course in hygiene in the Department of Anatomy, Physiology and Hygiene concurrently enrolled in Welsh's animal physiology course. Throughout the 1890s, the department's lecture course in hygiene and physiology remained embedded in the college's preliminary medical course in conjunction with four courses in the biology, chemistry and physics departments. Welsh remained on the faculty rosters of the departments of biology and anatomy and hygiene through 1908. Graduation requirements in science had been steadily increasing in the early decades of the twentieth century. From 1915 to 1934, one year of physics or chemistry was required of all students in addition to one semester each of biology, physiology, hygiene and psychology, [43] reflecting a general trend of 'advancing scientism' in American higher education. [44]

Welsh's goal for the course was to provide her students with the biological, chemical and physical concepts 'necessary to the understanding of hygiene and as applied science'. [45] The conclusions of female inferiority advanced by many

American and English scientists in the last half of the nineteenth century, including the work of an English psychiatrist 'who showed by painstaking measurements that the entire cross section of arteries going to the female brain is less than that going to the male' [46] were those that she tried to dispel among her students and in her work. The opening of Johns Hopkins medical school in 1892 also influenced the emphasis on science education at Goucher. In 1893 the course numbers within biology and anatomy, physiology and hygiene were rearranged for greater numerical and conceptual fluidity. In addition, the prerequisite of courses in biology, physics and chemistry for work in physiology and hygiene created an intersection between those two departments, and a connection with work done in preparation for entering medical school.

Welsh's 'Preventive' Curriculum and the Scientific Basis of Hygiene

When Lilian Welsh joined the faculty of Goucher College, her position incorporated three aspects: (1) to oversee and organize a programme of gymnastic exercises based on the Swedish system; (2) to teach required courses in hygiene; and (3) to provide laboratory work and lectures for a small number of advanced students in the basic elements of physiology and histology. Much of what is known about her early life comes from sources in the Goucher archives, her autobiography, *Reminiscences of Thirty Years in Baltimore* (1925) and her 1923 presentation on 'Fifty Years of Women's Education in the United States', which inaugurated the Lilian Welsh Lectureship at Goucher. What emerges is a picture of a woman deeply committed to the pursuit of health and higher education for women as well as to the growing public and preventive health movement. In 1889, with a medical degree from the Woman's Medical College of Pennsylvania, Welsh sought to pursue a doctoral degree in physiological chemistry from the University of Zurich, one of the few institutions willing to grant the PhD to women. [47] Difficult financial circumstances forced her to leave Zurich before completing her degree, whereupon she took a position as assistant resident physician in a hospital for the insane at Norristown, Pennsylvania, where she stayed for two years. She was then appointed professor of anatomy, physiology, hygiene and physical training at Goucher, succeeding Mary Mitchell.

The professional marginality of both the asylum and the women's college made them an option for medically trained women. Collegiate physical training programmes for women hired and promoted women – especially those with medical training – when other departments and medical institutions would not. At Goucher, for example, Hall, Mitchell and Welsh were the only women to hold professorships until 1904, when Eleanor Lord was promoted in the history department. Dr Frances Emily White, professor of physiology at the Woman's Medical College of Pennsylvania, lamented the fact that three of her students (Hall, Mitchell and Welsh) 'were wasting their talents and their medical education in teaching gymnastic movements to girls'. [48] However, neither Welsh nor her two predecessors were actively engaged in teaching gymnastics, nor was that the basis for their positions at Goucher. In addition, although she cared for ill students from her first day at Goucher, she was never compensated for this work and received no recognition as resident physician. [49] Promotion to the rank of full professor came only with her retirement in 1924 as professor emeritus of physiology and hygiene. [50]

Writing in her autobiography of 1925, Welsh recalled that

> A woman who accepted a position in a woman's college in 1890 to develop a department of hygiene entered an unworked field and could practically make of it what she pleased. She could expect little or no help from her colleagues in trying to give her department academic rank because the subject of hygiene as a dignified subject for department standing in a college of liberal arts was unheard of and a professor of physical training was given scant consideration by the early generation of doctors of philosophy who were rapidly filling the professorial chairs in colleges. [51]

When Welsh coordinated the academic and physical activity programmes at Goucher, the *Program* of courses noted that the Department of Anatomy, Physiology and Hygiene was 'closely associated' with that of physical training, a reiteration of departmental alliances that reflects both jurisdictional and academic issues. Continually striving to legitimize the work of the Department of Physical Training, she highlighted its achievements in the college yearbook:

> The Woman's College of Baltimore is the only college in the United States which, in its organization, provided for a department of physical training with a required course coordinate with the other departments of college work, and, with the exception of Amherst, is, so far as I know, the only college in America where the work of physical training has received this recognition. [52]

In 1925, she reminisced that she had initially viewed the gymnasium at Goucher College as a laboratory 'where one might study the effects of exercise and of mental work upon the health of girls and women'. [53] In those 'early days', she recalled, there were few students 'with a neurotic history or a neurotic tendency whose mind was not fixed upon her reproductive organs as the source of all her troubles'. [54] She remembered the last decades of the nineteenth century as a time when the female reproductive system was viewed 'as the source of most of their ills and the function of menstruation as a monthly recurrent disabling period, even if not accompanied by dysmenorrhaea' [*sic*]. [55] Emphasizing a curriculum that was *preventive* rather than *curative* became an important focus for Welsh, who established the role of medical inspection as the basis of the programme of physical training. The records kept on each student allowed her to determine that ill-health symptoms attributed to collegiate life were pre-existing. The unification of the Department of Physical Training and Hygiene meant that 'physical training, together with scientific instruction in anatomy, physiology, and hygiene were required of every student'. [56] She justified her lack of compensation for medical services she rendered as supportive of her philosophy of a 'preventive' rather than 'curative' approach to the health of young women.

Welsh balanced her efforts between developing the necessary physical activity components of the physical training programme and focusing her attention on expanding the required hygiene course (which included instruction in anatomy and physiology) from one hour to three hours per week in 1895 in an effort to increase its academic status among both students and her colleagues. [57] At that time, Welsh shifted her time away from the gymnasium activities that were now under the direction of instructors Eva Braun and Helene Gihl, graduates of the Gymnastic Institute at Stockholm; she was convinced that 'the Swedish system offered the best foundation for systematic formal gymnastics in classes'. [58] In 1894, Welsh spent five months observing teacher training programmes in Sweden, Germany and England and returned to the United States convinced of the value of the scientifically-based Swedish gymnastic method. [59] As director of the programme, she then hired Swedish and English instructors with few exceptions; the scientifically appropriate Swedish gymnastic system and English outdoor games were thought to add 'healthful activity of every organ and bring about symmetry of form and ease of movement'. [60]

Pre-requisite for enrolment in Welsh's elementary hygiene course was a background in basic sciences including biology because of her belief that the inner workings of the body must be understood in order to maintain its health. She taught her students the principles of healthy daily living and gave them 'the necessary biological, chemical and physical concepts necessary to the understanding of hygiene as an applied science [and] to thoroughly instill into their minds a respect for hygiene as a growing body of truths of fundamental importance to human life and human happiness'. [61]

Goucher students' rigorous grounding in laboratory histology, physiology and bacteriology as well as in the fundamentals of public and preventive health gave them a broad perspective on the human body. Laboratory study was still a relatively new concept among the nation's leading medical schools and scientific medicine was not yet thoroughly accepted as the best path for medical education. [62] Welsh's advocacy of laboratory work for undergraduates was a new method of scientific education. By the turn of the century, the major elective became increasingly laboratory oriented as an animal dissection was added to the course tasks. In addition, the course was extended from one-half of the term to the whole second term, the remaining time devoted to 'elementary work in cellular physiology and the physiology of nerve and muscle'. [63]

Welsh had been interested in physiological chemistry in medical school and with the course returned to her home department she regained full control of the course content. As the scientific foundation of the department expanded, she found the basis for offering a course in her subject of passion: physiological chemistry. In 1907–8 the course in animal physiology moved back to the Physiology and Hygiene Department as a lecture and laboratory course that included 'the study of nerve muscle physiology with experimental work, and the physiology of digestion and secretion with special reference to the chemistry of these processes'.

In 1910 and then again in 1911, Welsh was invited to deliver hygiene lectures to the students of Bryn Mawr College. Bryn Mawr president M. Carey Thomas moved the second year's lecture to freshman year, 'so that they may be as hygienic as possible for the rest of the year'. [64] She turned down the position as resident physician and professor of hygiene at Bryn Mawr offered her two years later for reasons that remain unclear. The offer of a salary of $2,500, well above the average income for an American family of four of $830, could not have been the reason. [65]

Welsh continued to teach hygiene and physiology courses, adding to her teaching responsibilities a course on the physiology of the nervous system that she taught in 1917. That same year, she separated the subject of 'community hygiene' from the course on family and communal hygiene. Topics included municipal, state and national methods for preventing disease and promoting health, another area of interest of hers given her association with the Maryland State Board of Health as a member of the commission studying the problem of tuberculosis in Maryland, her work as a founding member of the National Association for the Study and Prevention of Infant Mortality in 1912 and long-term membership on the board of managers of the Evening Dispensary for Working Women and Girls of Baltimore City.

In her 30-year affiliation with Goucher and the Baltimore medical and public health communities, Lilian Welsh advocated a variety of preventive health care methods, emphasizing the importance of education in the prevention of disease. At Goucher, she was particularly interested in educating women about their physiological and reproductive processes. As women became better informed about their functions, Welsh asserted, they would be less 'fixed upon [their] reproductive organs as the source' of all their troubles. [66] In this, she shared with Mosher the view that women are not biologically susceptible to ill-health.

Conclusions

Between 1888 and 1924, under its first three directors, Hall, Mitchell and Welsh, the Goucher Department of Physiology and Hygiene evolved from a programme based on hygiene and elementary physiology into one whose aims paralleled those of the growing public health movement by incorporating the modern principles of hygiene and bacteriology. At Stanford, the Department of Hygiene and Physical Training also developed into a rigorous, scientifically-based curriculum that provided students with the tools for healthful living.

Though both Mosher and Welsh integrated discoveries in the new fields of physiology and preventive medicine into their educational approaches, neither one was able to wholly discard a view that focused on the role of the reproductive system in determining female health. Mosher continued to assert that female health was the basis for motherhood, while Welsh advocated the use of science to dispel myths about female reproductive system inferiority and for the development and preservation of personal health. Ultimately both women became strong advocates for the role of physical activity and physical training in the improvement of female physical capacity and the prevention of disease.

Using physical training, physiology and hygiene as their tools, Welsh and Mosher also fought deeply ingrained notions of female capacity that in various ways had sabotaged their own careers. As Mosher overtly championed the rights of women to pursue both physical and intellectual training, she experienced, and likely suffered, from professional and employment inequities that exemplified the social context of the late nineteenth and early twentieth centuries. Welsh, too, aware of the limitations on her professional growth and progress, took advantage of opportunities within the broader community to utilize her medical and public health expertise.

Looking back over the half-century of development of women's higher education, Bryn Mawr president M. Carey Thomas could say with some confidence in 1907 that the 'battle' had been 'gloriously, and forever, won'. [67] Questions about intellectual capacity and the impact of college education on marriage and motherhood that had been prevalent in the decades before had been greatly, though not completely, dismissed. Looking back over the 30 years of professional service by these physician/physical educators, the impact of their insistence on a scientific basis for claims about the capacity of the female body and their advocacy of physical activity for the health of women is evident in the legacy of female physical educators who comprise the rank and file of the profession and hold positions at the highest levels of professional leadership.

In 1974, the re-named American Alliance for Health, Physical Education, Recreation and Dance (AAHPERD), the largest organization of professionals associated with the fields of physical and health education, instituted a policy of alternating female and male presidents, thus providing a secure leadership opportunity for female physical educators. [68] From its inception at the 1980 meeting of the Research Consortium of AAHPERD, female scholars have presented 12 of the 30 C.H. McCloy Memorial Lectures, an honour bestowed upon outstanding scholars and scientists, [69] and since 1941, 20 women have been elected to the annual term of president of the American Academy of Physical Education (now American Academy of Kinesiology and Physical Education, AAKPE), one of the profession's leading honorary societies. [70] Although there are signs that the increasing emphasis on the biomedical component of the field has reduced participation by female members – only 24 per cent of new members of AAKPE since 1981 are women [71] – physical education continues to be a site where female practitioners and scholars influence the ways in which the (moving) female body is viewed and understood.

Notes

[1] Hewlett *et al.*, 'Stopping the Exodus'.
[2] Quoted in Lisa Belkin, 'Diversity Isn't Rocket Science, Is it?', *New York Times*, 15 May 2008.

[3] This article is excerpted from Zieff, 'Medicalization of Higher Education'.

[4] Allen, 'Plain Words', 171.

[5] Clarke, *Sex in Education*.

[6] The numbers of female students increased fourfold to 40,000 from the 1870s to the 1880s. See Newcomer, *Century of Higher Education*, 46.

[7] Griego, 'A Part and Yet Apart', 81–2.

[8] One of her professors, the zoologist Charles Henry Gilbert, had been sufficiently impressed by her capacity for scientific research that he wrote her a letter of recommendation for a fellowship in 1896.

[9] Frederick Burk to Clelia Duel Mosher (n.d.), SCII, box 2, folder 2, Mosher Papers, Stanford University Archives (hereafter SUA).

[10] Griego, 'A Part and Yet Apart', 115–16.

[11] This account is taken from SCII, box 2, folder 2, Mosher papers, SUA, various notes.

[12] In a letter of support for Mosher's application for the Alice Freeman Palmer Fellowship he wrote in 1909, Stanford president David Starr Jordan noted that she 'has a great deal of valuable material, and she wishes to make this the subject of a monograph which shall be more important than other papers yet published on the subject': David Starr Jordan to Florence N. Cushing, Committee on Fellowships, 9 Jan. 1909, SCII, box 2, Folder 1, Mosher Papers, SUA.

[13] Stanford University, *Register* (1911–12), 148.

[14] Coolidge, 'Clelia Duel Mosher', 638.

[15] Stanford University (herafter SU), Register (1911–1912), 148.

[16] SU, *Register* (1912–13), 151.

[17] SU, *Register* (1916–17), 237.

[18] SU, *Register* (1917–18), 254.

[19] Clelia Duel Mosher to Ray Lyman Wilbur, 19 April 1923, SCII, box 1, folder 6, Mosher Papers, SUA.

[20] Quoted in Griego, 'A Part and Yet Apart', 157.

[21] Clelia Duel Mosher to Lou Henry Hoover, 25 Feb. 1925, box 1, Clelia Mosher papers, Hoover Institution Archives. Mrs Hoover refused to allow Mosher to resign her committee membership.

[22] Clelia Duel Mosher, Diary, 26 May 1926, SCII, Mosher Papers, SUA.

[23] Mosher, 'Concerning the Size', 54.

[24] Almost 30 years earlier, Claes Enebuske, director of the Boston Normal School of Gymnastics, commented that 'physical efficiency', referring to functional capacity 'measured by strength, endurance, and skill' improved in his students from their work in Swedish pedagogical gymnastics (Enebuske, 'Some Measurable Results', 222).

[25] Mosher, 'Some of the Causal Factors', 536.

[26] Ibid.

[27] At that time Mosher was stationed in Paris as associate medical director of the Bureau of Refugees and Relief, a division of the American Red Cross in France providing medical assistance to those affected by the war.

[28] Mosher and Martin, 'The Muscular Strength', 142.

[29] Mosher, 'Strength of Women', 18.

[30] Mosher, 'Schematogram', 645.

[31] Griego, 'The Making of a Misfit', 155.

[32] Mrozek, 'The Scientific Quest'.

[33] Mosher, 'Functional Periodicity'.

[34] Mosher, 'The Physical Training of Women', 4.

[35] Ibid., 9.

[36] Wright, 'Report on Exercise'.

[37] Mosher, 'Normal Menstruation', 179.
[38] George J. Engelmann to Howard Kelly, Feb. 1900, SCII, box 3, vol. 6, part 2, SUA
[39] Rossiter, *Women Scientists*, 76.
[40] Griego, 'A Part and Yet Apart', 84.
[41] With her companion, Dr Mary Sherwood, Welsh became a member of the board of managers of the Evening Dispensary for Working Women and Girls of Baltimore City, a clinic that dispensed clean milk to mothers with infants, among other services.
[42] Welsh, *Reminiscences*, 128.
[43] Knipp and Thomas, *The History of Goucher College*, 424.
[44] Veysey, *The Emergence of the American University*, 173.
[45] Welsh, *Reminiscences*, 128.
[46] Welsh, 'Fifty Years', 10.
[47] Welsh, *Reminiscences*, 46.
[48] Ibid., 116.
[49] The position of resident physician began in 1920 with the appointment of Dr S. Elizabeth Van Duyne. See Goucher College, *Catalogue* (1920–1921), 79, 81.
[50] Guth, 'Impressions of Lilian Welsh', 3.
[51] Welsh, *Reminiscences*, 115.
[52] Welsh, 'Physical Training', 58.
[53] Welsh, *Reminiscences*, 119.
[54] Ibid.
[55] Ibid.
[56] Knipp and Thomas, *The History of Goucher College*, 83.
[57] Welsh, *Reminiscences*, 128.
[58] Ibid., 121.
[59] King, 'A Tribute to Lilian Welsh'.
[60] Women's College of Baltimore, *Tenth Annual Program* (1898), 46.
[61] Ibid., 128.
[62] Starr, *The Social Transformations*, 112–16.
[63] Women's College of Baltimore, *April Bulletin* 2, no. 4 (April 1906), 5.
[64] M. Carey Thomas to Lilian Welsh, 26 Dec. 1911, SUA.
[65] Solomon, *In the Company*, 65.
[66] Welsh, *Reminiscences*, 119.
[67] Thomas, 'Present Tendencies', 64
[68] AAHPERD, 'AAHPERD Presidential Roster', Reston, VA: AAHPERD. Available online at http://member.aahperd.org/extranet/organizational_documents/AAHPERD_PastPres_LIST-complete_08.pdf, accessed 9 June2009.
[69] Research Consortium, 'The C.H. McCloy Research Lecture'. Available online at http://www.aahperd.org/research/template.cfm?template=pastLecturers_McCloy.htm, accessed 9 June 2009.
[70] AAKPE, 'Presidents: American Academy of Kinesiology and Physical Education'. Available online at http://www.aakpe.org/documents/Presidential_History_2008.pdf, accessed 9 June 2009.
[71] Park, '"An Affirmation"', 16.

References

Allen, Grant. 'Plain Words on the Woman Question'. *Popular Science Monthly*, Dec. 1889: 170–81.

Clarke, Edward Hammond. *Sex in Education; or a Fair Chance for Girls*. Boston, MA: Houghton, Mifflin and Co., 1873.

Coolidge, Mary Roberts. 'Clelia Duel Mosher, the Scientific Feminist'. *Research Quarterly* 12 (1941): 638.

Enebuske, Claes. 'Some Measurable Results of Swedish Pedagogical Gymnastics'. In *Proceedings of the American Association for the Advancement of Physical Education, Philadelphia, Seventh Annual Meeting 1892*. Springfield, MA: Press of Springfield Printing and Binding Co., 1893: 207–35.

Griego, Elizabeth Brownlee. 'A Part and Yet Apart: Clelia Duel Mosher and Professional Women at the Turn-of-the-Century'. PhD diss., University of California, Berkeley, 1983.

Griego, Elizabeth Brownlee. 'The Making of a Misfit: Clelia Duel Mosher, 1863–1940'. In *Lone Voyagers: Academic Women in Coeducational Institutions, 1870–1937*, edited by Geraldine Clifford. New York: The Feminist Press, 1989.

Guth, William W. 'Impressions of Lilian Welsh'. *The Goucher Alumnae Quarterly* 4 (Dec. 1924): 3–10.

Hewlett, Sylvia A., Carolyn Buck Luce and Lisa J. Servon. 'Stopping the Exodus of Women in Science'. *Harvard Business Review*, 2008: 22–4.

King, Jessie L. '*A Tribute to Lilian Welsh*'. Baltimore, MD: Goucher College, 1938.

Knipp, Anna and Thaddeus Thomas. *The History of Goucher College*. Baltimore: Goucher College, 1938.

Mosher, Clelia Duel. 'Normal Menstruation and Some of the Factors Modifying It'. *Johns Hopkins Hospital Bulletin*, 12 (April–May–June 1901): 178–9.

Mosher, Clelia Duel. 'Functional Periodicity in Women and Some of the Modifying Factors (Second Note)'. *California State Journal of Medicine* 9 (1911): 4–8, 55–8.

Mosher, Clelia Duel. 'The Physical Training of Women in Relation to Functional Periodicity'. Reprint from *The Woman's Medical Journal* 25 (April 1915): 71–74.

Mosher, Clelia Duel. 'The Schematogram – A New Method of Graphically Recording Posture and Changes in the Contours of the Body'. *School and Society* 1 (1915): 642–5.

Mosher, Clelia Duel. 'Concerning the Size of Women: Preliminary Note with Special Reference to Height'. *California State Journal of Medicine* 19, no. 2 (Feb. 1921): 53–4.

Mosher, Clelia Duel. 'Strength of Women'. In *Proceedings of the International Conference of Women Physicians*. New York: The Woman's Press, 1920: 160–77.

Mosher, Clelia Duel. 'Some of the Causal Factors in the Increased Height of College Women'. *Journal of the American Medical Association* 81, no. 7 (18 Aug. 1923): 535–8.

Mosher, Clelia Duel and Ernest Gale Martin. 'The Muscular Strength of College Women With Some Consideration of its Distribution: Preliminary Paper'. *Journal of the American Medical Association* 70 (1918): 140–2.

Mrozek, Donald J. 'The Scientific Quest for Physical Culture and the Persistent Appeal of Quackery'. *Journal of Sport History* 14 (1987): 76–86.

Newcomer, Mabel. *A Century of Higher Education for American Women*. New York: Harper & Brothers Publishers, 1959.

Park, Roberta J. '"An Affirmation of the Abilities of Woman": Women's Contributions to the American Academy of Kinesiology and Physical Education'. *Quest* 58 (2006): 16.

Rossiter, Margaret. *Women Scientists in America: Struggles and Strategies to 1940*. Baltimore, MD: The Johns Hopkins University Press, 1982.

Solomon, Barbara Miller. *In the Company of Educated Women*. New Haven, CT: Yale University Press, 1985.

Starr, Paul. *The Social Transformations of American Medicine*. New York: Basic Books, 1982.

Thomas, M. Carey. 'Present Tendencies in Women's College and University Education'. *Publication of the Association of Collegiate Alumnae Magazine*, series. 3 (Feb. 1908): 45–62.

Veysey, Laurence R. *The Emergence of the American University*. Chicago: The University of Chicago Press, 1965.

Welsh, Lilian. 'Fifty Years of Women's Education in the United States'. *Bulletin of Goucher College* 10, n.s. 2 (1923): 5–21.

Welsh, Lilian. 'Physical Training'. In *Donnybrook Fair*. Baltimore, MD: Goucher College, 1897.

Welsh, Lilian. *Reminiscences of Thirty Years in Baltimore*. Baltimore, MD: The Norman, Remington Co., 1925.

Wright, Elizabeth A. 'Report on Exercise as a Factor in the Relief of Menstrual Disturbances'. Mary Hemenway Alumnae Association of the Department of Hygiene. Wellesley College *Bulletin* (1917–1918).

Zieff, Susan G. 'The Medicalization of Higher Education: Women Physicians and Physical Training, 1870–1920'. PhD diss., University of California, Berkeley, 1993.

Empowering Women through Sport: Women's Basketball in Brazil and the Significant Role of Maria Helena Cardoso

Claudia M. Guedes

As historian June Hahner observes in her 1990 book Emancipating the Female Sex: The Struggle for Women's Rights in Brazil, 1850–1940, *'Although women have always comprised an essential element in the evolution of Brazil, their activities have received scant scholarly attention'. Major journals such as* Women's History *and the* International Journal of Women's Studies *seldom contain anything having to do with the experiences, much less the achievements, of women in Brazil. Therefore, few individuals have any understanding of how important the sport of basketball has been in helping foster their advancement. This article, which sets forth their involvement in this game from the time that it was brought to Brazil from the United States in 1896 to the present, is about more than sporting competitions. It also is about how sport can be – and has been – used to improve the lives of girls and women.*

Introduction

The two ludic [1] events for which Brazil is best known are carnival, founded in Rio de Janeiro in 1641, and football (soccer), introduced to the resident population by English and Scottish engineers who arrived in the late 1800s. During the 1960s and 1970s another sporting event rose to considerable prominence, the game of basketball. It was women's basketball that led the way. Things started in an international arena. On 6 October 1965 the following words appeared in the Spanish newspaper *Diario Desportivo La Marca*: 'Everything is ready for the match this afternoon at the Palacio de los Desportes. The Brazilian and Czechoslovakian girls are confident they will play an impeccable game.' The writer, journalist

José M. Fernandez, was referring to the third of three games that had been scheduled to take place in Madrid between women's teams from Brazil and Czechoslovakia during the 1965 World Club Tournament of the Federación Internacional de Baloncesto Amateur. [2] The winning team was Brazil.

Little has been written about the history of this event or about how, and why, the game quickly became of considerable interest to Brazilians. [3] Even less is known about the importance that some members of the 1965 team subsequently would have in providing positive experiences for girls from economically depressed backgrounds whose lives otherwise might have turned in negative directions. The story of the rise to prominence of women's basketball in Brazil, then, is about much more than competitive sports.

Setting the Context

'Although women have always comprised an essential element in the evolution of Brazil, their activities have received scant scholarly attention.' [4] These words appeared in the preface to June Hahner's 1990 book *Emancipating the Female Sex: The Struggle for Women's Rights in Brazil, 1850–1940*. By the 1980s, relevant information was only beginning to appear in books such as *Vivência Historia and Sexualidade* [*Experience: History and Sexuality*]; *Imagens Femininas: Mulher, Sociedade e Estado no Brasil* [*Female Images: Women, Society and Politics in Brazil*] and *Ideologia e Voto Feminino no Brasil* [*Idelology and Women's Vote in Brazil*]. [5] Since then there has been some moderate growth in research regarding such matters as is evidenced in the bibliographies of *Reinventing the Culture of Womanhood in America and Brazil* (2002) and *Gender Politics in Brazil and Chile* (2006). [6] However, very little has been published in English. Major journals such as *Women's History* and the *International Journal of Women's Studies* seldom contain anything having to do with the experiences, much less the achievements, of women in Brazil. Moreover, with the exception of Mourão and Votre's short chapter dealing with physical activities and sports that have involved Brazilian girls and their informative chapter dealing with Maria Lenk, who reached the semi-finals at the 1936 Berlin Olympics and was first Brazilian of either sex to set a world record in swimming, [7] almost nothing is available to the English reader regarding the achievements that they have attained in and through sports.

The women's suffrage movement in Brazil, which had begun in the early 1900s, gained an important advance when in 1927 Rio Grande do Norte became the first state to grant women the right to vote. In 1932 the franchise was extended throughout the country, which allowed them to vote in the 1933 national elections. In very small numbers they slowly began to attain local, then state and ultimately a few national offices. However, there still are many areas in which women in Brazil remain far from being equal with men. These inequities typically are attributed to the legacy of traditional values that placed males in a position of power and authority and held that the proper, and for many the only, role of women was motherhood and subordination to their husbands. [8] Even so, in spite of many obstacles a few women attained opportunities to express, and sometimes graphically demonstrate, their abilities. With regard to the latter, sport was especially important. In fact, a few girls and women in Brazil were engaging in basketball much earlier than most people realize.

The Rise and Expansion of Basketball in Brazil

Basketball was played in Brazil for the first time in 1896 at the Mackenzie College, [9] an educational institution that had been established in 1871 in São Paulo City by George Whitehall Chamberlain, a Presbyterian minister who had arrived from the United States. Popularly known as the 'American School', Mackenzie College was quite different from other contemporary Brazilian schools. It had mixed-sex classrooms and provided daily physical education for girls as well as for boys. This pedagogical approach, which brought boys and girls together, was severely criticized by conservative Brazilian society. The physical education classes received particular disapproval from Catholic families because of fears that the more comfortable clothing needed to engage in gymnastic exercises might reveal certain parts of the body. [10] However, the high standard of education and the successful outcomes that were attained by the Mackenzie students, in comparison with those who graduated from Catholic schools, would become increasingly attractive to rich families, whose interest in the school's academic excellence began to replace earlier concerns about its 'innovations'.

During the late 1800s large numbers of immigrants were arriving in Brazil from numerous countries. The new arrivals, especially those from Germany and Great Britain, began to modify the intense social restrictions that had been imposed upon Brazilian society since colonial times by the Catholic Church. Both Rio de Janeiro and São Paulo became more urban and cosmopolitan, and in several locations immigrants created opportunities for sport and other forms of exercise that they had brought with them from their native lands. [11] The German Society for Turnverein, for example, was established in São Paulo in 1870. This club held classes of gymnastics and other events for German immigrants. Wealthy Brazilians were invited to attend and participate. [12]

Among the Brazilian population activities such as cockfights, traditional music and dance presentations predominated. A few local residents began watching Scottish and English immigrants as they engaged in football in the courtyards of factories that they had established. The São Paulo Athletic Club, which still exists today, was established in 1885 by British immigrants who also introduced cricket, golf and other sports to the resident population in various parts of Brazil. Of all the sports that the British introduced, football (soccer) would become the most prominent. A small number of native-born Brazilians were playing the soccer game as early as 1893. [13]

During the 1890s and early 1900s activities such as bicycle riding, spending afternoons watching soccer games, and attending cricket matches at the English Club became some of the most popular entertainments among the inhabitants of São Paulo city. [14] The sportive lifestyle increasingly became both an entertainment and one of the ways for the higher levels of society to demonstrate their economic status and power. Introduced forms of sportive activity had become so popular by 1900 that traditional schools established by Jesuits and Benedictines were beginning to include in their curricula various types of sports such as soccer, fencing, basketball and gymnastics.

Some types of physical activities also began to be provided for girls. In this case Americans and the Protestant church led the way. Anthropologist Gilberto Freire is among those who have written about the importance to Brazil of 'challenges of the educational reform influenced by Protestant curricula improvement'. [15] The individual behind this 'challenge' was George Whitehall Chamberlain, who was making the curriculum of the *Escola Americana* (American School) the strongest influence on educational reform in the state of São Paulo. This 'Protestant curricula improvement' for Brazilian schools was made possible in 1889 when the State of São Paulo invited Chamberlain and his team of American teachers to help direct reforms that would occur the following year when the State of São Paulo established a 'system for elementary school public instruction'. [16]. The reforms included daily physical education classes – a motivation that surely came from the Americans.

For the system for elementary school public instruction to become effective it was necessary to also establish a system for training local public school teachers. This training was provided by Brazilian-born Marcia Brown and Maria Guilhermina Loureiro, both of whom had graduated from the Boston Normal School of Gymnastics. They were the first women to assume important positions at the Normal School of São Paulo, which had been established by the government on 16 March 1846. Maria Guilhermina became the school's administrative director and Marcia Brown became its academic director. Their appointments were crucial to the development of the educational reform project that Chamberlain had proposed because as the head directors they were responsible for guiding the training for the teachers needed by the schools.

Chamberlain continued to build Mackenzie College, and to expand its work he invited a number of Americans to come to Brazil. [17] One of these was August Farnham Shaw, a teacher of art history who had graduated from Yale University. Shaw brought with him not only books but also a basketball, and on the school's patio he erected a basket and began to play basketball with some of the students in his spare time. [18] According to the *Minutes of the Brazil Mission of the Presbyterian Church of the USA* [19], the first basketball game among the boys is reported to have taken place around 1896. The same article notes that a girl's team also had been created. According to the *Brazil Mission Minutes Magazine*, the first picture of a male team appeared in 1899; [20] however, it was not until the 1920s that the first picture of a women's team was published, no doubt because it would have been considered improper to publish photographs of females playing such a game. [21]

Other factors were of consequence in introducing the game of basketball to Brazilians. One of these was the establishment of a YMCA in São Paulo in 1902. [22] Initially games were played after the practice of gymnastic exercises. [23] In 1915 the YMCA organized the first local 'basket ball' championship in the city of Rio de Janeiro, which at the time was the capital of Brazil. [24]

Another influence was Oscar Thompson, who served as Director of Public Instruction for the State of São Paulo from 1901 to 1911. In 1906 Thompson introduced basketball at the Normal School of São Paulo at the request of American teachers who recently had been hired to develop kindergartens in the city's schools. According to the *Brazil Mission Minutes Magazine*, from 1907 to 1912 many games between the women teachers from the Normal School and those from Mackenzie College took place. The popularity of basketball among young Brazilian teachers who had been trained at both of these institutions helped spread the sport among youth throughout the state of São Paulo and elsewhere. [25]

Women's Basketball Emerges

In the of city Casa Branca, which is near São Paulo, in the early 1900s a club called Centro de Atividade Fisica (which had been established in 1871) hosted the first basketball teams to be created by both male and female classroom teachers. Apparently the two sexes sometimes played against each other. The women's team that started practising regularly in 1910 played competitively against male teams composed of Presbyterian seminary students from the towns of Rio Claro and Piracicaba. However, some individuals held strongly to the view that basketball was 'a vulgar and dangerous activity' that could harm a female. [26] Therefore, games that involved both women and men were not usual in São Paulo, the capital of the state in which conservative religious views were especially strong.

The rules of basketball were translated into Portuguese in 1916 and published by Stampa Editors Associated. [27] This helped extend the game beyond the American influence. Yet, with few exceptions until well into the 1920s, women's tournaments were restricted to being held in female schools and to special events that were carefully monitored within the facilities of large clubs. [28]

Opportunities for Girls and Women Grow

During the 1930s, the number of opportunities in sport for girls increased, in part because wealthy Brazilians often sought to mirror events and developments in female education that were occurring in Europe and the United States, [29] where women had been playing basketball since 1892. It was the Amateur Athletic Union's (AAU) first sponsorship of a national women's basketball championship in 1926 that inspired Antonio Paolillo to create the first official and public tournament for women in Brazil. This took place in 1930 in São Paulo city. The Brazilian women primarily followed the rules of men's basketball but with the adaptation of four quarters played for ten minutes each with three minute breaks in between. This first tournament involved Club Esperia, Associação Atlética de São Paulo, and the City Bank Club. [30]

By the early 1940s modest advances were apparent and the first women's National Team was organized by the Confederacão Brasileira de Basquete, whose president was Paulo Martins Meira. The women's first national team played in the South American Tournament in 1946 against Peru, Argentina, Chile, Paraguay and Uruguay – and brought to Brazil the first of what would become many silver and gold medals in basketball. (All the players had been selected by their physical education teachers, who suggested their names to clubs and coaches throughout the state of São Paulo.) Although it now is rarely noted, the Brazilian women's basketball national team has held important titles since it was established. [31]

Even so, the game was not always viewed as a feminine activity, and many individuals continued to consider the competitions to be unladylike and vulgar. Coaches often had difficulty securing a family's permission for a daughter to play, and occasionally they resorted to bringing the entire family to the games to prove that the girl would be far removed from boys and protected the entire time. [32] In addition to the issue of morality and decency, the women had to deal with the limited attention given in the media to their sport in comparison with that given to men's soccer, which was ascending to ever greater heights of popularity.

Political events of the 1960s had a significant effect upon Brazilian sports, most notably soccer, which by this time held the dominant and overwhelming interest of the Brazilian population. The events of the 1960s also began to open more opportunities for girls and women. In 1964 a military *coup d'état* led by the Brazilian military deposed the democratically elected president of Brazil, João Goulart. Four years later a movement of resistance against this dictatorial government, strongly influenced by the French students' political movement of 1968, gained increasing attention among students in Brazil. Searching for strategies to contain the students, the military government started creating sports facilities and encouraging youth to participate in sports, highlighting the soccer team which had won many championships and blazed the name of Brazil all over the world. [33].

The growing sense of invincibility and national identity that men's soccer promoted was influential throughout the educational system, but mainly at the universities. The government invested money that was coming from the United States such as USAID-1970 to create Olympic centres in the major universities. The so-called Olympic centres were sports facilities that were open to the undergraduate students. These were intended, in large measure, to promote sport and deflect attention from political agendas. During the decade of the 1970s Brazil's government gave incentives to all types of sport initiatives throughout the country. The most famous programme was 'Sport for All', a concept that was brought from Norway by Lamartine Pereira Da Costa. [34] The seeming invincibility of the men's national soccer team, demonstrated by its successes in World Cup competitions, enhanced Brazilian national identity and self-esteem rose. Despite living under an oppressive government, many individuals came to believe that it was possible to be patriotic. It was within these contexts that women's basketball would capture the attention of the Brazilian population. [35]

News of the games between the Brazilian and the Czechoslovakian women's teams at the 1965 Federación Internacional de Baloncesto Amateur World Championship had cheered considerable numbers of Brazilians. They were even more delighted when they learned that the sixth FIBA women's basketball tournament would be hosted by the city of São Paulo in May 1971. For the first time in Brazil, a women's basketball game received the attention of approximately 15,000 enthusiastic fans. The hymn that had been sung for Brazil at the 1970 soccer World Cup, whose lyrics were intended to inspire hope for a better future, also became adopted as the hymn for the women's basketball team at the sixth FIBA World Tournament in 1971. [36]

This period also marked the beginning of a new era in the ways that Brazilian television, radio, newspapers and magazines covered the accomplishments of the nation's female athletes. A person of particular importance to women's basketball in Brazil during this period was Maria Helena Cardoso.

The Important Role of Maria Helena Cardoso

Maria Helena Cardoso, who had been a member of the Brazilian Women's National Basketball Team since 1956, participated in all the international tournaments in which the team engaged until 1972. After retiring as a player, she became a coach whose work helped win several titles for Brazilian women's basketball. These included winning the Pan-American Games in 1991, the World FIBA Tournament in 1994 and a silver medal at the 1992 Olympic Games. Besides being an accomplished athlete and coach, Maria Helena was a visionary who developed a variety of opportunities for girls and women throughout Brazil, the largest country in Latin America. Some of the most athletically talented with whom she worked became well known players. These included Hortência Marcari and Maria Paula Goncalves da Silva, who became members of the Springfield College Class Basketball Hall of Fame in 2002 and 2006 respectively.

A remarkable player, coach and teacher, Maria Helena Cardoso became part of Brazilian national history as the captain of the national team that had played against Czechoslovakia during the 1965 FIBA world tournament in Madrid. (The tournament had been organized in an attempt to convince the International Olympic Committee that females could play basketball at the Olympic level.) She would go on to lead, as the head coach, the Brazilian women's national team to the world championship in 1991 and bring Brazil to the level that it could be classified, for the first time, as eligible for the Olympic Games of 1992. The work of other women who had played for Maria Helena also was noteworthy. Especially important contributions were made by those who recruited girls from the impoverished countryside to play basketball and thereby enabled them to have experiences that would lead to a life with greater opportunities.

Born in Descalvado in the State of São Paulo in 1940, Maria Helena Cardoso grew up with sisters and a brother who all were extraordinary athletes. The oldest sister, Maria Aparecida Cardoso, played on the ntional basketball team from 1951 to 1954. Her other three sisters also took to the basketball courts. These five young women created their own basketball team with the support of their older brother, who had become a professional soccer player. When Maria Helena was 15 years old she was recruited for the first time to play in the tournament called Open Games of Piracicaba. [37] A year later she left the countryside to go to the state capital to join her sister Maria Aparecida Cardoso on the State of São Paulo team. As part of the Paulista team she met teammates with whom she would share experiences on the national team.

Although Descalvado was a small town, it was full of sports opportunities for youth. These included hosting several championship basketball teams, especially for women. The city government supported the residents' enthusiasm for basketball, and as a consequence Descalvado holds several first-place finishes in state and national basketball championships. Maria Helena's physical education teachers also were basketball players; and they sometimes served as coaches for teams located outside the city. They soon discovered that Maria Helena was talented, and in 1955 they recommended that she play for the Pinheiros Club in São Paulo. [38] This was the starting-point for the person who over the next two decades would become the best female player in Brazil.

To be eligible to play for sport clubs as well as for city, state and national teams, the national sports league association – the Conselho Nacional do Desporto (CND) – specified that an athlete must have a formal job with regular salary. [39] Maria Helena and the other players incorporated work, study and practice into their daily routines. Many worked as kindergarten teachers in the public schools, an educational occupation that necessitated attending a normal school to obtain the appropriate training. By the late 1960s, most of the female basketball players on the national team were attending university and majoring in physical education. The empowerment that came from being part of a team and travelling throughout the country and sometimes overseas brought to these women experiences and leadership skills that would change their futures. Experiences such as these were the main inspiration for Maria Helena, who became a coach in 1972.

As a basketball coach she travelled throughout the state of São Paulo to find the best players – girls and young women with whom she would form her first team in Piracicaba. She never used scouts, only her own experience and wisdom. This was how she found Hortencia and Paula (the first Brazilian women athletes to be inducted to the Basketball Hall of Fame in Springfield, Massachusetts). Her goals extended beyond offering basketball opportunities to the girls whom she met in the regions around São Paulo, where the game became increasingly popular. She wanted very much to bring to them a different view of the world – one in which hard training and discipline brought real-life results and accomplishments.

When Maria Helena began her work in the 1970s, women in Brazil still suffered discrimination in the workforce, often being denied jobs because of the belief that the proper and, according to many individuals, the only proper female role was that of home-maker and caretaker of the family. Equal opportunities would not emerge until 1988 with the new Federal Constitution that established equality of sexes by law. [40] By this time society was changing in a number of other ways. In 1990 75 per cent of all Brazilians lived in cities and there were about 52 million boys and girls under the age of 19. The most heavily populated region was south-eastern Brazil, where São Paulo and Rio de Janeiro were located and several million children were living in poverty. In many places females were especially vulnerable to risks such as drug abuse and pregnancy. School drop-out rates for girls were high and many fell prey to violence, alcoholism and sexual abuse.

Although the situation had been somewhat less serious in the 1970s than in the1990s, it had so deeply troubled Maria Helena that she decided to use her knowledge of basketball and the lessons that it could teach to create an educational project that might bring to girls such as these a sense of dignity and respect. [41] Even before graduating from the Universidade Metodista de Piracicaba with majors in physical education and pedagogy, she had begun to design an educational programme with her teammate Maria Helena Campos (Heleninha). This soon was attracting girls from regions around the city of Piracicaba. [42] Called '*Basketball Nucleos*', it used basketball as the main tool to attract, educate and empower young girls and teenagers. Their goal was to disseminate educationally oriented *Basketball Nucleos* (Basketball centres) throughout the country.

Funds to start the programme had been obtained from the government of the City of Piracicaba. A request for further funds was made in 1982 to a government initiative entitled 'Sport for All', When the needed money was not forthcoming, the commercial bank Finasa assumed the sponsorship of the city's basketball team, and with its support Maria Helena and Heleninha were able to develop several centres. By 1986 the two leaders had in operation ten *Basketball Nucleos* in Piracicaba and elsewhere in the state of São Paulo. These provided important experiences for more than 600 girls ages nine to 13, many of whom came from impoverished and difficult backgrounds. By 1997 there were at least 12 *Basketball Nucleos*, located throughout the city of São Paulo alone. Centres also had been created in Guaruja and in Osasco. Many of the girls and teenagers who participated in these programmes credit the positive and uplifting experiences they had with changing their lives and have gone on to become teachers, lawyers, medical doctors and other professionals.

Although now retired, Maria Helena Cardoso remains an active contributor to these programmes and often is asked for advice by former participants as well as by a variety of organizations and community groups. Her work has been the model and inspiration for most of the female basketball coaches throughout the country. Financial institutions (for example National Credit Bank [BCN], Bradesco and Banco do Brasil), commercial brands (such as Spaldini and Champion) and governmental institutions such as Eletrobras (the electricity company of Brazil) have all adopted Maria Helena's model for bringing young girls into a more positive lifestyle by means of the game of basketball.

In 2005, Eletrobras, in partnership with Spaldini and with the support of the Basketball National League (CBB – *Confederacao Brasileira de Basketball*), established 'Basketball of the Future'. The aim of this programme is to develop in each state a basketball '*nucleo* of initiation' for youth of both sexes ages seven to 17. Today 24 of these *nucleos* are actively disseminating their work. Others are being built in São Paulo, Ceara and Tocantins; and more are planned to start by the end of 2009. The collective mission is to educate and socialize teenagers by means of their basketball experiences and to continue to spread this approach to the sport of basketball throughout Brazil.

To further emphasize the educational mission, coaches are called 'educators' or 'teachers'. They engage regularly in career development programmes, and twice a year they meet in Rio de Janeiro for lectures, to exchange experiences and to update their pedagogical training. Today the director of the Coaches Department of the Female Division of the National League of Basketball (*Diretora do Departamento Tecnico – Divisao feminine* – CBB) is former player Hortencia Marcari, who was Maria Helena Cardoso's best player. [43]

As a consequence of her efforts to enhance the lives of young women and men through sport, Maria Helena Cardoso remains an inspiration to most of the young basketball players in Brazil. There is a widespread belief that Maria Helena Cardosa was the best woman basketball player Brazil ever had as well as the best coach, and that her work has resulted in positive experiences for thousands of players. She continues to fight whenever necessary to keep the practice of basketball safe, and to promote sport as a way for girls to have a better life.

Notes

[1] For an interesting examination of ludic aspects of carnival and American football see: Langman, 'Culture, Identity and Hegemony'.
[2] José M. Fernandez in *Diario Deportivo La Marca*, 6 Oct. 1965.
[3] Priore, *Historia das Mulheres no Brasil*.
[4] Hahner, Emancipating *the Female Sex*, xi.
[5] Bruschini and Rosemberg, *Vivência*; Barroso, *Mulher, Sociedade e Estado no Brasil*; Alves, *Ideologia e Voto Feminino*.
[6] Westfield, *Reinventing the Culture of Womanhood* ; Macaulay, *Gender Politics*.
[7] Mourão and Votre, "Brazilian Women and Girls in Physical Activities"; Votre and Mourão, 'Ignoring Taboos'.
[8] See for example, http://womenshistory.about.com/library/ency/blwh_brazil.htm, accessed 10 Nov. 2009
[9] Sims, 'Histórico do Basket Ball no Brasil'.
[10] Freyre, Order *and Progress*.
[11] Mota, 'À procura das Origens do Mackenzie'. Useful information regarding the larger social contexts can be found in books such as Azevedo, *Brazilian Culture*; Barman, *Citizen Emperor*; and Fletcher, *O Brasil e os Brasileiros*.
[12] See for example, Nicolini, *Tietê: O Rio do Esporte*.
[13] Sevcenko, *Orfeu Extático na Metrópole*.
[14] Ibid.

[15] Freyre, *Order and Progress.*

[16] Garcez, *O Mackenzie.*

[17] Oliveira, *Destino (não) Manifesto.*

[18] *Revista Comemorativa dos Cem Anos do Basquetebol.*

[19] *Minutes of the Brazil Mission of the Presbyterian Church .*

[20] Ibid.

[21] *São Paulo State Set of Rules for General Discipline.*

[22] The YMCA of São Paulo was established on 23 December 1902.

[23] Daiuto, *Basquetebol.*

[24] The championship was held at the Island of Villegagnon. Besides the YMCA there were teams from the America Foot-Ball Club; Club Internacional de Regatas; Colégio Sylvio Leite; Club Gymnastico Portuguez; and Corpo de Marinheiros Nacionaes de Willegagnon. TheYMCA attained first place. Its players were: Itagiba R. Novaes, Romulo Alexandro, Lysias de Cerqueira Leite, Victor Mussafir, Sylvio Vianna, Victor A. Auguste and Renato Eloy de Andrade. The head coach was Henry J. Sims.

[25] See *Revista Educação Physica, Rio de Janeiro*, 73 (1938), 15–19.

[26] Hahner, *A Mulher Brasileira.*

[27] Sims, 'Histórico do Basket Ball no Brasil'.

[28] The project was under the supervision of a committee formed by Itagiba R. Novaes, D.F. Moutinho, Victor Auguste and Henry J. Sims (director of physical education of the YMCA of Rio de Janeiro).

[29] 'Mulheres na Sala de Aula', in Priore, *História das Mulheres no Brasil*, .443–81.

[30] Confederação Brasileira de Basquetebol [Brazilian League of Basketball], Year Reports from 1920 to 1950. CBB Archives, Rio de Janeiro, Brazil, Box 1–10.

[31] At the South American tournaments the Brazilian women's national team won gold medals in 1954, in 1958, from 1965 to 1974, from 1978 to 1981 and from 1983 to 2003. It won silver medals in the 1946, 1952, 1960, and 1975. At the Pan American Games the Brazilian women's team won gold medals in 1967, 1971, and 1991 – and silver medals in 1959, 1963, and 1987. At the FIBA World Championship, the Brazilian women's national team won the bronze medal in 1971 and the gold medal in 1994. At the Olympic Games, it won a bronze medal in 2000 and a silver medal in 1996.

[32] Louro and Trindade, *Clotildes ou Marias*, 37.

[33] See Gaspari, *A Ditadura Envergonhada.*

[34] Valente, *Perspectivas Históricas.*

[35] See Guedes, *Mulheres a Cesta.*

[36] The lyrics of 'Millions in Action', composed by Miguel Gustavo in 1969 and introduced during the 1970 FIFA World Cup, declare: '90 millions in action, go ahead Brazil from my heart. All together moving forward. Hail to the National Team. Suddenly is the wave moving forward. Seems that we are all holding hands, all connected in one emotion. All are one heart. All together moving forward Brazil. Brazil: hail to the National Team.'

[37] This is a tournament that involves all Olympic sports and is open to all clubs and schools.

[38] The Pinheiros Club was established on 7 September 1899 by Hans Nobling under the name Sport Club Germania.

[39] Brazilian Decree-Law 3.199 de 14.04.41 established amateur 'fair play' rules, and athletes who received money or gifts were considered professional and not eligible for Olympic Games or world competitions.

[40] According to Article 5 of the Brazilian Constitution of 1988 all people are equal, with no discrimination, assuring to all Brazilian citizens and aliens residents the right to life, freedom, equality, safety and ownership. Men and women are equal in rights and obligations.

[41] Cardoso, 'Youth Risk-Taking Behavior in Brazil'.

[42] Maria Helena Campos also graduated from the Universidade Metodista de Piracicaba in 1971 with an emphasis in pedagogy and physical education.
[43] Much of the information for this section was obtained from personal interviews with Maria Helena Cardoso and her colleagues from 2002 to 2005.

References

Alves, Branca Moreira. *Ideologia e Voto Feminino no Brasil*. Petrópolis: Vozes, 1980.

Azevedo, Fernando de. *Brazilian Culture: an Introduction to the Study of Culture in Brazil*. New York: The Macmillan Co., 1950.

Barman, Roderick J. *Citizen Emperor: Pedro II and the Making of Brazil, 1825–91*. Stanford, CA: Stanford University Press, 1999.

Barroso, Carmen, *Mulher, Sociedade e Estado no Brasil*. Sao Paulo: Editora Brasiliense, 1982.

Bruschini, Maria Cristina A. and Fúlvia Rosenberg, eds. *Vivência: Historia and Sexualidade, e Imagens Femininas Mulher*. Sao Paulo: Editora Brasiliense, 1980.

Cardoso, Ana Rute. 'Youth Risk–Taking Behavior in Brazil: Drug Use and Teenage Pregnancies'. Washington, DC: Federal Research Division of the Library of Congress (Copy sent to San Francisco State University Library in May 2009).

Daiuto, Moacyr. *Basquetebol: Origem e Evolução*. Sao Paulo: Iglu, 1991.

Fletcher, James C. *O Brasil e os Brasileiros*. Rio de Janeiro: Editora Nacional, 1857.

Freyre, G. *Order and Progress, Brazil from Monarchy to Republic*. New York: Alfred A. Knopf, 1970.

Garcez, Benedicto Novaes. *O Mackenzie*. São Paulo: Casa Editora Presbiteriana, 1970.

Gaspari, Elio. *A Ditadura Envergonhada*. São Paulo: Cia. das Letras, 2002.

Guedes, Claudia Maria. *Mulheres a Cesta: O Basquetebol Feminino no Brasil (1892–1971)*. São Paulo: Miss Lilly, 2009.

Hahner, J. *A Mulher Brasileira e suas Lutas Sociais e Políticas. 1850–1937*. Translated by Maria Thereza P. de Almeida. São Paulo: Brasiliense, 1981.

Hahner, June. *Emancipating the Female Sex: The Struggle for Women's Rights in Brazil, 1850–1940*. Durham, NC: Duke University Press, 1990.

Langman, Lauren, 'Culture, Identity and Hegemony: The Body in a Global Age'. *Current Sociology* 51 (May/June 2003): 223–47.

Louro, G.L. and E.M.C. Trindade. *Clotildes ou Marias: Mulheres de Curitiba na Primeira República*. Curitiba: Fundação Cultural, 1996.

Macaulay, Fiona. *Gender Politics in Brazil and Chile*. New York: Palgrave Macmillan, 2006.

Minutes of the Brazil Mission of the Presbyterian Church in the U. S. of A., vol. IV. Rio de Janeiro: First Brazilian Presbyterian Church, 1900.

Mota, Jorge Cesar. 'À procura das origens do Mackenzie'. In *Edições comemorativas dos 100 anos Mackenzie*, Special Centennial Issue (1970): 30–55.

Mourão, Ludmilla and Sebastião Votre. 'Brazilian Women and Girls in Physical Activities and Sport'. In *Sport and Women: Social Issues in International Perspective*, edited by Ilse Hartmann-Twes and Gertrud Pfister. London: Routledge, 2003: 179–91.

Nicolini, Henrique. *Tietê: O Rio do Esporte*. Sao Paulo: Phorte Editors, 2000.

Oliveira, Ana Maria Costa. *Destino (não) Manifesto – Os imigrantes Norte- Americanos no. Brasil*. São Paulo: União Cultural Brasil-Estados Unidos, 1995.

Priore, Mary Del, ed. *Historia das Mulheres no Brasil*. Sao Paulo: Contexto, 1997.

Revista Comemorativa dos Cem Anos do Basquetebol 1891–1991 [Centennial Issue on Basketball]. São Paulo: Associação Crista de Mocos (YMCA).

São Paulo State Set of Rules for General Discipline in Public and Private Educational Institutions, 1850–1900. São Paulo: Estado de São Paulo Publishing House, 1972.

Sevcenko, Nicolau. *Orfeu Extático na Metrópole. São Paulo, Sociedade e Cultura nos Frementes anos 20*. São Paulo: Cia das Letras, 2000.

Sims, Henry J. 'Histórico do Basket Ball no Brasil'. *Educação Physica: Revista Technica de Esportese Athletismo* 1 (1932): 53–9.

Valente, Edison Francisco. *Perspectivas Históricas sobre o Movimento Esporte para Todos. Dissertação de mestrado em Educação Física*. Campinas: Unicamp, 1993.

Votre, Sebastiãoand Ludmilla Mourão. 'Ignoring Taboos: Maria Lenk, Latin American Inspirationalist'. In *Freeing the Female Body: Inspirational Icons*, edited by J. A. Mangan and Fan Hong. London and Portland, OR: *Frank* Cass, 2001: 196–218.

Westfield, Alex Huxley. *Reinventing the Culture of Womanhood in America and Brazil, An Anthropological Perspective: Models for the 21st Century*. Lanham, MD: University Press of America, 2002.

Strong, Athletic and Beautiful: Edmondo De Amicis and the Ideal Italian Woman

David Chapman and Gigliola Gori

Edmondo De Amicis (1843–1908) was one of Italy's most popular writers, and perhaps more than any other figure in post-Risorgimento Italy, he reflected the common hopes, dreams and prejudices of his countrymen. De Amicis was particularly interested in gymnastics and physical education, and he wrote about them frequently. His most famous work on these subjects is his novella Amore e ginnastica [Love and Gymnastics] (1892) which explores female fitness, sexual stereotypes and gender roles in nineteenth-century Italy. This opus, along with two others (a lecture and a magazine article), can help modern readers understand the role of female sport and gender expectations in post-Risorgimento Italy. In addition to exploring women's gymnastics, De Amicis was also interested in female mountain climbing. By examining the activities and physical appearance of lady mountaineers, the author reveals his personal criteria for the perfect woman. When these are combined with the gymnasts in the earlier work, we can distill the writer's own particular attitudes toward gender and female perfection. For De Amicis a woman was required to be athletic, beautiful, modest, faithful, loving and with just a soupçon of uncertainty about her sexuality to make her interesting.

Fort, sportif et beau : Edmondo De Amicis et la femme italienne idéale

Edmondo De Amicis (1843–1908) fut l'un des écrivains les populaires d'Italie et, peut-être davantage que toute autre figure de l'Italie post- Risorgimento, il refléta les espoirs communs, les rêves et les préjugés de ces concitoyens. De Amicis était particulièrement intéressé par la gymnastique et l'éducation physique à propos desquelles il écrivit fréquemment. Son œuvre la plus connue sur ces sujets est sa nouvelle *Amore e ginnastica* [Amour et gymnastique] (1892) qui explore le bien-être féminin, les stéréotypes sexuels et les rôles sexués dans l'Italie du dix-neuvième siècle. Cet opus, avec deux autres textes (une conférence et un article de magazine), peut aider les lecteurs contemporains à comprendre le rôle du sport féminin et des attentes de genre dans l'Italie post- Risorgimento. En plus de l'explorer la gymnastique des femmes, De Amicis s'intéressa aussi à l'alpinisme féminin. En examinant les activités et les apparences physiques des femmes alpinistes, l'auteur révèle ses critères personnels définissant la femme parfaite. Lorsqu'ils sont combinés avec les gymnastes de son œuvre antérieure, il devient alors possible d'appréhender les postures particulières de l'écrivain au regard du genre et de la perfection féminine. Pour De Amicis, une femme était supposée être athlétique, belle, modeste, fidèle, aimante et avec juste un soupçon d'incertitude à propos de sa sexualité pour la rendre intéressante.

Fuerte, atlética y bella: Edmondo de Amicis y la mujer italiana ideal

Edmondo de Amicis (1843–1908) fue uno de los escritores más populares de Italia y, quizás en mayor medida que cualquier otra figura de la Italia del post-Risorgimento, reflejó las esperanzas, los sueños y los prejuicios comunes de sus compatriotas. De Amicis estaba particularmente interesado en la gimnasia y la educación física, temas sobre los que escribió a menudo. Su obra más celebre sobre estos temas es su novela *Amore e ginnastica* (1892), centrada en la salud femenina, los estereotipos sexuales y los roles de género en la Italia del siglo XIX. Esta obra, junto con otras dos (una conferencia y un artículo de revista), puede ayudar a los lectores contemporáneos a entender el papel del deporte femenino y de las expectativas de género en la Italia del post-Risorgimento. Además de explorar el tema de la gimnasia femenina, De Amicis estaba interesado en el alpinismo femenino. Mediante una revisión de las actividades y de la apariencia física de las montañeras, el autor revela sus criterios personales sobre la mujer perfecta. Cuando estos criterios se proyectan en las gimnastas en su trabajo inicial podemos deducir las actitudes personales del escritor en relación con el género y la perfección femenina. Para De Amicis una mujer, para resultar interesante, debía ser atlética, bella, modesta, fiel, cariñosa y con una pizca de ambigüedad en cuanto a su sexualidad.

Stark, Athletisch und Schön: Edmondo de Amicis und die perfekte italienische Frau

Edmondo De Amicis (1843–1908) gehörte zu Italiens berühmtesten Schriftstellern und spiegelte die gemeinsamen Hoffnungen, Träume und Vorurteile seiner Landsleute wider wie vielleicht kein anderer des Italiens der nach-Risorgimento Epoche. De Amicis war besonders an der Gymnastik und Leibeserziehung interessiert und schrieb regelmäßig darüber. Seine bekannteste Abhandlung über diese Bereiche ist die Novelle Amore e ginnastica (Liebe und Gymnastik) (1892), die die weibliche Fitness, sexuelle Stereotypen und Geschlechterrollen im Italien des 19. Jahrhunderts untersucht. Dieses Werk kann, neben zwei weiteren (einer Vorlesung und einem Zeitschriftenbeitrag), dem modernen Leser helfen, die Rolle des Frauensports und geschlechtergebundener Erwartungen im nach-Risorgimento Italien zu verstehen. Neben der Erforschung der weiblichen Gymnastik interessierte sich De Amici auch für das weibliche Bergsteigen. Durch das Untersuchen der Aktivitäten und des Erscheinungsbildes weiblicher Bergsteigerinnen enthüllt der Autor seine persönlichen Kriterien für die perfekte Frau. Werden diese kombiniert mit den Gymnastinnen der früheren Arbeiten, kann man die besonderen Einstellungen des Autors hinsichtlich Geschlechterrolle und weiblicher Perfektion herausfiltern. Für De Amicis musste eine Frau athletisch, schön, bescheiden, gläubig, liebend und mit einem Anflug von Unsicherheit bezüglich ihrer Sexualität ausgestattet sein, um sie interessant zu machen.

坚强，运动与美丽：埃德蒙多．德．亚米契斯与理想意大利女性

埃德蒙多．德．亚米契斯（1843-1908）是意大利最负盛名的作家之一，可以说他比任何后意大利复兴运动时期的作家都要受欢迎，他表达出了他的同胞们共同的希望，梦想与偏见。亚米契斯尤其对体操与体育教育感兴趣，他的写作经常涉及到这些内容。他关于这些题材最有名的作品是小说Amore e ginnastica [爱与体操]（1892），小说探讨了意大利十九世纪的女性健身，性偏见与社会性别角色。这部名著，与其他两个作品（一篇演讲稿与一篇杂志文章）一起，能够帮助现代的读者了解意大利后复兴运动时期的 女性体育和社会性别期望。除了女性体操，亚米契斯还对女性登山运动感兴趣。通过考察登山活动与女登山者的外形，作者透露了其完美女性标准。将女登山者和早期作品的体操运动员结合起来，我们可以提炼出作者自己对于性别和完美女性的独特看法。对于德亚米契斯来说，一个女人应该是运动的，美丽的，谦逊的，忠诚，富有爱心，对自己的性征不确定使她更有吸引力。

Introduction

Every age and country has at least one figure who sums up the national psyche, a figure who understands and comments on the shared values and dominant issues of the time; sometimes they are political leaders, sometimes popular heroes, but often they are writers who can combine the clear-sighted vision of a journalist with the eloquence of a wordsmith in order to hold a mirror up to society. In nineteenth-century Italy such a man was the novelist and essayist Edmondo De Amicis (1843–1908). In addition to journalistic reports on the social and political issues of the day, De Amicis deftly used both humour and pathos in his novels and short stories to point out the foibles, faults and beauties of his world. Although De Amicis wrote about many subjects connected to the middle-class world of northern Italy that he knew so well, one of his strongest and most abiding interests was sport and physical culture. Even more unusual for a writer of his time, he was fascinated with women's health and exercise. Some of his most important literary creations deal with this subject, and by examining three key works (a lecture, a novel and a magazine article) we can gain an insight into women's gender roles and the way that these concepts affected middle and upper-class men in nineteenth-century Italian society.

Edmondo De Amicis was born in the little Italian Riviera community of Oneglia on October 21, 1843, but his family soon moved to Turin where the author's father was the proprietor of a tobacconist's shop. After a stint in the army where he saw action in several battles in support of the *Risorgimento*, Italy's fight to achieve independence and unification, De Amicis settled into a career as a journalist and travel writer. The author was witness to the great age of Italian patriotism, and like most of his fellow citizens, he rejoiced when the country was finally united in 1861. The one exception to Italy's total unification was the city of Rome, which was still under the control of the Pope. This changed on September 20, 1870 when the Italian army, led by General Raffaele Cadorna, blasted through the ancient walls and liberated Rome from the rule of the Holy See. This was significant both politically and socially since it meant that Italy would never more submit either to the dictates of foreigners or the Catholic Church. In one action Italy had become an independent, modern, secular state; this separation also meant that writers like De Amicis would be free to express themselves with little worry about church censorship.

The *Risorgimento* brought about a tremendous upsurge of patriotic feeling among the upper and middle classes throughout the country, and these emotions were especially strong in the North and central regions of Italy. Despite the good feelings, unification was often a difficult task in a country that had been divided by foreign powers, petty princes, cultural diversity and linguistic variations. In many of his literary works from this time, De Amicis sought to show that such diverse Italian groups as Milanese merchants and Sicilian farmers were united by many of the same aspirations and desires, and they ought to think of themselves as brothers rather than merely inhabitants of the same peninsula. It is this great lesson of moral, spiritual and secular fusion that appears over and over in the author's work.

Nowhere is the theme of Italian unification better presented than in *Cuore* [Heart], a work that De Amicis published in 1886; it later became by far his most favourite and renowned novel. Subtitled, 'A book for children,' this is an account of an entire school year told in the form of a schoolboy's journal (with occasional moral and patriotic stories thrown in for good measure) which became for many children a guide to becoming fully engaged and integrated Italian citizens. Several of the episodes exploit the tender emotions of the audience, and it was a hard-hearted reader who would not shed one or two tears in the reading. Because of this, one scholar has accused De Amicis of using 'a didactic of weeping' in order to teach his messages of heroism, patriotism and sacrifice for the fatherland. [1] Despite its lachrymose tactics, *Cuore* is a sweet and sentimental book full of sympathetic characters who must face circumstances that test their pluck and love of country, but the book's principal goal is to bring together young Italians in order to celebrate the same kind of nationalistic ardor that the author felt. The best place for this reconciliation was in schools and among the young who would become Italy's future citizens.

Cuore is a book about Italian school children–male children. It would take a few more years before De Amicis would write about the education of girls. The only females who appear in the book are affectionate, caring mothers who behave with proper middle-class decorum. Although the women in *Cuore* never stray too far from their traditional roles as wives and mothers, they often show enough spunk and vivacity to indicate that the author did not expect them merely to be a bunch of submissive, domestic drones. Still, very few shots were fired in the battle for female equality or independence. Women remained at the periphery of Italian society and politics (as well as in the novels and articles of De Amicis). Their plight would have to wait until De Amicis and his fellow citizens had the time and understanding to tackle it. In the meantime, there were other more pressing problems to attack.

In the midst of the progressive, liberal Italian state there was still much misfortune, and De Amicis began to be deeply affected by the poverty and backwardness that afflicted many of his fellow citizens. Because of this, he was drawn to socialism as a political and economic philosophy, and in 1890, he began to identify himself more and more with the radical elements of Italian politics. His most profound statement on the subject came in the novel that he began in the early 1890's and which he continued to work on for almost a decade: *Primo Maggio* [Mayday]. The work revolves around two Mayday demonstrations in 1890 and 1891. During the second and more violent of the two, one of the protagonists, a socialist teacher, goes down into the piazza to show his solidarity with the anarchists, and there he is killed. The story was too dark and too pessimistic for readers in fin-de-siècle Italy, so it could only be published posthumously a century later. Fortunately, De Amicis was a very prolific writer, and he continued to publish popular works.

Perhaps because of the great success of *Cuore*, and his increasingly socialist views De Amicis discovered that he still had several things to say about education and the schooling of children, but this time the results were anything but a children's book. In 1890 he published a slightly disenchanted look at the teaching profession in his novel, *Il romanzo d'un maestro* [A Teacher's Story], but it was not until 1892 that his most acerbic, sexually suggestive and maliciously amusing work was published in book form. *Amore e ginnastica* [Love and Gymnastics] was part of a group of novellas and brief sketches in the anthology *Fra scuola e casa* [Between School and Home]. [2]

Despite the early successes of his literary life, De Amicis's later personal life was not so happy; in 1898 his beloved eldest son Furio committed suicide by shooting himself in the neck. The loss of his son caused a deep rift between himself and his wife, and the writer was never quite the same afterward. Indeed, the suicide drove the author to despair and hastened his wife's eventual madness. Financial reverses and the death of his wife in 1900 caused a further breakdown in his physical and mental state. One of the few places where the author could find solace was high in the Italian Alps, and the cool, mountain air and rugged surroundings helped bring him out of his depression.

Finally, on 11 March 1908, Edmondo De Amicis died of a cerebral haemorrhage at his home in Bordighera not far from his birthplace. Until the end of his life, De Amicis had remained one of Italy's most well liked writers, a witness to his country's unification as well as the rising prosperity of its middle class. With the changing values and economic status, he still retained a healthy sympathy for the working classes. It was this mixture of benevolence and patriotism that endeared him to the Italian public. Finally, in October of 1923 on the eightieth anniversary of his birth, the people of Turin erected an impressive statue and monument to De Amicis in the park across from the main railway station. At its dedication hundreds of school children filed past the statue while waving flags, carrying bouquets and giving the Fascist salute (Figures 1 and 2). [3]

Figure 1. Inauguration of the monument to Edmondo De Amicis in Turin, 1923. Many of the city's schoolchildren marched past carrying flags and floral tributes and giving the Fascist salute to honor the author of *Heart*. The monument is directly across from Turin's principal railroad station.

Figure 2. Edmondo De Amicis died on 11 March 1908, and this commemorative issue of *Il Secolo XX* [The Twentieth Century] was issued shortly thereafter. Although the author's reputation was based on his popular children's novel *Cuore* [Heart], he wrote many other books with adult themes.

It is quite certain that the children passing by the monument to De Amicis in the autumn of 1923 had not read – indeed, had not been allowed to read – *Love and Gymnastics*, a book that deals with themes and subjects that were certainly deemed more appropriate for the adult world. The novel tells the story of a thirty-year-old seminary dropout who comes to Turin to live with his wealthy uncle and becomes the older man's accountant and rent collector. Mr. Celzani, is physically weak and pathetically unworldly, but as mischievous fate would have it, he falls in love with one of his uncle's tenants, Maria Pedani, a very beautiful physical education teacher at a local school, whose muscles are steely and unyielding, and her intellect brilliant. Poor Celzani is distraught when the object of his affection, who looks upon him as little more than an inconvenient aggravation, repeatedly rebuffs him. Miss Pedani's one true love is gymnastics, and she has no time or interest in the love of a man, especially a groveling little weakling like Celzani. But the diminutive suitor is as determined to prevail as the Junoesque object of his affection is to avoid him. In order to ingratiate himself in the eyes of his beloved, he enrols in a gymnastics class, begins to read sporting journals and constantly manages to encounter the woman as if by accident. As a result the mild-mannered accountant begins to assume a more masculine role, while Pedani slowly settles into a more traditional female role. When he sees all his efforts thwarted, Celzani decides to leave the city and contemplates immigrating to America. However, his constant attention and the almost canine affection that he has shown seem to have gradually and unexpectedly worn down the woman's defences. As he is about to bid Pedani a final farewell, she grabs him forcefully and kisses him passionately. Celzani becomes giddy with pleasure and can only exclaim 'Great God!' before he is swept off his feet into a whirlwind of ardor.

De Amicis had a genius for translating the issues of the day into flesh-and-blood situations, and in *Love and Gymnastics* we have both a human and a theoretical drama that plays out in the streets and inner corridors of Turin. In essence the book is a cautionary tale about the problems of gender roles, strength and weakness. Fortunately, there is enough humanity and humour in the book to save it from being an artless tract or a shrill political diatribe. The famed Italian critic and novelist Italo Calvino has suggested that a better title for this book would have been 'Eros and Ideology' because of its unusual mixture of theoretical gymnastics with the steamy passions and amorous intrigues that lace its pages. [4] As Historian Suzanne Stewart-Steinberg explains, 'Celzani falls both into love and into ideology,' and if he wants to win Miss Pedani's love, he must accept the theories and values that are so sacred to her. [5] These athletic theories form the philosophical centre of the novel and are derived from the writings of two giants of Italian gymnastics, Obermann and Baumann, and are constantly quoted, debated and bickered over.

The Swiss instructor Rudolf Obermann (1812–1869) was the first to propose a system of scientific physical education as early as 1833 when he came to Turin to teach gymnastics to the Piedmontese army. Obermann adapted the Turnverein, or German gymnastics system, of Friedrich Ludwig Jahn (1778–1852) to the requirements of his employers in Turin; he also fit the techniques and philosophies of such men as Adolf Spiess (1810–1858), Johann Guts-Muths (1759–1839) and Heinrich Pestalozzi (1746–1827) to the needs of the army of the House of Savoy, hereditary rulers of Piedmont. In less than a decade, the Swiss immigrant had impressed many military leaders, and his form of exercise became an important part of army training. Thanks to this important groundwork, when the Casati laws of 1859 introduced 'educational gymnastics' for the first time to all the schools in the territory annexed by Piedmont, it was Obermann's system that was used. His methods were also popular with non-military athletes; in 1844 several former army members as well as a group of civilian pupils asked him to open a school of gymnastics for the general public. Thus the *Reale Società Ginnastica di Torino* [Royal Gymnastics Society of Turin] was formed, the first such organization in Italy. Obermann wanted to promote physical education for all ages and both sexes, but his interest in more strenuous exercise as well as his inevitable connection to the army made him more popular with military men than any other group. Emilio Baumann (1843–1917), on the other hand, was a more eclectic figure who based his system on an amalgam of the Swedish gymnastic system of Per Henrik Ling, Obermann's military gymnastics and his own personal ideas. His system was more 'natural,' emphasizing walking, marching, climbing, jumping and other body movements.

The interaction between these theories and the characters who espouse them forms the narrative basis for *Love and Gymnastics*, but there is much more at work in the novel than simply this. In addition, the book touches on two important issues: first the draconian administration of Italian national gymnastics, and second the problems attendant specifically to Italian women's exercise. The views and opinions that De Amicis expresses in *Love and Gymnastics* are later reflected in two other shorter works that touch on women's sport. It is therefore important to understand this book because it illuminates not only the writer's attitudes and prejudices, but it also helps to understand the real-life women who are reflected in the works.

Several Italian scholars have wondered if De Amicis based his fictional character of Miss Pedani on a specific person. Although she is almost certainly an amalgam of several real-life women, historian Renata Freccero suggests that according to recent research in the archives of Turin, there is a strong probability that Miss Pedani was inspired by an instructor named Luisa Rebecca Faccio. Although little is known about her, Faccio seems to have been active as a gymnastics teacher in Turin around the turn of the century. Her first recorded publication appeared in the early twentieth century, but she was almost certainly known before then. If she was indeed the model for the fictional Maria Pedani, then she must have been a familiar figure in Turinese gymnastics circles around 1891 while De Amicis was writing his novel. Despite the scanty biographical information, we can say with little doubt that Faccio was the first Italian to produce an exercise book for women by a woman, *Cinquanta giuochi ginnastici, in uso presso le sezioni femminili della società ginnastica di Torino* [Fifty gymnastic games in use by the women's section of the Gymnastics Society of Turin] which appeared in 1908. According to Renata Freccero, Luisa Rebecca Faccio embodies the 'sympathetic pedantry' and originality that are found in De Amicis's heroine. [6] Maria Pedani is an original, and her flesh-and-blood inspiration was probably much better off not being as eccentric or as inimitable as the fictional creation. Female exercise remained one of De Amicis's favorite topics, and he was loath to abandon it.

In addition to his novel *Love and Gymnastics*, De Amicis aired his views on women and physical education in another work, a lecture that was given to a mainly female audience in Campiglia Cervo, a popular mountain resort in 1891, the same year that he was writing his more famous novel. The title of the speech is '*Non si sgomentino le signore …*' [Ladies, Don't Be Alarmed …] and in it De Amicis warns his audience not to be shocked because big changes were in store for Italian women when it came to their physical fitness. Laws requiring universal physical education had been in Italy's legal codes for nearly three decades, but it was a requirement that was not strictly or universally applied. In 1878 Minister of Education Francesco De Sanctis pushed new legislation through parliament which made gymnastics compulsory in all Italian schools, whether public or private; more importantly, it stated that 'In female schools at every level gymnastics will have an exclusively educational character and will be regulated by special rules.' [7] Although De Amicis was generally in favour of the new attitudes toward women's exercise, he tempered his agreement with a couple of serious concerns.

First, he worried about the way the new laws would impact Italian schools because now they would have to find enough qualified teachers to instruct the children adequately. To this end new normal schools for physical education teachers were opened in several Italian cities, but there was another problem. By making gymnastics obligatory in all schools, De Amicis worried that this could cause serious problems in certain cases, especially in religious institutions. The author considers the serio-comic results when 'cloistered nuns who teach elementary schools, are forced to learn gymnastics and to submit themselves to examinations by governmental commissions … You can imagine the difficulty, the resistance and the scruples that would be encountered in this austere, timid little world by the introduction of physical exercises.' He imagines an especially embarrassing time when the sisters will have to lift up their black habits a bit in order to demonstrate to the inspectors that they can move their feet in the required way. It would be, as he says, 'a spectacle that is more sad than it is comic.' [8]

Even teachers in state-run public schools have problems reconciling traditional academic learning with what many considered to be little more than acrobatics. De Amicis quotes a former minister of public instruction who registered his discontent with the systems of both Baumann and Obermann. 'We have only two kinds of gymnastics in Italy just now: one for kiddies and the other for acrobats.' [9] The author then goes on to say that this analysis is wrong on both counts, but it points out the controversies and confusions inherent in the dueling systems. Exercise for girls is one of the matters that cause the greatest divisions and which has paralyzed the system.

> I hesitate to say that one of the issues of major disagreement among the two schools is that of female gymnastics, which Baumann would like to make more masculine and freer, while his adversaries for reasons of decency no less than for hygienic reasons, want to reduce to moderate and more seemly exercises. This contrast occasioned endless arguments centering on female dignity and modesty and to certain drawbacks and dangers of an extremely delicate nature; arguments that delighted the curious and malicious public for a time, and frightened a lot of mothers. In the end, girls' gymnastics has remained pretty much the same as it was. [10]

Despite the seeming political and educational intransigence, De Amicis concludes by saying that both Baumann and Obermann have an equal right to the nation's gratitude if for no other reason than their insistence on the importance of physical education for Italy's girls and for instilling a love for gymnastics that extends beyond the confines of theories and philosophies.

> It is very true that for twenty years Italian youth has turned with hitherto unknown enthusiasm to every sort of physical exercise, and mountain climbing, bicycling and rowing have flourished, long-distance walking races are growing, and new gymnastics clubs are forming every day, and gymnastics meets and festivals are becoming more frequent and more beautiful every year. [11]

But, De Amicis quickly adds, the picture is not entirely rosy. Gymnastics in the public sector had certainly not kept up with school gymnastics; worse yet, physical education in schools was in grave danger of extinction. All the promises of speedy fitness and instant strength had not, in fact, been kept, and this discouraged many participants. De Amicis does not wonder at this failure. With only two hours of gymnastics per week, the exercises conducted in schools were simply not sufficient to fulfill the potential that had been promised. In addition, the students had to undergo interminable lessons in exercise theory that were too detailed and verbose; instead of being a time when young bodies could get out and enjoy the freedom of motion and physical activity, physical education had turned into just another boring lesson. Unless something was done to remedy the situation, gymnastics which had 'arisen amidst deliriums of enthusiasm,' would 'die amidst yawns.' [12] The situation was, if anything, even worse in secondary schools where both the teachers and the students considered gymnastics to be inadequate, infrequent and a waste of time. 'Oh, poor De Sanctis,' laments the author at the end of his address, 'your life's work has come to this!' [13]

Despite the drawbacks to the system, De Amicis continued to be concerned with girl's gymnastics because if young ladies did not receive instruction in the early years, they were not very likely to receive it at all. As important as girls' physical education was to De Amicis, he still had another reservation linked to female exercise. This one was more closely linked to cultural and sexual worries since the author fretted about the reaction that a squad of bouncing, jiggling girls might have on the Italian male.

As envisioned by late nineteenth century Italians, gymnastics was not a competitive activity; sporting games were seen as divisive since they pitted one Italian against another. Group gymnastics, on the other hand, were considered a unifying force in which everyone moved together at the same time. Thus, all students were required to participate in these community-building activities and to do calisthenics and other bodybuilding exercises on a regular basis. In order to make the gymnastics exercises more interesting and to show off their newfound agility, the students would sometimes give performances called 'saggi' [exhibitions or recitals] in which large numbers of female gymnasts would demonstrate their abilities in unison. Many of these exhibitions were open to the public, and this is where De Amicis has some qualms because he feels that many male spectators were there for distinctly impure reasons. This is the sensuous description of a saggio consisting of 150 girls that De Amicis gives in *Love and Gymnastics*: 'All those beautiful arms and tiny hands in the air, those thick braids falling on rosy necks and on slender torsos, three hundred slender, arched feet, and the indefinable grace of those movements somewhere between dancing and leaping. And those long dresses that gave them the appearance of a chaste corps de ballet. It was new and seductive without a doubt!' [14]

Novel it might have been; seductive it certainly was. The author wonders how many of the sober, white-haired community leaders in the audience were there simply to support gymnastics. The answer seems to be very few, indeed. De Amicis implies strongly that it is the backing of these old perverts who enjoy seeing healthy young girls bounce and bobble in front of them who kept the demonstrations going far beyond what was necessary. There is certainly no doubt why Old Celzani, the main character's wealthy uncle in *Love and Gymnastics*, never misses a saggio when there are young girls performing. As one of the novel's more worldly characters remarks slyly about the elderly man and others of his type, 'Female gymnastics has been an incomparable discovery for these gentlemen, a true consolation of their old age, a source of the most delicious cerebral delights of which we ordinary people can have but a faint inkling.' [15] Whenever the old man contemplates gymnastic performances, he invariably falls into a trance-like state of reverie where his perverse dreams play over and over in his mind like some sort of mental pornographic film. [16]

De Amicis was not alone is his worries about the motives of many Italian men who attended gymnastics displays. Even Miss Pedani's great ideal, Emilio Baumann had fretted about how best to protect Italian female gymnasts from predatory males. Running about and exercising in public might be all well and good in certain northern countries, he argues, but Italian women were not quite ready for such freedom. 'We [Italians] cannot understand a lady who capers about, turns somersaults, lifts heavy weights, handles weapons or wrestles, or even performs any exercise that causes her clothing to fly about. We can understand a little girl who scrambles around, but not a woman, because even if nothing is revealed, it will awaken erotic images in those men who are present.' [17]

Voyeurism is just one of the diverse sexual activities in which the characters indulge in *Love and Gymnastics*. De Amicis has his creations display a wide variety of passions including masochism and lesbianism. Such variations of the sexual urge seem to indicate that the author was perhaps more open to alternative expressions of love than his disapproval of women's gymnastics displays might indicate. Maria Pedani, the central character in *Love and Gymnastics*, represents both the best and the worst qualities of Italian womanhood as Edmondo De Amicis saw them. She is constantly described as being 'virile' or 'masculine' in her appearance and activities. She is portrayed as a 'tall and strong lass of twenty-seven 'wide of shoulder and narrow of waist' … who would have been extremely beautiful if her nose had been a little finer and her facial expression and gait a bit less manly.' [18] There is a very strong implication that Miss Pedani is the dominant partner in a lesbian relationship with her silly, flighty, more conventionally feminine roommate, Miss Zibelli.

Although Miss Pedani is apparently too masculine for traditional tastes, she measures up quite well in the eyes of the other protagonist, Mr. Celzani. The little man rather likes the prospect of being dominated by a strong, muscular woman, and as the story progresses, the more hard-hearted and abusive she becomes, the better Celzani seems to like it. He continually refers to himself as Miss Pedani's servant or slave; he denigrates himself and looks forward to the time when she will make him grovel under her lovely but brutal heel. As Pedani's fame and respect grow in the world of physical culture, Celzani's masochism increases, and he fantasizes about being the husband of such a well known and admired woman: 'It rather seemed to him that his happiness would be so much sweeter and deeper precisely because he was small and unimportant next to her, nothing more than a husband, forgotten at certain times (even for most of the day); kept like a servant, a tool, a plaything, an overgrown house pet.' [19] The lady would go out into the world and do great and wonderful things while the man would stay in the background, to be used as a virtual sex slave whenever he was wanted. This is hardly the part that Italian women were supposed to play in domestic arrangements, and the reversal of roles forms part of the interest and piquancy of the novel.

The role reversal reaches its peak of intensity when Pedani finally decides to let her suitor taste the delights that she has withheld for the entire novel. In the final scene of the novel, Celzani encounters Pedani on the stairway of the building to admit his utter defeat by telling the woman one last goodbye.

> But he had not finished his words when he felt a powerful hand on the nape of his neck and two fiery lips on his mouth; and in the delirious joy that invaded him in the midst of that immense dark paradise where he felt himself lifted up as if by a whirlwind, he could only emit a strangled cry: 'Oh, Great God!' [20]

Thus, when Pedani pulls her persistent and ultimately successful suitor into her arms and kisses him passionately, it is she who initiates the action, and Celzani who nearly swoons with emotion. This is quite the opposite from traditional male/female functions, and it is just this element that makes the novel more interesting and revolutionary in terms of gender roles. At first glance De Amicis seems to lay out a traditional heterosexual ending where the two characters will get married and live happily ever after. One Italian scholar has interpreted this last scene as a reconciliation of traditional gender roles and the values of socialist equality.

> In the end it is Celzani's constancy and his capacity to suffer that succeeds in breeching Miss Pedani's 'manly heart,' and this time the couple is more balanced in their respective roles, and will find their just and legitimate realization in matrimony, family and the fundamental and indispensable values of De Amicis the socialist. [21]

But perhaps Pedani's conversion is not quite so complete. It is true that both characters have edged nearer to the traditional sex roles that Italian society revered, but on closer inspection, Pedani surrenders only a tiny amount of ground when it comes to her usual 'masculinity' since she is still the aggressor. One might also argue that she is merely exchanging one companion, Miss Zibelli, for another slightly less feminine one in the expectation that the relationship will stay more or less the same. Whatever the real reasons for her seeming capitulation to societal norms, we can be certain that Celzani and Pedani will have a decidedly unconventional relationship.

In 'Non si sgomentino le signore' the author considers the theoretical plusses and minuses of female physical education, and in Love and Gymnastics he gives those theories human faces and physiques. Toward the end of his life De Amicis became fascinated with another form of exercise, mountain climbing, and it was not long before he began to write about a woman's role in this activity, also.

The suicide of Furio, De Amicis's son, in November of 1898 was a defining moment for the entire family. After Furio's death the family dynamics were irrevocably changed by the tragedy, and the family members worked through their grief in different ways. Teresa, the boy's mother spiralled downward into madness and legal separation from her husband; De Amicis' grief was inconsolable, and for many weeks thereafter he could not bring himself to write or resume his normal life; Ugo, the younger brother, sought solace in the open air and devoted himself more and more to mountain climbing as a way to redirect his own unhappiness. Since Turin, the long-time home of the De Amicis family, sits at the base of the Alps, it was not a great inconvenience for devotees of climbing or winter sports to escape to higher altitudes. One of Ugo's favourite locations was the comfortable Hotel Giomein in the Val d'Aosta, set up above the tree line at the foot of the Matterhorn; it was from here that the young man began many of his excursions into the rocky heights. It was also here that starting around 1900 De Amicis came to be with his son and to enjoy the both the mountains and the colourful people who came and went at the Alpine hotel.

By 1902 De Amicis had accumulated a wealth of material at this location, and he completed his first set of Alpine sketches which were later published as *Nel regno del Cervino: Gli scritti del Giomein* [In the Realm of the Matterhorn: Writings from Giomein]. Among the various characters that he encounters at the hotel are a German couple, Theodor Wundt and his wife Maud. De Amicis is immediately drawn to the man, a major in the German army, by his tall stature, his expansive personality and his rugged appearance; he is described as 'a rocky crag in human form which the alpine winds have infused with life.' [22] But even more fascinating to the author is Wundt's energetic wife, Maud. She is a dutiful wife and mother, but she is also a superb athlete who can scale the highest peaks along with her husband and can out-climb almost any man on the mountain. Maud was born and raised in England, but she came to Stuttgart in order to learn German and to study music. It was there that she met and fell in love with her mountain-climbing husband. It is immediately clear to De Amicis that Maud is an extraordinary woman who is game for almost any challenge. He is astounded to learn that they spent the first night of their honeymoon 'in [one of] the rough Alpine huts at more than three thousand meters above sea level, in the midst of ice and snow where two human creatures had perhaps never before exchanged a lover's kiss.' [23]

De Amicis continues his fascination with both Maud Wundt and female climbers in an article that was first published in April 1903 called '*Le grandi alpiniste tedesche*' [Great German Lady Mountaineers] (Figures 3 and 4). The piece was inspired by an article written in the German magazine *Die Woche* by Frau Wundt called '*Berühmte Bergsteigerinnen*' [Famous Lady Mountaineers], and it describes the activities of female mountain climbers in the German-speaking world. Rather than do a simple translation of the article, De Amicis decided to 'write a few pages as a sort of 'variation' as a musician might do on the theme that has so moved me.' [24] The article is a gloss on the original with the author's thoughts, digressions and opinions taking centre stage rather than the lady mountain climbers. The Teutonic ladies offer De Amicis an opportunity to contemplate the nature of femininity, the effects of mountain climbing on women and, most importantly, what constitutes an ideal 'look' for athletic women.

LE GRANDI ALPINISTE TEDESCHE.

1. Sig.ª Rose Friedmann, nata Rostborn (Vienna).   2. Sig.ª Maud Wundt (Heilbronn) (L'autrice
dell'articolo della *Woche*).   3. Sig.ª Hermine Tauscher-Ceduly (Presburgo).
4. Sig.ª Mabel Rickmers (Vienna).   5. Contessa di Ortenburg (Castello Tambach, Franconia).
Sig.ª Henriette Terschak (Cortina).

Figure 3. Illustration of some of the women in the article 'Le grandi alpiniste tedesche' [Great German Lady Mountaineers], from *Il Secolo XX*, April 1903. Portrait number 2 (top middle) is Maud Wundt, the author of the original article upon which De Amicis based his essay, 'Le alpiniste tedesche' [German Lady Mountaineers].

Figure 4. Strong, athletic and (shocking for the time) wearing trousers, a group of women ascend an alpine peak in the title illustration to 'Great German Lady Mountaineers' from the April 1903 issue of *Il Secolo XX*.

The author is greatly impressed by the sheer number of climbs that the German women have accomplished – and not just young and apparently fit girls for one of them is sixty years of age and still climbing. The author is surprised to learn that virtually every peak in the central and eastern Alps (and a good many in the western section) have been conquered by women. After attesting to the skill and perseverance of the ladies he describes, De Amicis is not slow to question the femininity of a woman who displays such masculine attributes as strength, courage and fitness. He recognizes that an Italian male reader might balk at such things, but he reminds his audience how sexy strong women can be. 'You might well be able to say that the nerve of these virile women irritates you, but you cannot deny that you would take great pleasure in seeing a line of them stretching out ahead of you, and many times during the procession you might (at least mentally, if in no other way) put your fingertips to your pursed lips and stretch out your hand as if you were throwing a kiss.' [25] Frau Wundt herself feels the need to ask her correspondents whether they think that mountain climbing is appropriate for women. A majority replies that in general, men have 'a greater vigor, resolution and astuteness as well as an intuitive knowledge of the mountains,' but women have greater dexterity, stamina and tenacity. [26] Besides, women neither drink nor smoke, nor are they picky about the food that they eat, so those traits alone would put women ahead of men.

An avid proponent of women's physical activity that he is, De Amicis still reflects many of the common prejudices of his day. He recommends that women abstain from overly long, arduous ascents. 'The principal rule of female mountaineering must be, in essence, that they should avoid excessive fatigue.' De Amicis reminds his readers approvingly that women are naturally more kind-hearted than men, and he repeats that no matter how strong or masculine looking they might be, women cherish and nurture children far more frequently than men. [27] Another curious prejudice is revealed in this sentence: 'We should also observe the morality of the German lady mountaineers, for almost all of them made their expeditions with their husbands with whom they shared a common passion for the mountains; either that, or they did so with a sister or a brother.' [28] No self-respecting middle-class lady would think of going off on an adventure like mountain climbing alone. A husband or suitable relative must accompany her lest her reputation suffer. The days when a woman, no matter how strong or independent, could run off at a moment's notice to do whatever she wanted (with whomever she wanted) were far in the future.

As important as all these ideas are, the most prominent feature of 'German Lady Mountaineers' is the emphasis that De Amicis places on the physical appearance of the women in the article. Portraits of the lady alpinists accompanied the original piece, and De Amicis makes much of this feature. The first thing that he notices are that all the women look like typical Germans: 'solid heads, wide and bony faces, heavy bodies, eyes with a proud and bold look that seem to stare into the face of a challenge on the tops of distant mountains.' How many of them, he wonders, have muscular arms beneath their shirtsleeves. He describes one formidable lady as very 'buxom,' a regular 'Juno of the Alps,' and says that another 'has the torso of a wrestler and who holds her hands behind her back as if she is hiding a club.' Another has 'a square forehead, two deep-set eyes and a stubbornly closed mouth – enough to remove anyone's temptation to cross her on a whim.' These rather fearsome ladies are joined by others of a more conventional femininity who 'possess a delicacy of features and a softness of expression that, were you to see them elsewhere, it would never occur to you that they were bold mountaineers.' [29]

One of the most exciting things about the photos of lady athletes for De Amicis is their apparel; in their photographs they all wear trousers. Many of them also sport short hair and assume masculine poses with wide stances, often grasping sturdy alpenstocks or ice axes. Women who wear men's clothing always seemed to excite the author. The suggestion of a strong, dominating woman is both sexy and frightening to De Amicis, as is the subtle whiff of lesbianism. As if to prove this, the author states that he envies the guide who has the good luck to prop up one of the ladies on a difficult climb, no doubt imagining in his cerebral cinema (much like Uncle Celzani) the delights of applying a gentle nudge to the be-trousered rear end of one of these alpine amazons.

For De Amicis, the Matterhorn was a place of refuge where he could escape from his grief and unhappy home life; it was a place of heroism, of purity and of isolation. When women enter this world they must be pure and strong, too. These are Eves in an icy, primordial male Eden. De Amicis was an ardent socialist, and there are echoes of this in the mountains. The Alps also form a rare arena where gender, class and economic conditions are relatively unimportant, where only skill determines rank. It is a realm where men and women are equal, where the dangers and delights are open to all.

There is only one glaring omission in this otherwise fascinating article: where are the Italian lady mountaineers? De Amicis claims that he would have preferred to write an article on the exploits of his fellow countrywomen, but he could only find four of them. If he had looked a little harder, he certainly would have encountered a great number of Italian female alpinists. Perhaps De Amicis was reluctant to imagine Italian ladies in trousers, leaving their fathers and husbands behind to clamber up the Alpine peaks.

When we examine the three works here under discussion, we can distill certain traits of De Amicis's ideal woman (Figure 5). She is beautiful (as is Miss Pedani); modest and moral (like the German ladies who will not venture out without a male relative); faithful (like Pedani who is steadfast to her ideals and Frau Wundt to her

Figure 5. Four students at the government's school for female gymnastics instructors attached to the Royal Gymnastics Society of Turin. The photographer is Mario Gabino, and the picture was taken in 1894. These were the real-life models for the fictional Maria Pedani, protagonist of *Love and Gymnastics*. Photo courtesy of the Royal Gymnastics Society of Turin.   Further images and information on the history of Italian gymnastics are available at the website www.museorealeginnastica.it

husband); strong, courageous and athletic (although not excessively so, like certain of the German lady mountaineers); caring and nurturing (like the good mothers in *Cuore*; and finally, imbued with enough personal and sexual ambiguity to keep a man intrigued. Naturally, these facets are rarely found in the same woman, but they are present to one degree or another in De Amicis's literary heroines. It is the man who must sort out the contradictory values and characteristics that he finds in his beloved, and even then he is very often deceived by what he sees.

The muddled interaction between men and women is a theme that De Amicis returns to again and again. When the two genders reverse their proper roles, the results will include confusion, disorder, comedy and (sometimes) true love. It is still a subject of endless fascination, and although De Amicis can only give us his particular perspective as a nineteenth-century Italian male, more often than not his attitudes and mores reflect those of the times. Defining the proper behaviour for men and women constantly intrigues him; it is this fascination with the eternal questions of male and female which keeps his works sparkling and interesting a century later. For him, men will never really understand women (and almost certainly vice versa). Men can only judge a woman by her appearance and by the emotions that she stirs up in a man's soul. Or, as he says more eloquently in *Love and Gymnastics*, 'A girl is always a mystery; one can only trust in her face and the inspiration in one's own heart.' [30] Beyond that she is an enigma.

Notes

[1] Giovanni 'Appunti per una lettura critica del pensiero educativo di Edmondo De Amicis', 73.

[2] According to Bruno Traversetti, Love and Gymnastics is meant to be the reverse of the educational coin for which Heart is the more palatable side (see Traversetti, *Introduzione a De Amicis*, 95).

[3] *La Domenica del Corriere*, 4 November 1923, cover illustration.

[4] 'Nota Introduttiva' to *Amore e ginnastica*, originally published in the 1971 edition of the novel by publisher Einaudi, Turin.

[5] Stewart-Steinberg, *Pinocchio Effect*, 172.

[6] Freccero, *Amore e Ginnastica*, 17. Although Freccero quotes no sources to substantiate her claim that Faccio is the model for Pedani, she does quote extensively from the 1924 edition of Faccio's book. Luisa Rebecca Faccio had undoubtedly been teaching and working on her first book long before its publication. Her next book (1912) was expanded to 100 games for women, and in 1924 she published 125 games for children.

[7] Quoted in Gori, *Italian Fascism and the Female* Body, 40.

[8] De Amicis, *Non Si Sgomentino*, 11–12.

[9] Ibid., 16. The original is, 'Non abbiamo per ora in Italia che due ginnastiche: una da marmocchi e l'altra da saltimbanchi.'

[10] Ibid., 16–17. The 'dangers of a delicate nature' almost certainly refers to menstruation.

[11] Ibid., 17.

[12] Ibid.

[13] Ibid., 19.

[14] De Amicis, *Amore e Ginnastica*, 29. This sentence is used almost word-for-word in the lecture 'Non si sgomentino le signore.'

[15] Ibid., 34. The speaker, Engineer Ginoni, probably echoes most closely the views of the author.

[16] The idea of a 'cerebral cinema' had been explored in 1907 by De Amicis in 'Cinematografo cerebrale' in which a fictional character imagines himself in all sorts of bizarre scenarios which he 'watches' with his mind's eye.

[17] Baumann, *Ginnastica e Scienza*, 349–350. This book was originally published in 1910.

[18] *De Amicis, Amore e ginnastica*, 9.

[19] *De Amicis, Amore e ginnastica*, 57–58.

[20] *De Amicis, Amore e ginnastica*, 117.

[21] Brambilla, *De Amicis*, 108.

[22] De Amicis, *Nel Regno del Cervino*, 49–50.

[23] Ibid., 48.

[24] De Amicis, 'Le Alpiniste Tedesche,' 86.

[25] Ibid., 89.

[26] Ibid., 90.

[27] Ibid., 90.

[28] Ibid., 88.

[29] Ibid., 93–94.

[30] *Amore e ginnastica*, 54. The original is, 'Una ragazza è sempre un mistero; non c'è che fidarsi al suo viso e all'ispirazione del proprio cuore.' This epigrammatic sentence has become the most quoted line in the entire novel.

References

Baumann, Emilio. *Ginnastica e Scienza: La Ginnastica Italiana e le Scienze Affini (Anatomia, Fisiologia, Igiene, Meccanica Umana) Con Riferimento Alla Ginnastica Medica, Ortopedica, e Pedagogica*. Venice: La Cultura Fisica, 1950.

Brambilla, Alberto. *De Amicis: Paragrafi Eterodossi*. Modena: Mucchi, 1992.

De Amicis, Edmondo. *Amore e Ginnastica (con una nota introduttiva di Italo Calvino)*. Milan: Mondadori, 1996.

De Amicis, Edmondo. *Amore e Ginnastica (edizione commentata a cura di Renata Freccero)*. Turin: Levrotto & Bella, 2000.

De Amicis, Edmondo. 'Nel Regno del Cervino: Gli Scritti del Giomein; A Cura di Pietro Crivellaro. Turin: Vivalda, 1998.

De Amicis, Edmondo. 'Le Alpiniste Tedesche'. In *Pagine Allegre*. Milan: Treves, 1906.

De Amicis, Edmondo. *Non Si Sgomentino le Signore: Conferenza Sull'educazione Fisica; Letta e Commentata da Pino Boero, Maria Cristina Ferraro Bertolotto e Giovanni Ricci*. Genoa: Tilgher, 1984.

Freccero, Renata. *Amore e Ginnastica* (annotated edition). Turin: Levrotto & Bella, 2000.

Gori, Gigliola. *Italian Fascism and the Female Body: Sport, Submissive Women and Strong Mothers*, London: Routledge, 2004.

La Domenica del Corriere (Illustrated supplement to the *Corriere della Sera*), XXV, no. 44 (1923).

Ricci, Giovanni. 'Appunti per una lettura critica del pensiero educativo di Edmondo De Amicis'. In Non Si Sgomentino le Signore: Conferenza Sull'Educazione Fisica; Letta e Commentata da Pino Boero, Maria Cristina Ferraro Bertolotto e Giovanni Ricci. Genoa: Tilgher, 1984.

Stewart-Steinberg, Suzanne. *The Pinocchio Effect: On Making Italians (1860–1920)*, Chicago: University of Chicago Press, 2007.

Traversetti, Bruno. *Introduzione a De Amicis*. Rome/Bari: Laterza, 1991.

Women as Leaders: What Women Have Attained In and Through the Field of Physical Education

Roberta J. Park

In her 1792 treatise A Vindication of the Rights of Woman, *Mary Wollstonecraft proclaimed that when girls were allowed to take the same exercise as boys the fiction of the 'natural superiority of man' would be exposed. A century later, as growing numbers of women began engaging in sports and achieving a place of distinction in the profession of physical education, her assertion became a reality. Few people today know that women were serving as presidents of the inclusive American Physical Education Association decades before any became the president of organizations such as the American Medical Association or the American Historical Association – or how early they had achieved other leadership positions. Although a considerable number of informative books now exist regarding what women have achieved in and through sporting competitions, to date the only comprehensive treatment of what women once attained in and through physical education has been Shelia Fletcher's book* Women First: The Female Tradition in Physical Education in English Physical Education, 1880–1980. *This article sets down foundations for bringing about better understandings of the American experience.*

Introduction

Although 'woman's rights' movements had appeared earlier in a number of countries, the 1960s were especially significant in bringing about greater opportunities for members of the female sex. During the 1970s 'women's history' became a formalized field of endeavour. [1] Initially those topics that received the greatest attention from feminist and other scholars were matters relating to economic independence, political struggles and enfranchisement. Interest then turned to biological and medical matters focused largely around the *presumed* weaknesses – both physical and intellectual – of females. As early as 1974 four American physical educators whose areas of research were physiology, social psychology, motor skill acquisition and history published *The American Woman in Sport*, which opens with the statement: 'Why have we written a book on women in sport? First and foremost, to answer the need for information. Sport for American women has been a neglected phenomenon – both in terms of providing adequate opportunities for varied participation and in regard to the scholarly study of the sportswoman.' [2] By the 1980s other positive examinations of the past experiences of women were appearing. Some of the more interesting – and informative – dealt with what they had attained in and through sporting activities. [3] The 1990s would witness a considerable growth in the number of such works. [4] However, the only comprehensive treatment of what women once attained in and through physical education has been Shelia Fletcher's book *Women First: The Female Tradition in Physical Education in English Physical Education, 1880–1980.* [5] No such work yet exists regarding the United States. This article seeks to set down foundations for bringing about better understandings of the American experience.

In 1979 a small monograph entitled *Women as Leaders in Physical Education and Sports* which had emanated from a series of lectures sponsored by the Department of Physical Education and Dance at the University of Iowa was published. In the introduction co-editor Mary Hoferek stated: 'Over one hundred thousand women in this country [the United States] occupy leadership positions in physical education and sport. We are teachers of physical education, coaches, instructors, and administrators. We work in colleges, universities, public and private schools, recreation programs, camps, institutions, sport clubs, and other settings.' A less encouraging statement followed: 'The percentage of women athletic directors for women's sports declined from sixty-one percent in 1976 to fifty-five percent in 1978.' [6]

This was not the only decrease that would occur in leadership roles that American women once had attained in and through physical education and sport. Few individuals today seem to realize how much they had achieved. A better understanding of such matters requires a reevaluation of the nine decades following the creation of the Association for the Advancement of Physical Education in 1885, and the unforeseen consequences of a very important piece of federal legislation that was enacted as part of the 1972 Education Amendments – Title IX – which states that 'No person in the United States shall on the basis of sex be denied the benefits of, or subjected to, discrimination under any education program or activity receiving Federal financial assistance'.

Although Title IX specified nothing relating to athletics, it was of enormous importance in bringing about opportunities for females in schools and colleges to participate in sports on a level commensurate with that which males had enjoyed for over a century. [7] The growth of intercollegiate and interscholastic programmes for women and girls and increasingly higher levels of performance for those who wanted to become members of competitive teams has been quite remarkable. An unanticipated result of Title IX has been the striking decline of women who now serve as the coaches of such teams and as athletic directors. A decline in the number of women who served as chairs of departments of physical education (now often called kinesiology or exercise science) also occurred. Moreover, it is possible that Title IX unwittingly contributed to the decline of school-based physical education that has occurred since the 1970s, and to such things as the percentage of women who annually are elected to membership in honorary organizations such as the American Academy of Kinesiology and Physical Education.

Everyone knows, or thinks they know, what physical education is and what its goals have been. This has seldom been the case. Even less is known about its history, or that within their profession American female physical educators attained leadership roles much earlier, and much more frequently, than did women in the American Medical Association and other professional organizations. Since the 1970s there has been a tendency to denounce the stance that some, but certainly not all, took against commercialized forms of sports for girls and women. However, it is doubtful that critics know – or perhaps even care – that when the Women's Division of the National Amateur Athletic Federation held its first meeting in 1923 concerns about excesses in men's intercollegiate athletics were intensifying and the Carnegie Foundation for the Advancement of Teaching was about to initiate a major investigation. [8]

Antecedents of Late Nineteenth and Early Twentieth Century Physical Education

The importance of exercise as a component of health, which had been acknowledged since antiquity, was given renewed attention during the 1700s in books such as Scottish-born physician George Cheyne's *Essay on Health and Long Life* and Swiss physician Simon Andre Tissot's *Avis au Peuple sur sa Santé*. [9] The 1800s would witness growing interest in such matters. The following words appeared in a five-page article entitled 'Physical Education' that was published in the January 1826 issue of William Russell's *American Journal of Education*: 'The time we hope is near, when there will be no literary institution unprovided with proper means of healthful exercise and innocent recreation.' [10] Commentaries relating to the importance of exercise and physical education continued to appear. The November 1826 issue of the *American Journal of Education*, for example, included 'Gymnastic Exercises for Females', an article reprinted from *The Boston Medical Intelligencer* in which William B. Fowle (founder of the Boston Monitorial School) expressed hope that 'the day is not far distant when gymnasiums for women will be as common as churches in Boston'. [11]

From the 1830s to the outbreak of the Civil War (1861–65) health, hygiene, exercise and physical education received extensive attention in publications such as the *Common School Journal*, the *American Journal of Education*, the *Boston Medical and Surgical Journal* (today known as *The New England Journal of Medicine*) and *Boston Health Journal and Advocate of Physiological Reform* [12] as well as in a spate of books such as Charles Caldwell's *Thoughts on Physical Education* (1834) and physician Elizabeth Blackwell's *The Laws of Life, With Special Reference to the Physical Education of Girls* (1852). [13] Given the times, a remarkable amount of the attention was directed to girls and women.

At all-male Amherst College, a Department of Physical Culture was established in 1860. Named its director in 1861, Edward Hitchcock, MD, would become the first president of the Association for the Advancement of Physical Education (today known as the American Alliance for Health, Physical Education, Recreation, and Dance). Physical education also became an important part of the many women's colleges that were being established. Founded in 1865 by Matthew Vassar, the stated purpose of Vassar Female College was 'to accomplish for young women what our colleges are accomplishing for young men'. The initial prospectus declared that 'good health is essential to the successful prosecution of study'. [14] Graduates were expected to 'go forth physically well-developed, vigorous, and graceful women, with enlightened views and wholesome habits as regards the use and care of their bodies'. From the beginning students engaged in 'light gymnastics' and 'healthful female sports in the open air' under the direction of an experienced female instructor. A qualified 'lady physician' oversaw the programme and gave instruction in anatomy, physiology and the 'laws of health' (i.e. hygiene). [15] Similar arrangements would be made at other early women's colleges such as Goucher and Mount Holyoke. Health, hygiene and physical education also received attention at the first coeducational college in the United States, Oberlin College, which opened in 1833. Oberlin subsequently would have a significant role in preparing individuals who became leaders of the new field of physical education. [16]

Following the Civil War the sanitary movement strengthened, and important a growing number of health-oriented organizations such as the American Public Health Association were established. [17] As greater numbers of young men and women began to enter institutions of higher learning the adage *mens sana in corpore sano* found concrete expression in the growth of departments of physical training (then the more frequent term). At coeducational institutions it was typical to form separate units, often headed by an individual who held a medical degree, for male and female students. The curriculum focused upon prescribed exercises typically derived from the German or Swedish 'system' (preferred for females) or that designed by Dudley Allen Sargent, MD, director of the Harvard Gymnasium. The faculty's major responsibility was teaching physical education classes, usually required during the freshman and sophomore years. With the rise of the high school at the turn of the century the need for qualified gymnastics (i.e. physical education) teachers increased, and teacher training became the next most time-consuming part of the curriculum.

Male Directors of Physical Education Confront 'An Unholy Alliance'

Baseball, football and other intercollegiate men's sports, which rose to prominence during the last years of the nineteenth century, initially were controlled by students.

[18] Physical educators had little or no connection with these activities. In 1900 Clark Hetherington (who was at the University of Missouri) was one of only two men who were serving as both professor of physical training and director of athletics. [19] Increasing numbers of deaths in the American game of football [20] brought about the December 1905 meeting that led to more faculty oversight and the formation of the Intercollegiate Athletic Association of the United States. Soon renamed the National Collegiate Athletic Association, this became the major rule-governing body. [21] Contemporary college and university presidents were of two persuasions. Whereas Yale's president Arthur T. Hadley asserted that he and his faculty were content to leave everything to Walter Camp (Yale's noted football coach), Harvard's president Charles William Eliot (an oarsman during his college days in the 1860s) repeatedly denounced intercollegiate athletics. [22]

By the First World War, as matters relating to psycho-social as well as physiological health were becoming a significant goal of physical education, the curriculum turned increasingly to games and sports. Hetherington's *School Program in Physical Education* (1922) and *The New Physical Education* (1927), by Thomas Denison Wood, MD, and Rosalind Frances Cassidy, are two of the more influential books that reflect the trend. [23] Hetherington also was instrumental in creating an Athletic Research Society to study social and moral aspects of rapidly expanding school, college and other athletic programmes and, hopefully, improve how these were being conducted. [24] In 1925 the Athletic Research Society would affiliate with the American Physical Education Association (the name the AAPE had adopted in 1906). [25] The Carnegie Foundation for the Advancement of Teaching already had launched its major investigation of the many problems associated with intercollegiate athletics. [26]

Following the First World War, as problems related to intercollegiate athletics intensified, men who headed departments of physical education became increasingly aware of the necessity to define what the relationship of an athletic programme should be to a physical education programme. Addressing the annual meeting of the all-male Society of Directors of Physical Education in Colleges in 1921, Edgar Fauver, MD (director, Wesleyan University) spoke for many of his contemporaries when he declared: 'I can find no place for intercollegiate athletics, as at present conducted in most colleges, in a physical education program. ... Physical education considers the individual and through a wise selection of activities, gymnastics, and more especially athletic sports, endeavors to give him health, neuro-muscular training, and physical strength.' By contrast the aim of intercollegiate athletics was 'the winning of games'. [27] George Meylan, MD (director, Columbia University) pointed to the 'sharp contrast' between commercialized intercollegiate athletics and the educational emphasis to be found in intramural sports. [28]

In a 1922 article published in the *Educational Review* John Sundwall, MD (head of student health services at the University of Michigan) cited as the first of his five major objections to the way that intercollegiate athletics were being conducted the fact that a university's facilities and equipment typically were given over to 'a few selected athletes'. Therefore, the needs of 'the rank and file of students' were neglected. [29] These three important contemporaries were by no means alone!

The matter received even greater attention at the 1922 meeting of the Society of Directors of Physical Education in Colleges. Fauver was especially emphatic: 'I believe to-day that the proper settlement of the intercollegiate athletic problem is the most serious question before the members of this society.' [30] Although many, but not all, male directors were of a similar opinion, various members of their faculties would have been happy to serve as coaches (or assistant coaches) for major intercollegiate sports (e.g. football, baseball). Some, in fact, were teaching physical education classes and also coaching so-called 'minor sports' (e.g. gymnastics, swimming).

Female Physical Educators 'Hear the Call' and Make Unrelenting Efforts to Avoid 'An Unholy Alliance'

What is usually recognized as the first women's 'field day' (track, basketball and other sports were included) had taken place at Vassar College in September 1895. [31] By the early 1900s women's field days were culminating the year's activities at many other institutions. Before the First World War opportunities for women and girls to engage in sporting competitions grew modestly; however, nowhere did they equal those available to males. Yet in some places competitive events for girls were accorded considerable approval – most notably in basketball in the state of Iowa. [32] With some exceptions, things would change markedly beginning in the 1920s.

The American Physical Education Association's Committee on Women's Athletics [33] (which had evolved from a Women's Basketball Committee that had been organized in 1899) was well aware of discussions that its male counterparts were having regarding excesses in men's intercollegiate sports. The fact that both sexes belonged to a single organization (the American Physical Education Association) and subscribed to the same journal (the *American Physical Education Review*) was helpful in this regard. Joan S. Hult's well-documented account of the role that female physical educators performed in the governance of athletics for girls and women from 1899 to 1949 includes relevant words from a letter that Blanche Trilling (director of physical education for women, University of Wisconsin) wrote to Lou Henry Hoover (chair of the newly created Women's Division – National Amateur Athletic Federation) in 1923: 'It seems to me ... that unless a very definite stand is taken ... we will find ourselves fighting the same vicious system that the men are doing, and that our women will be having commercially sponsored athletics.' [34] An overview of discussions that had occurred at the meeting when the Women's Division of the NAAF was formed was even published in the 1923 *Report of the International Health Education Conference of the World Conference on Education.* [35]

Why did Trilling and other female physical educators object so vehemently? One reason was that as educators they believed that educational, not competitive, goals must be paramount. They also were well aware that outside of departments of physical education there were very few women on the faculties of institutions of higher learning. Many were apprehensive that if they were to initiate intercollegiate athletics for female students the coaching might be taken over by men and that this might lead to men taking over the physical education curriculum as well. They did not want to lose what they had laboured so hard – and successfully – to attain. The Women's Division of the National Amateur Athletic Federation [36] provided them with a number of opportunities to exercise control over sports, especially those conducted within educational institutions. [37]

It would be difficult to deny that in many instances their efforts were excessive. However, the antipathy that since the 1970s has been directed at female physical educators such as Trilling and Mabel Lee needs to be reconsidered in light of what the situation was like in 1923 when Trilling wrote to Hoover and Lee (then director of physical education for women at Beloit College) addressed the Middle West Society of College Directors of Physical Education for Women on the topic 'The Case for and Against Intercollegiate Athletics for Women As it Stands Today'. In her address Lee acknowledged that intercollegiate athletics might have benefits (e. g., participants were like likely to develop more vigour and 'even quickness of thought'; contact with 'girls' from other schools could broaden their social skills). However, she felt certain that problems that infected men's intercollegiate athletics were 'sure to creep in'. Because the teaching staff's time would become consumed with training a small number of the most talented individuals, intramural and inter-class activities for large numbers of girls and women would be in jeopardy. [38] Lee's views reached a wider audience when 'The Case for and Against Intercollegiate Athletics for Women As it Stands Today' was published in the *American Physical Education Review*. [39]

Similar concerns were being raised regarding interscholastic athletics for high-school girls. The 1928 report of the Pennsylvania Athletic Association, for example, included among its 11 objections 'the development of star players and winning school teams', the 'tendency to neglect the "many"' and the fact that male coaches already were too often 'in charge of girls' athletics'. Instead, the emphasis should be on intramural programmes that promote 'better health through exercise' and 'stimulate enjoyment' in participation. When these goals were pre-eminent then it could be acceptable for the semester's or year's activities to culminate in properly organized and conducted 'county field days'. [40]

As did most of their male counterparts, female physical educators typically dedicated considerable time to creating and conducting intramural sports programmes as well as teaching the physical education curriculum. Because participation was deemed more important than winning, the preferred model (at least by the faculty) was the round-robin, not the elimination, tournament. By the 1930s they also had begun to initiate carefully controlled, smaller (and limited) more competitive inter-class programmes for those students who desired somewhat more challenging experiences. These extracurricular sports programmes were conducted under the auspices of a student organization – usually called the women's athletic association or women's recreation association – that was closely watched over by one or more female faculty advisers. Although carefully controlled, the WAA/WRA did provide many young women with a variety of sporting activities and well as opportunities to develop a number of leadership skills.

Dance was another important extracurricular activity. Folk and aesthetic dancing had become a part of the physical education curriculum in the early 1900s. During the 1920s the type of 'modern' dance that Margaret H'Doubler (University of Wisconsin) was creating was embraced by many departments of physical education for women. Extracurricular student groups modelled after Orchesis, which H'Doubler had started at her university, developed annual events to which the general student body, parents and friends were invited. These performances typically included contributions from beginning as well as advanced students. A different approach emerged, usually in connection with units such as a department of dramatic arts. Here the focus was upon small numbers of highly skilled dancers, not events that included beginning as well as accomplished individuals. [41]

'Which Approach Shall We Women Physical Educators Take – Inclusive, Single-Sex or Both Types of Organization?

The Seneca Falls Convention of 1848 had launched the woman's rights movement in the United States. Dissatisfied that the Fifteenth Amendment to the Constitution contained nothing that would extend the franchise to members of the female sex, in 1869 Susan B. Anthony and the ever-assertive Elizabeth Cady Stanton established the National Woman Suffrage Association. That same year the American Woman Suffrage Association was begun by Lucretia Mott and other more conservative women. The two groups would merge in 1890. For over two decades each had pursued a different approach. [42] Late nineteenth and early twentieth century female medical doctors also were of two persuasions – those who wished to see women included in male organizations as rapidly as possible and those who 'concentrated on the building of separate institutions in order to preserve and strengthen female spheres of influence within the profession'. [43] Within physical education both approaches may be found.

Fletcher's *Women First: The Female Tradition in English Physical Education* provides an interesting, and useful, examination of how 'at a time when women were trying very hard to make their way into men's professions' the single-sex women's physical training college became the standard in Britain. The first was Dartford Physical Training College, established in 1895 by Martina Berman-Österberg; five similar institutions were in existence by 1914. The Ling Association, established in 1899 and open to women trained at Dartford or the Stockholm Central Gymnastic Institute, further perpetuated a 'world' in which virtually all power rested with women. Dorette Wilkie (who arrived from Bavaria and subsequently founded Chelsea College of Physical Training) and only a few others had connections with the men's National Society of Physical Education or the other two small physical education organizations that existed in Britain at the turn of the century. [44]

In the United States women took an approach that in some ways was similar to developments in Britain but in other ways differed. In America from the beginning they capitalized upon opportunities to become recognized, even respected, members of the Association for the Advancement of Physical Education. They also created their own organizations within which they exerted total dominance. This approach helped ensure employment and careers, gave them a certain amount of status in what was then 'a man's world' and unquestionably developed and honed their leadership skills.

On 20 June 1888 the *Philadelphia Medical Times* announced that Dr Mary Willits, 'a lady in every way worthy of the distinction', recently had been elected the first female member of the Philadelphia Medical Society. [45] Not insignificantly, three years earlier six women had been among the 49 individuals who met to form the Association for the Advancement of Physical Education. Helen Putnam, who had taught gymnastics at Vassar College before graduating from the Women's Medical College of Philadelphia, was named vice president – and served in that capacity until 1888. Carolyn Ladd and Eliza Mosher, both of whom also were physicians, were two other early vice presidents. Although the vice presidency was largely a nominal position, it did bring the women into association with male officers. Apparently, when Mosher stated that she intended to step down from the position of first vice president of the AAAPE, male members had asked her to remain. Women also served frequently as the secretary – and occasionally as the president – of the many local physical education societies that were formed during the late 1800s and early 1900s; men also sometimes served as secretaries of these local associations.

Physical Education's Early Intersections with Medicine

Whereas female physicians encountered many obstacles in the field of medicine, physical education provided them with a number of opportunities. Alice T. Hall, a graduate of the Women's Medical College of Pennsylvania, became the first director of the Department of Hygiene and Physical Training at all-female Goucher College in 1891. Prior to beginning her duties she had visited Vienna, Berlin, Paris and Zurich to learn more about medicine as well as Stockholm to learn about Swedish gymnastics. As was typical of the times, both Hall and her successor resigned when they married. In 1894 Lilian Welsh, also a graduate of the Women's Medical College of Pennsylvania and who had studied histology and bacteriology at the University of Zurich (one of the few European institutions that was open to women), became professor of anatomy, physiology, and physical training at Goucher and served in that position for 30 years.[46] Although Welsh never became a member of the APEA, Mosher (an 1875 graduate of the University of Michigan's medical school) served as president of the Michigan Physical Education Society as well as a vice president of the national organization. In 1896 she returned to the University of Michigan as the first female faculty member – dean of women and professor of hygiene – and initiated a programme of exercises for the women students. Over a long and productive career she held a variety of other positions, contributed to several other organizations, and conducted a private medical practice. [47]

Prior to receiving a medical degree from the University of Michigan Delphine Hanna had completed a year of work at the physical education training school established by Dudley Allen Sargent, MD. Destined to become a significant contributor to the profession, shortly after she became director of the Women's Department of Physical Training at Oberlin College in 1887 Hanna conducted a class that included three men who would make major contributions to physical education: Fred Leonard, Luther Halsey Gulick and Thomas Denison Wood (who credited Hanna with nurturing his interest in physical education as a 'vital branch of education'). [48] All three men went on to earn medical degrees.

At the outbreak of the First World War women accounted for nearly a quarter of the members of the national council of the American Physical Education Association. As Mabel Lee makes clear in *Memories Beyond Bloomers* (a personal account of her experiences in the years from 1924 to 1954), it required tact as well as determination for them to advance their particular views and causes. As was the case throughout society, most of the male members initially were accustomed to working only with men. Fortunately, there were important exceptions such as Frederick W. Maroney, MD, who upon being elected president in 1929 set about bringing more efficiency to the workings of the APEA. Lee writes of how an initial misunderstanding between the two of them turned into a professional friendship of nearly 30 years. [49] She became the first woman president of the Middle West Society of Physical Education in 1929, and the first woman president of the APEA in 1931. By 1942–3 four other women had held that position. [50] Since 1946–7 they have served alternatively with men as president. This is far better representation than what women were able to achieve within the American Historical Association, where only three had served as president before 2000; before 1971 only 15 women had served on the AHA's national council. The American Physiological Society did not elect a woman president until 1975 [51]; and it was not until 1997 that the American Medical Association did so. In fact, in 1970 less than five per cent of the members of the AMA were female physicians [52]; and as late as 1995 women accounted for less than four per cent of the chairs of medical schools in the United States. [53]

Whereas the national, district, stat, and local physical education societies performed a useful role in bringing female members into contact with male members, the single-sex organizations that the women created provided other opportunities. When the Society of Directors of Physical Education in College was founded in 1897, membership had been limited to those men who held director positions. In 1933 membership was extended to any man who taught in college health and physical education programmes and the name was changed to the National

College Physical Education Association for Men. Female physical educators would adopt a similar approach when forming the Association of Directors of Physical Education for Women in Colleges and Universities in 1924. Membership opportunities subsequently would be extended to any female physical educator who taught at the college or university level.

Beliefs about the frailty and intellectual limitations of females had been prevalent when Boston philanthropist Mary Hemenway founded the all-female Boston Normal School of Gymnastics (BNSG) in 1889 and appointed Amy Morris Homans as its director. It was Hemenway's goal was to 'further the serious study of gymnastics and physical activity to improve and benefit the lives of women'. Under Homans's competent leadership the BNSG developed an excellent two-year academic programme that included lectures by members of the Harvard University faculty as well as classes in chemistry, physiology and biology taught at the Massachusetts Institute of Technology. In 1909 the BNSG became the Department of Physical Education at Wellesley College. The course of study soon was increased to four years; and a master's degree programme was added in 1919. [54]

The BNSG/Wellesley College Department of Hygiene and Physical Education had high academic standards and Homans was adept at arranging for the best graduates to be hired throughout the country. By 1936 more than 200 directed or taught in physical education programmes for women at colleges and universities. [55] Graduates also held leadership in positions in a variety of other organizations. Ethel Perrin's many accomplishments, for example, included supervisor of physical culture for the Detroit public schools and associate director of health education for the American Child Health Association. In 1917 she had served as the first woman president of the Mid-West District of the American Physical Education Association. [56] By 1935 four other BNSG/Wellesley graduates had served, or were serving, as presidents of other district physical education associations. [57]

In 1910 Homans had invited directors from several New England women's colleges to Wellesley to discuss matters of concern and interest. The group met annually, and in 1915 organized as the Association of Directors of Physical Education for Women – renamed in 1920 the Eastern Society of College Directors of Physical Education for Women. The Middle West [later renamed Mid-West] Society of College Directors of Physical Education for Women was established in 1917; the Western Society of College Directors of Physical Education for Women in 1921. The three organizations soon came to an agreement, and the Association of Directors of Physical Education for Women in Colleges and Universities held its first meeting in 1924. [58] By 1946, when Dorothy Ainsworth wrote a brief account of the organization for the *Journal of Health and Physical Education*, three more sectional societies had been created, membership had been extended to all qualified female faculty and the name had been changed to the National Association of Physical Education for College Women. [59] It would not be until 1978–9 that the NAPECW would join with the National College Physical Education Association for Men to form the present National Association for Physical Education in Higher Education.

Interest in, and Opportunities for, Research

At the inaugural 1885 meeting of the Association for the Advancement of Physical Education, E.P. Thwing (president of the New York Academy of Anthropology) had declared that physical education was a subject deserving of 'thorough, scholarly consideration' and one that could be beneficially approached from several perspectives. [60] Five years later Luther Halsey Gulick described it as *a new profession* 'involving for its fullest appreciation a profound knowledge' derived from physiology, anatomy, psychology, history and philosophy. At the international congress on education that was held during the 1893 Chicago International Exposition, Thomas Denison Wood, MD, pointed out that physical education was a field that required both research and the means to put the best findings of research into practice. [61] The latter (i.e., pedagogical matters) would remain the dominant focus until the 1960s.

Although a few early members did engage in research and publish the results of their investigations, a persistent dilemma confronting the profession of physical education has been how to accommodate both scholarly/research interests and the 'practical/applied' needs of a large portion of the membership. When the *American Physical Education Review* was launched in 1896 only a few members of the AAAPE were engaging in any kind of research. The *Review*'s first editor, George Fitz, MD, [62] (whose research also appeared in publications such as the *Journal of Experimental Medicine*) succinctly summarized a recurring complaint when he declared in 1905: 'The criticism is frequently made that the *Review* is too scientific, that it does not apply to the 'practical teacher of gymnastics' (i.e., physical education). [63] However, during its 33 years of existence the *American Physical Education Review* (*APER*) did publish many research accounts as well as professional articles, articles reprinted from the *Journal of the American Medical Association* and other publications, papers read at local and district physical education meetings, a variety of reports (including those of the Athletic Research Society), presentations that had been made at annual conventions of the National Collegiate Athletic Association (many of which expressed views similar to those that Fauver and others were asserting in the 1920s), [64] book reviews (both domestic and foreign) and more.

Although the number of articles by women was small in comparison to those written by men, many did contribute. In an article in the September 1897 issue of the *APER* Alice Bertha Foster, MD (Bryn Mawr) declared that it was appropriate for girls and women to play basketball provided they had received the approval of 'a competent [medical] examiner'. [65] Another early example was an 1898 article by Harriet Ballintine (Vassar College) that stated that basketball had been of considerable value in 'stimulating interest and effort' among the young women. Although she believed that girls required 'a certain amount of healthful excitement', Ballintine considered comparing 'records made by women with those of men to be absurd'. [66] One of the more frequent early contributors was Jessie Hubbell

Bancroft, who has been described by Ellen Gerber as a person who 'indefatigably brought physical education – the new profession – to the public, school administrators, teachers, business men, and anyone she could reach through articles, speeches, and demonstrations'. [67] In 1903 Bancroft became assistant director of physical training in the New York public schools (Gulick was the director), and held that position for 25 years. Several points made in her *APER* article 'Some Essentials of Physical Training in Public Schools', published in 1898, are as pertinent today as they were more than a hundred years ago. [68]

During the 1920s the *American Physical Education Review* would continue to publish professional articles, papers read at physical education meetings, a variety of reports (including those of the Women's Division of the National Amateur Athletic Federation), book reviews and other information. More research articles also began to appear. Some were written by physical educators, some by individuals in other fields – for example, J. Anna Norris, MD, 'A Method of Testing the Strength of the Abdominal Muscles'; Vivian D. Collins and Eugene C. Howe, 'The Measurement of Organic and Neuromuscular Fitness'; Coleman R. Griffith, 'Psychology and Its Relation to Athletic Competition'. [69] (Norris was director of physical education for women at the University of Minnesota; Collins and Howe were with the Wellesley College Graduate Department of Hygiene and Physical Education; Griffith was a professor of psychology at the University of Illinois.)

An important step in advancing research was taken when the *Research Quarterly* was launched in 1930. (Henceforth, professional articles, most reports, commentaries, announcements and other items would be published in the *Journal of Physical Education* – later renamed the *Journal of Health, Physical Education, and Recreation.*) Female physical educators became involved more frequently than often is realized. Of the contributions to the *Research Quarterly* in 1934 39 per cent were authored or co-authored by women; the figure was 38 per cent in 1935; 42 per cent in 1936; 46 per cent in 1937; 35 per cent in 1938; and 25 per cent in 1939. [70] Moreover, 40 per cent of the chapters that comprised the first edition of *Research Methods Applied to Health, Physical Education* (1949), which was a harbinger of advances that soon would take place, were prepared by committees headed by a woman. [71]

The 1960s ushered in major changes throughout higher education. One was increasing demands that faculty become more involved in research. These matters did not escape the notice of physical educators. Joy Kistler chose 'Future Directions in Physical Education' as the topic of his 1961 presidential address before the National College Physical Education Association for Men. Because its bases range from biology and psychology to sociology, Kistler observed, physical education 'probably encompasses a broader field of knowledge than any other single discipline'. [72] Eight months previously, the *Research Quarterly* had published a special issue dealing with 'Contributions of Physical Activity to Human Well-Being'. Three of the six articles were written by female physical educators: 'Psychological Development' (M. Gladys Scott, University of Iowa); 'Skill Learning' (Dorothy R. Mohr, University of

Maryland); 'Growth' [Motor Development] (Anna S. Espenschade, University of California). [73]

A Sterling Example of an 'All-Around' Physical Educator [74]

Anna Espenschade was an example of those women who rightfully could be called 'all-around' physical educators. A 1924 graduate of Goucher College, where she had majored in Spanish, been president of the athletic association and earned a coveted sweater 'with a blue and gold G' for her athletic accomplishments when only a freshman, she received a master's degree in hygiene and physical training from Wellesley College in 1926. While at Wellesley she joined the Boston Field Hockey Association, and in 1925 was named left halfback on the United States Field Hockey Association's reserve team. Field hockey, a game that she played for decades, was only one of many sports at which she was very adept. As a woman in her 50s she could perform all 20 flexibility, strength, and coordination items of the Brace Test, which was something that only the best young women majors could do. Well into her 80s she was travelling to Australia and elsewhere to compete in lawn bowling tournaments.

Although many female physical educators were athletically accomplished, they tended not to focus their participation on only one sport. (That would not have been in keeping with the 'A sport for every girl/every girl in a sport' ideal that was widely enunciated in the 1920s and 1930s.) The women-only United States Field Hockey Association and its several sectional and many local associations offered an especially valuable arena for those who wanted to hone their athletic talents. Few men in the United States played or were interested in the game, which was not the case in Great Britain, Australia, New Zealand or even certain European countries. Also, field hockey matches typically took place in carefully controlled settings and were of no particular interest to the general public. Selection of the national team – indeed the game itself – traditionally had been deeply embedded in a number of 'frames' that symbolically, if not literally, proclaimed unity and cooperation as well as competition. All that would begin to change in the mid-1970s. [75]

Following two years on the faculty at the University of Syracuse, Espenschade joined the Department of Physical Education for Women at the University in California, where her responsibilities included teaching a variety of physical education classes (e.g., swimming, tennis), first aid, tests and measurements (required of all majors), and theory of group athletics (required of all women majors). She also coached the field hockey team and served as adviser to the WAA, the women's 'C' Society, and other student groups. Invited by Professor Harold Jones (director of UC Berkeley's Institute of Child Welfare) to join a longitudinal study of adolescence, she went on to earn a PhD in psychology and became an internationally recognized authority in the area of motor development. In 1949 she would be elected a fellow of the American Psychological Association. Although her departmental responsibilities now were teaching upper division and graduate classes and supervising the research of master's and doctoral degree students, Espenschade would continue to work with extracurricular student groups for another decade.

Her extensive service to professional organizations included: president of the San Francisco Bay Counties Board of Women Officials; chair of the Pacific Southwest Section of the United States Field Hockey Association; chair of the American Association for Health, Physical Education, and Recreation's National Section on Women's Athletics; president of the Western Society of Physical Education for College Women; vice president of the National Association of Physical Education for College Women; and president of the American Academy of Physical Education. Although retired, in the early 1970s she continued to speak at meetings of the International Association of Physical Education and Sports for Girls and Women and other gatherings.

During the 1950s and 1960s her time had been especially consumed by leadership roles brought about by the 'physical fitness' furores that had been stimulated by articles in the public press such as 'What's Wrong With American Youth?' and 'The Report That Shocked the President'. [76] The California Physical Fitness Project's Committee on Measurements, which she chaired from 1957 to 1967, gathered extensive data and created the battery of tests that became the bases for those issued by the President's Council for Physical Fitness, with which she also worked. [77] In 1963 Genevie Dexter (California state consultant in physical education) wrote: 'Without Dr. Espenschade's leadership it would have been impossible to gather the data necessary for the development of the tests.' [78] Her book *Motor Development*, published in 1967, has been described as the first comprehensive text dealing with the topic. Jerry M. Thomas (a motor behaviour authority) has stated that this area of investigation 'might well have died out' had it not been for the work of Espenschade, G. Lawrence Rarick (who become her colleague at the University of California following a productive career at the University of Wisconsin) and Ruth Glassow (University of Wisconsin). [79]

Women and the American Academy of Kinesiology and Physical Education [80]

Election to the American Academy of Physical Education has been one of the profession's highest honours. Although no woman had been included in the small academy that existed between 1904 and the First World War, they were destined to become a significant presence in the one that was formally established in 1930 and continues today as the American Academy of Kinesiology and Physical Education. Summarizing that organization's early years, Mabel Lee makes the following observation:

> The 78-year old Woman's Suffrage Movement had ended in victory in 1920 and opened the doors to women in a man's world. Thus the Academy opened its doors to its first woman member, Jessie Bancroft, who for many years had been head of girls' physical education for the public schools of Greater New York City. [81]

The event to which Lee was referring was the cordial invitation to become member number 8 that 60-year-old Bancroft had received from Clark Hetherington, the academy's first president. [82] As of November 1930 three more women had been elected: Amy Morris Homans (number 12), J. Anna Norris (number 24), and Elizabeth Burchenal (number 28). The following year Arthur Steinhaus nominated Mabel Lee (number 30), giving particular attention to the quality of her work as president of the Middle West Association of Physical Education and having been 'one of the individuals most responsible for bringing about more happy relations between the Mid-West and National bodies'. [83] Early female members seem to have been as likely to nominate men as they were women. In 1933, for example, Norris recommended Eugene Howe and Ethel Perrin. Charles H. McCloy recommended as one of his five nominees Agnes Wayman, [84] whose contributions would include presidency of the APEA from 1935 to 1936. With the addition of Wayman (number 35) and Rosalind Cassidy (number 40), by 1938 females accounted for seven of the 40 individuals who had been elected to academy membership. Although some members were engaged in research, from the 1930s through to the 1950s the typical achievements of those individuals who were nominated for academy membership (men as well as for women) were contributions to professional organizations, editorships, the production of textbooks and articles in the *American School Board Journal*, the *Journal of Physical Education and Health* and similar publications. [85] By December 1941 46 individuals, ten of whom were women, had been elected.

The Second World War brought large numbers of women into occupations and fields that previously had been considered provinces for men. They quickly demonstrated their considerable abilities and leadership capabilities. When in 1944 new academy members were elected for the first time since 1941, nearly 42 per cent were women. In 1950 women accounted for slightly more than fifty-three percent of the Academy's new members. During the 1950s the appointment of women to presidential and standing committees was about proportional to their membership. From 1949 to 1960, except for three instances (1953–4, 1954–5, and 1956–7), they accounted for at least one half of the academy's officers. Elected president in 1941, Mabel Lee was the first of 16 women who would hold that office by 1990. [86]

Hoping to help all members of the profession become better informed about the contributions of physical education to health, education and American life, Frederick W. Cozens (who had become president in 1949) arranged for academy members to write eight articles. These were published in the *Journal of Health, Physical Education and Recreation* between 1949 and 1951. Four were written by women: Mabel Rugen (health education); Dorothy Ainsworth (community agency programmes); Rosalind Cassidy (democratic citizenship); and Ann Schley Duggan (dance in the school physical education programme). Additionally, Josephine Rathbone co-authored 'The Contributions of Physical Education to Medicine' with David Lamb and Peter Karpovich. [87]

The *American Academy of Physical Education Professional Contributions*, which consisted of papers and reports presented at annual meetings, was launched in 1951 under the editorship of Donna Mae Miller and Elwood Craig Davis. Of the 15 contributors to issue 1, which dealt with 'Recent Research of Significance', seven were women: psychology (Anna Espenschade and Mabel Rugen); sociological research (Elizabeth Halsey); group dynamics (Martha Deane, Dorothy Nyswander and Elizabeth Halsey); and cultural anthropology (Ruth Abernathy). During the next decade, in only two instances (1952 and 1961) did females account for less than one-third of the contributing authors.

Changes in the 1960s and Turbulence During the 1970s, and 1980s

Changes that had begun to occur within higher education following the Second World War were given greater impetus by the Soviet Union's successes in space. The launching of Sputnik in 1957 intensified anxieties that already existed regarding the quality of American education. Greater amounts of government funding were directed to certain lines of research and specialization increased rapidly. All of these matters – and more – had a significant impact upon the field of physical education, which soon was struggling to define itself as an 'academic discipline' and determine how disciplinary matters should, and could, be related to those of a professional nature.

The preface to the comprehensive 1960 book *Science and Medicine of Exercise and Sport* opened with the statement: 'In recent years great progress has been made in the scientific study of exercise and sports.' [88] In 1963 the National Association for Physical Education of College Women and the National College Physical Education Association for Men jointly initiated *Quest*, a publication that would become of considerable importance for the profession. Its first editor was Donna Mae Miller (University of Arizona); men and women served in equal numbers of the editorial board. Franklin Henry's 1964 article 'Physical Education: An Academic Discipline' [89] was especially influential. (The article had evolved from a successful response that he and his colleagues at the University of California – Anna Espenschade, Pauline Hodgson and Carl Nordly – had prepared to counter California Senate Bill 57, which sought to classify physical education and certain other subject-matter areas as non-academic.)

More individuals associated with the field of physical education (increasingly referred to as kinesiology or exercise science) become productive scientists and scholars. The growth of quality research was a positive and much-needed development; however, change often results in unforeseen consequences. As physical educators, who now often referred to themselves as exercise scientists, sport psychologists and other more specific terms, became more specialized it became increasingly apparent (at least to some individuals) that the need to bring unity to a field that draws upon a wide array of disciplinary areas was becoming intense. Additionally, there seemed to be a failure on the part of many researchers to recognize that their findings needed to be linked to intelligent practice. Citing as examples departments of engineering and architecture, in an insightful 1979 article published in *Quest* (the journal of the National Association for Physical Education in Higher Education) Elizabeth Bressan challenged readers to think more comprehensively about whether or not in a 'productive discipline' there really was a dichotomy between scholars and practitioners. [90]

Appearing in the same volume of *Quest* was Jean Perry's presentation of problems that were arising as a consequence of increasing mergers of formerly separate men's and women's departments of physical education. [91] That same year (1979) *Women As Leaders in Physical Education and Sports* was published. Its introduction begins with the telling observation: 'As women's and men's physical education departments are combined across the country, women have lost the major administrative positions in disproportionate numbers.' Moreover, although intercollegiate programmes for women were growing, 'the proportion of women athletic directors and women coaches' was declining. [92] The decline of female directors and coaches would continue. [93] Could it be that Mabel Lee and her contemporaries were correct?

Other causes for concern were to be seen in Margaret Safrit's 1979 *Quest* article 'Women in Research in Physical Education'. Between June 1977 and June 1978 men had submitted more than three-and-a-half times as many manuscripts as had women to the *Research Quarterly*. [94] Moreover, women now accounted for less than one quarter of the AAHPER's Research Consortium. Five years later Safrit reported that the status of women as scholars in physical education had not improved. [95] Additionally, whereas from 1961 to 1970 females had accounted for nearly 45 per cent of the American Academy of Physical Education's new members, that number also began to decline. [96]

As the field that once was almost universally known as physical education struggled to re-identify itself during the 1980s, articles such as Shirl Hoffman's 'Specialization + Fragmentation = Extermination: A Formula for the Demise of Graduate Education' and Jerry Thomas's 'Physical Education and Paranoia – Synonyms' raised perceptive and troubling questions. [97] In 1991 Don Hellison, an authority on teaching and curricular physical education, offered compelling arguments regarding why 'putting theory and research into practice' had become an urgent matter. [98] The 1996 *Report of the Surgeon General of the United States* declared that 'Scientists and doctors have known for years that substantial benefits can be gained from regular physical activity'. [99] However, an article published in the *Journal of Physical Activity and Health* in 2006, which referred repeatedly to this report, pointed out that although 70 per cent of 'all measurement or surveillance studies of PA [physical activity]' conducted during the last four decades had been published since 1996, applications of the information they contained had been 'inadequate and ineffectual'. [100] The number of students participating in daily physical education had begun to decline in the 1970s – and the decline continues today. [101] Is it possible that warnings set forth in the 1920s by Lee and others might have been accurate about an overemphasis on high performance sports weakening programmes for the general student? Is it possible that the 'athletic' potential of Title

IX was so captivating that many female physical educators turned away from creating broad-based programmes?

And what about the decline of women engaged in research that Safrit reported? Is it possible that many younger women began to concentrate so much effort on trying to equalize athletic programmes (as meritorious as this may be) that they ceased preparing themselves to have an important role in research? As reflected in the American Academy of Physical Education's annual *Professional Contributions*, women had accounted for nearly 33 per cent of the papers and responses presented at annual meetings between 1950 and 1961. From 1962 to 1971 the number that appeared in the renamed *Academy Papers* rose to 44 per cent. It then declined to 37 per cent for the period 1972 to 1981. From 1982 to 1991 there was a further decline to 25 per cent. Moreover, between 1981 and 2006 fewer than 25 per cent of newly elected American Academy of Kinesiology and Physical Education members were women. [102] *Quo Vadis* 2015?

Notes

[1] Hartman and Banner, *Clio's Consciousness Raised*, xii.
[2] Gerber *et al.*, *The American Woman in Sport*, v.
[3] For example, Mangan and Park, *From 'Fair Sex' to Feminism*.
[4] For example, Guttmann, *Women's Sports*; Cahn, *Coming on Strong*; Fan Hong, *Footbinding, Feminism and Freedom*.
[5] Fletcher, *Women First*.
[6] Scott and Hoferek, *Women as Leaders*, 2.
[7] 'Athletics' quickly became its 'public face' as feminists and others who had been advocating greater opportunities for females seized upon it to advance their cause.
[8] Savage, *American College Athletics*.
[9] See for example Park, 'Concern for Health and Exercise'.
[10] 'Physical Education'.
[11] Fowle, 'Gymnastic Exercises for Females'.
[12] Three informative books regarding these matters are: Whorton, *Crusaders for Fitness*; Green, *Fit for America*; and Grover, *Fitness in American Culture*.
[13] Caldwell, *Thoughts on Physical Education*; Blackwell, *The Laws of Life*.
[14] *Prospectus of Vassar Female College, 1865*, 3.
[15] *First Annual Catalogue of the Officers and Students of Vassar*, 28. See also Ballintine, *The History of Physical Training at Vassar College*.
[16] See Gerber, *Innovators and Institutions*, 325–31.
[17] Duffy, *The Sanitarians*, ch. 9.
[18] Smith, 'Preludes to the NCAA'; Smith, *Sports and Freedom*.
[19] Gerber, *Innovators and Institutions*, 391. The other was Amos Alonzo Stagg at the University of Chicago.
[20] On football injuries see, Park, 'Mended or Ended?'
[21] Lewis, 'Theodore Roosevelt's Role in the 1905 Football Controversy'.
[22] Correspondence between Eliot and Hadley located in the Archives at Harvard University and Yale University is quite informative. See also 'Football and Its Distorted Values', 147.
[23] Hetherington, *School Program in Physical Education*; Wood and Cassidy, *The New Physical Education*.

[24] 'The Athletic Research Society'. On Hetherington, see Gerber, *Innovators and Institutions*, 389–93.

[25] Since its establishment the national physical education organization has had seven names: Association for the Advancement to Physical Education (1885); American Association for the Advancement to Physical Education (1886–1903); American Physical Education Association (1903–37); American Association for Health and Physical Education (1937–8); American Association for Health, Physical Education, and Recreation (1938–74); American Association for Health, Physical Education, Recreation, and Dance (1974–9); American Alliance for Health, Physical Education, Recreation, and Dance (1979–present).

[26] 'Announcement of the Research Section'; Clarke, 'History of the Research Section'.

[27] Fauver, 'The Place of Intercollegiate Athletics'.

[28] Meylan, 'Intercollegiate Athletics'.

[29] Sundwell, 'Relation of Athletics to Physical Education'.

[30] Fauver, 'The Need for a Definite Formulation'.

[31] 'Vassar Girls in Athletics: The First Field Day in the College's History', *New York Times*, 21 Oct. 1895.

[32] See Beran, 'Playing to the Right Drummer'; Beran, *From Six-on-Six to Full Court Press*.

[33] The title would change five more times by 1974: Section on Women's Athletics (1927–31); Rules and Editorial Committee (1931–2); National Section on Women's Athletics (1932–53); National Section on Girls' and Women's Sports (1953–6); Division for Girls and Women's Sports (1957–74).

[34] Letter from Blanche M. Trilling to Lou Henry Hoover, 2 Feb. 1923, cited in endnote 25 of Hult, 'The Governance of Athletics for Girls and Women'.

[35] Bunting, 'The Washington Conference on Athletics for Girls'.

[36] In 1922 the Secretary of War and the Secretary of the Navy had called representatives of various athletic associations to Washington, DC, in the hope of creating an organization that might promote and improve men's amateur sports. The result was the creation of the National Amateur Athletic Federation – and soon the Women's Division of the NAAF. See for example Lucas and Smith, *Saga of American Sport*, 351–3.

[37] Sefton, *The Women's Division of the National Amateur Athletic Federation*. They had less influence in the broader sporting arena.

[38] Lee, 'The Case for and Against Intercollegiate Athletics'; *Wellesley College, 1923–24 Bulletin of the Mary Hemenway Alumnae Association, Graduate Department of Hygiene and Physical Education*, 1–12.

[39] Lee, 'The Case for and Against Intercollegiate Athletics'. Lee had sent a questionnaire to female directors of 50 'leading' colleges and universities asking for information about what types of activities were offered and the respondent's opinion of the advantages and disadvantages of intercollegiate athletics. One individual who responded also expressed concern that there would be a tendency to employ the 'coach type' of woman – a person who did not have an 'educational attitude' toward her work.

[40] 'Report of the Advisory Committee on Athletics for High School Girls'.

[41] See for example H'Doubler, *Dance*; Gray and Howe, 'Margaret H'Doubler'; Park, 'Creating From Minds and Bodies'; Vertinsky, 'Mothers of the Dance'.

[42] Flexner, *Century of Struggle*.

[43] Morantz-Sanchez, *Sympathy and Science*, 3–7.

[44] Fletcher, *Women First*, 4–5. This single-sex sphere of influence was strengthened because there were no physical training colleges for men in Britain before the 1930s.

[45] 'Female Physicians', *Philadelphia Medical Times*, 12 July 1888, 597–8.

[46] For more information regarding Welsh, see Zieff, 'Leading the Way in Science'.

[47] For more information regarding Mosher see, Wrynn, 'Eliza Maria Mosher'.

[48] Gerber, *Innovators and Institutions*, 325–31.

[49] Lee, *Memories Beyond Bloomers*, 88–96.

[50] Mary C. Coleman (1933–4); Agnes R. Weyman (1935–6); Margaret Bell (1939–40); Ann Schley Duggan (1941–2). For an account of the presidents see Lee and Bennett, 'This Is Our Heritage'.

[51] In 1943 Nellie Neilson served as the first female president of the AHA: 'Presidents of the American Historical Association, 1884–1984'.See also www.historians.org/info/ahahistory.cfm (accessed March 2009). Bodil M. Schmidt-Nielsen, daughter of the noted Danish physiologists August and Marie Keogh, became the first women president of the APS. See Brobeck *et al.*, *History of the American Physiological Society*.

[52] This information was kindly sent to the author in 2005 by Laura L. Carroll, AMA Archivist.

[53] Moore, *Restoring the Balance*.

[54] Spears, 'The Influential Miss Homans'.

[55] See Spears, *Leading the Way* for the most detailed account.

[56] Gerber, *Innovators and Institutions*, 368–73. According to Gerber, Perrin was 'one of the few leaders who approved of competition' (at least controlled competition) for girls.

[57] The Mid-West District Association and other '*district associations*' should not be confused with the single-sex Middle West Society of College Directors of Physical Education for Women and other '*district societies*' of physical education.

[58] Hill, *The Way We Were*, 6–7.

[59] Ainsworth, 'The National Association of Physical Education for College Women'. A Southern section was added in 1935; and in 1936 the Middle West Society divided into Central and Midwest societies.

[60] *Proceedings of the Association for the Advancement of Physical Education at Its Organization at Brooklyn*, 3–4.

[61] Gulick, 'Physical Education'; Wood, 'Some Unsolved Problems in Physical Education'.

[62] Regarding Fitz see Park, 'Rise and Demise of Harvard's BS Program'.

[63] 'Editorial Note and Comment'.

[64] For example, McCormick, 'College Athletics from the Viewpoint of the President of a University' (McCormick was Chancellor of the University of Pittsburgh).

[65] Foster, 'Basket Ball for Girls'.

[66] Ballintine, 'Out-of-Door Sports for College Women'.

[67] Gerber, *Innovators and Institutions*, 357–62.

[68] Bancroft, 'Pioneering in Physical Education'; Bancroft, 'Some Essentials of Physical Training'.

[69] Norris, 'A Method of Testing'; Collins and Howe, 'Measurement of Organic and Neuromuscular Fitness'; Griffith, 'Psychology and Its Relation to Athletic Competition'.

[70] In instances where only the letters of the first and middle names appear it is sometimes difficult to determine the gender. The author's college or other affiliation can help.

[71] American Association for Health, Physical Education, and Recreation, *Research Methods*.

[72] Kistler, 'Future Directions in Physical Education'.

[73] 'The Contributions of Physical Activity to Human Well-Being'.

[74] This section draws upon Park, '"Time Given Freely to Worthwhile Causes"'.

[75] See Park, 'Symbol, Celebration, and the Reduction of Conflict'.

[76] 'What's Wrong With American Youth?' *US News and World Report*, 19 March 1954, 35–6; 'The Report That Shocked the President', *Sports Illustrated*, 15 Aug. 1955, 30–3; 72–3.

[77] For an overview of these matters see, Park, *Measurement of Physical Fitness: A Historical Perspective*. The tests were criticized by some as being inefficient. However, because much of the testing had to be done by teachers who had no training in physical education they had to be simple.

[78] Genevie Dexter to Carl Nordly (Chair of the Department of Physical Education, University of California), 25 Feb. 1963. University of California, Bancroft Library Archival Collections, Hearst Gymnasium Historical Collections.

[79] Thomas, 'Motor Behavior', 242–3.

[80] This section draws upon Park, '"An Affirmation of the Abilities of Woman"'.

[81] Lee, *Memories Beyond Bloomers*, 268.

[82] Clark Hetherington, personal communication, 24 June 1927, Archives of the American Academy of Kinesiology and Physical Education, Special Collections, Pennsylvania State University, State College, PA (hereafter Archives of the AAKPE).

[83] Arthur Steinhaus, personal communication, 14 Nov. 1931, Archives of the AAKPE.

[84] Charles McCloy, personal communication, 25 Jan. 1935, Archives of the AAKPE.

[85] This information can be gleaned from annual 'Biographical Sketches of Candidates' located in the Archives of the AAKPE.

[86] Mabel Lee (1941–3); Rosalind Cassidy (1950–1); Anna S. Espenschade (1955–6); Helen Manley (1959–60); M. Gladys Scott (1961–2); Eleanor Metheny (1964–5); Margaret G. Fox (1967–8); Laura J. Huelster (1968–9); Ruth M. Wilson (1970–1); Ann E. Jewett (1973–4); Leona Holbrook (1975–6) ; Marguerite A. Clifton (1978–9); Aileene S. Lockhart (1980–1); Margaret J. Safrit (1986–7); Waneen Spirduso (1988–9); Roberta J. Park (1990–1).

[87] Rugen, 'Physical Education's Contributions to Health Education'; Ainsworth, 'Contributions of Physical Education to the Social Service Agency'; Cassidy, 'Contributions of Physical Education to Democratic Citizenship'; Duggan, 'The Place of Dance'; Lamb *et al.*, 'The Contributions of Physical Education to Medicine'.

[88] Johnson, *Science and Medicine of Exercise and Sport*, viii.

[89] Henry, 'Physical Education – An Academic Discipline'.

[90] Bressan, '2001: The Profession Is Dead'.

[91] Perry, 'Merging Departments'.

[92] Scott and Hoferek, *Women As Leaders in Physical Education*, 2.

[93] According to a recent longitudinal study the number of women athletic directors dropped from more than 90 per cent in 1972 to 21.3 per cent in 2008 – in Division I, women accounted for only 8.4 per cent. The number who coached women's teams also had lowered from more than 90 per cent in 1978 to 42.8 per cent in 2008 – the number of head coaches now was only 20.6 per cent. See 'Women in Intercollegiate Sport: A Longitudinal, National Study, Thirty One Year Update, 1977–2008', available at http://www.acostacarpenter.org/ 2008%20Summary, accessed March 2009.

[94] Safrit, 'Women in Research in Physical Education'.

[95] Safrit, 'Women in Research in Physical Education: A 1984 Update'.

[96] See Park, 'An Affirmation of the Abilities of Woman'.

[97] Hoffman, 'Specialization + Fragmentation = Extermination'; Thomas, 'Physical Education and Paranoia – Synonyms'.

[98] Hellison, 'The Whole Person in Physical Education Scholarship'.

[99] US Department of Health and Human Services, *Physical Activity and Health*, v.

[100] Kohl *et al.*, 'Physical Activity and Public Health'.

[101] According to the Center for Disease Control's recent 'Guidelines for School Health Programs to Promote Physical Activity', the percentage of high-school students who attended daily physical education classes dropped from 42 percent in 1991 to 33 per cent in 2005. The same report states that the percentage of overweight children ages six to 11 rose from 6.1 per cent in 1974 to 15.1 per cent in 1999. For those ages 12 to 19 the increase was from 6.5 per cent in 1976 to 14.8 per cent in 2000. (The fact that large numbers of children and youth now fail to engage in anything approaching adequate amounts of physical activity is very troubling, for it is during childhood and adolescence that proper habits regarding exercise are most likely

to be developed.) See www.cdc.gov/HealthyYouth/physicalactivity/guidelines/summary.htm, accessed March 2009.

[102] See Park, 'An Affirmation of the Abilities of Woman'.

References

Ainsworth, Dorothy S. 'The National Association of Physical Education for College Women'. *Journal of Health and Physical Education* 17 (1946): 525–6, 575–6.

Ainsworth, Dorothy S. 'Contributions of Physical Education to the Social Service Agency'. *Journal of Health, Physical Education, and Recreation* 21 (1950): 325, 367–8.

American Association for Health, Physical Education, and Recreation. *Research Methods Applied to Health, Physical Education, and Recreation.* Washington, DC: AAHPERD, 1949.

'Announcement of the Research Section'. *American Physical Education Review* 33 (1928): 678–80.

Ballintine, Harriet I. *The History of Physical Training at Vassar College.* Poughkeepsie, NY: Lansing and Brothers, 1915.

Ballintine, Harriet I. 'Out-of-Door Sports for College Women'. *American Physical Education Review* 3 (1898): 38–43.

Bancroft, Jessie H. 'Some Essentials of Physical Training in Public Schools'. *American Physical Education Review* 3 (1898): 281–7.

Bancroft, Jessie H. 'Pioneering in Physical Education – An Autobiography'. *Research Quarterly* 12 (1941): 666–78.

Beran, Janice A. 'Playing to the Right Drummer: Girls' Basketball in Iowa, 1893–1927'. *Research Quarterly for Exercise and Sport*, Special Centennial Issue (1985): 78–85.

Beran, Janice A. *From Six-on-Six to Full Court Press: A Century of Iowa Girls' Basketball.* Ames, IA: Iowa State University Press, 1993.

Blackwell, Elizabeth. *The Laws of Life, With Special Reference to the Physical Education of Girls.* New York: George P. Putnam, 1852.

Bressan, Elizabeth S. '2001: The Profession Is Dead – Was It Murder or Suicide?' *Quest* 31, no. 1 (1979): 77–82.

Brobeck, John R., Orrin E. Reynolds and Toby A. Appel, eds. *History of the American Physiological Society: The First Century, 1887–1987.* Bethesda, MD: The American Historical Association, 1987.

Bunting, Helen. 'The Washington Conference on Athletics for Girls'. In *Report of the International Health Education Conference of the World Conference on Education, San Francisco, CA, June 28–July 6, 1923.* New York: American Child Health Association, 1923, 248–53.

Cahn, Susan. *Coming on Strong: Gender and Sexuality in Twentieth Century Women's Sport.* New York: Free Press, 1994.

Caldwell, Charles. *Thoughts on Physical Education: Being a Discourse Delivered to a Convention of Teachers in Lexington, Ky.* Boston, MA: Marsh, Capen and Lyon, 1834.

Cassidy, Rosalind. 'Contributions of Physical Education to Democratic Citizenship'. *Journal of Health, Physical Education, and Recreation* 21, no. 4 (1950): 218–19; 264–65.

Clarke, H. Harrison. 'History of the Research Section of the American Association for Health and Physical Education'. *Research Quarterly* 9, no. 3 (1938): 25–36.

Collins, Vivian D. and Eugene C. Howe. 'The Measurement of Organic and Neuromuscular Fitness'. *American Physical Education Review* 29, no. 2 (1924): 64–70.

Duffy, John. *The Sanitarians: A History of American Public Health.* Urbana, IL: University of Illinois Press, 1990.

Duggan, Ann S. 'The Place of Dance in the High School Program'. *Journal of Health, Physical Education, and Recreation* 22, no. 3 (1951): 26–9.

'Editorial Note and Comment'. *American Physical Education Review* 10 (1905): 61–4.

Fan Hong. *Footbinding, Feminism and Freedom: The Liberation of Women's Bodies in Modern China*. London: Frank Cass, 1997.

Fauver, Edgar. 'The Place of Intercollegiate Athletics in a Physical Education Program'. *American Physical Education Review* 27 (1922): 272–6.

Fauver, Edgar. 'The Need of a Definite Formulation of the Aim and Scope of Intercollegiate Athletics'. *American Physical Education Review* 28 (1923): 255–60.

First Annual Catalogue of the Officers and Students of Vassar Female College, 1865–66. New York: John A. Gray and Green, 1866.

Fletcher, Shelia. *Women First. The Female Tradition in English Physical Education*. London: The Athlone Press, 1984.

Flexner, Eleanor. *Century of Struggle: The Woman's Rights Movement in the United States*. Cambridge, MA: Belknap Press of Harvard University, 1975.

'Football and Its Distorted Values'. *The World's Work* 11, no. 1 (1905).

Foster, Alice Bertha. 'Basket Ball for Girls'. *American Physical Education Review* 2 (1897): 152–4.

Fowle, William B. 'Gymnastic Exercises for Females'. *Boston Medical Intelligencer* 3, no. 1 (1825): 130.

Gerber, Ellen W. *Innovators and Institutions in Physical Education*. Philadelphia, PA: Lea and Febiger, 1971.

Gerber, Ellen W., Jan Felshin, Pearl Berlin and Waneen Wyrick. *The American Woman in Sport*. Reading, MA: Addison-Wesley Publishing Co., 1974.

Gray, Judith A. and Dianne Howe. 'Margaret H'Doubler: A Profile of Her Formative Years, 1898–1921'. *Research Quarterly for Exercise and Sport*, Centennial Issue (1985): 93–101.

Green, Harvey. *Fit for America: Health, Fitness, Sports and American Society*. New York: Pantheon Books, 1986.

Griffith, Coleman. 'Psychology and Its Relation to Athletic Competition'. *American Physical Education Review* 30 (1925): 193–9.

Grover, Kathryn, ed. *Fitness in American Culture: Images of Health, Sport, and the Body, 1830–1940*. Amherst, MA: University of Massachusetts Press, 1989.

Gulick, Luther Halsey. 'Physical Education: A New Profession'. In *Proceedings of the Fifth Annual Meeting of the American Association for the Advancement of Physical Education*. Ithaca, NY: Andrus and Church, 1890: 59–66.

Guttmann, Allen. *Women's Sports: A History*. New York: Columbia University Press, 1991.

H'Doubler, Margaret N. *Dance: A Creative Art Experience*. New York: Crofts and Co., 1940.

Hartman, Mary S. and Lois Banner, eds. *Clio's Consciousness Raised: New Perspectives on the History of Women*. New York: Harper & Row, 1974.

Hellison, Don. 'The Whole Person in Physical Education Scholarship: Toward Integration'. *Quest* 43 (1991): 307–18.

Henry, Franklin M. 'Physical Education – An Academic Discipline'. *Journal of Health, Physical Education, and Recreation* 35, no. 7 (1964): 32–3, 69.

Hetherington, Clarke W. *School Program in Physical Education*. New York: World Book Co., 1922.

Hill, Phyllis. *The Way We Were: A History of the Purposes of the NAPECW, 1924–1974*. A Publication of the National Association for Physical Education of College Women, December 1975.

Hoffman, Shirl. 'Specialization + Fragmentation = Extermination: A Formula for the Demise of Graduate Education'. *Journal of Physical Education, Recreation, and Dance* 56, no. 6 (1985): 19–22.

Hult, Joan S. 'The Governance of Athletics for Girls and Women: Leadership by Women Physical Educators, 1899–1949'. *Research Quarterly for Exercise and Sport*, Special Centennial Issue (April 1985): 64–77.

Johnson, Warren R., ed. *Science and Medicine of Exercise and Sport*. New York: Harper and Brothers, 1960.

Kistler, Joy W. 'Future Directions in Physical Education'. In *Proceedings of the 65th Annual Meeting of the College Physical Education Association, December 27–30, 1961*. Washington, DC: American Association for Health, Physical Education, and Recreation, 1962, 1–11.

Kohl, Harold W., Min Lee, Ilkka M. Vuori, Fran C. Wheeler, Adrian Bauman and James F. Sallis. 'Physical Activity and Public Health: The Emergence of a Subdiscipline. Report from the International Congress on Physical Activity and Public Health. April 17–21, 2008, Altanta, Georgia, USA'. *Journal of Physical Activity and Health* 3, no. 4 (2006): 344–64.

Lamb, David., Josephine L. Rathbone and Peter V. Karpovich, 'The Contributions of Physical Education to Medicine'. *Journal of Health, Physical Education, and Recreation* 21, no. 2 (1950): 68–9, 98–9.

Lee, Mabel. 'The Case for and Against Intercollegiate Athletics for Women as it Stands Today'. *American Physical Education Review* 19 (1924): 13–19.

Lee, Mabel. *Memories Beyond Bloomers: 1924–1954*. Washington, DC: American Alliance for Health, Physical Education, and Recreation, 1978.

Lee, Mabel and Bruce L. Bennett. 'This Is Our Heritage: 75 Years of the American Association for Health, Physical Education, and Recreation'. *Journal of Health, Physical Education, and Recreation* 31, no. 4 (1960): 25–116.

Lewis, Guy M. 'Theodore Roosevelt's Role in the 1905 Football Controversy'. *Research Quarterly* 40 (1969): 717–24.

Lucas, John A. and Ronald A. Smith. *Saga of American Sport*. Philadelphia, PA: Lea and Febiger, 1978.

McCormick, Samuel Black. 'College Athletics from the Viewpoint of the President of a University'. *American Physical Education Review* 17 (1912): 137–45.

Mangan, James A. and Roberta J. Park. *From 'Fair Sex' to Feminism: Sport and the Socialization of Women in the Industrial and Post-Industrial Eras*. London: Frank Cass, 1987.

Meylan, George. 'Intercollegiate Athletics and the Department of Physical Education'. *American Physical Education Review* 27 (1922): 268–71.

Moore, Ellen S. *Restoring the Balance: Women Physicians and the Profession of Medicine, 1850–1995*. Cambridge, MA: Harvard University Press, 1999.

Morantz-Sanchez, Regina. *Sympathy and Science: Women Physicians in American Medicine*. New York: Oxford University Press, 1985.

Norris, J. Anna. 'A Method of Testing the Strength of the Abdominal Muscles'. *American Physical Education Review* 29, no. 6 (1922): 343–4.

Park, Roberta J., 'Concern for Health and Exercise as Expressed in the Writings of 18th Century Physicians and Informed Laymen (England, France, Switzerland)'. *Research Quarterly* 47 (1976): 756–67.

Park, Roberta J. 'Symbol, Celebration, and the Reduction of Conflict: Women's Field Hockey, a Game in Transition'. In *The Many Faces of Play*, edited by Kendall Blanchard. Champaign, IL: Human Kinetics, 1986: 232–47.

Park, Roberta J. *Measurement of Physical Fitness: A Historical Perspective*. Washington, DC: US Department of Health and Human Services, 1988.

Park, Roberta J. 'The Rise and Demise of Harvard's BS Program in Anatomy, Physiology, and Physical Training: A Case of Conflicts of Interest and Scarce Resources'. *Research Quarterly for Exercise and Sport* 63 (1992): 1–15.

Park, Roberta J. '"Time Given Freely to Worthwhile Causes": Anna S. Espenschade's Contributions to Physical Education'. *Research Quarterly for Exercise and Sport* 71 (2000): 99–115.

Park, Roberta J. "'Mended or Ended?": Football Injuries and the British and American Medical Press, 1870–1910'. *The International Journal of the History of Sport* 18 (2001): 110–33.

Park, Roberta J. 'Creating From Minds and Bodes: The Spring Dance Concert'. *Chronicle of the University of California* 6 (2004): 77–88.

Park, Roberta J. "'An Affirmation of the Abilities of Woman": Women's Contributions to the American Academy of Kinesiology and Physical Education'. *Quest* 58 (2006): 6–19.

Perry, Jean L. 'Merging Departments: A Unique Opportunity for Research'. *Quest* 31, no. 1 (1979): 83–6.

'Physical Education'. *American Journal of Education* 1, no. 1 (1826): 19–23.

'Presidents of the American Historical Association, 1884–1984'. *American Historical Review* 89 (1984): 1016–36. Available online at http://www.historians.org/info/ahahistory.cfm, accessed Jun. 2009.

Proceedings of the Association for the Advancement of Physical Education at Its Organization at Brooklyn, NY, November 27, 1885. Brooklyn: Rome Brothers, 1885.

Prospectus of Vassar Female College, 1865. Arlington, NY: Special Collections, Vassar College Libraries, 1865.

'Report of the Advisory Committee on Athletics for High School Girls'. *American Physical Education Review* 23 (1928): 254–60.

Rugen, M.E. 'Physical Education's Contributions to Health Education'. *Journal of Health, Physical Education, and Recreation* 22, no. 6 (1951): 25–8.

Safrit, Margaret J. 'Women in Research in Physical Education'. *Quest* 31, no. 2 (1979): 158–71.

Safrit, Margaret J. 'Women in Research in Physical Education: A 1984 Update'. *Quest* 36, no. 4 (1984): 103–14.

Savage, Howard J. *American College Athletics*. New York: The Carnegie Foundation for the Advancement of Teaching, 1929.

Scott, M. Gladys and Mary J. Hoferek. *Women As Leaders in Physical Education and Sport*. Iowa City, IA: The University of Iowa, 1972.

Sefton, Alice A. *The Women's Division of the National Amateur Athletic Federation*. Palo Alto, CA: Stanford University Press, 1941.

Smith, Ronald A. 'Preludes to the NCAA: Early Failures of Faculty Intercollegiate Athletic Control'. *Research Quarterly for Exercise and Sport* 54 (1983): 372–82.

Smith, Ronald A. *Sports and Freedom: The Rise of Big Time College Athletics*. New York: Oxford University Press, 1988.

Spears, Betty. 'The Influential Miss Homans'. *Quest* 29 (1978): 46–57.

Spears, Betty. *Leading the Way: Amy Morris Homans and the Beginnings of Professional Education for Women*. New York: Greenwood Press, 1986.

Sundwell, John. 'The Relation of Athletics to Physical Education'. *Educational Review* (March 1922): 198–210.

'The Athletic Research Society'. *American Physical Education Review* 17 (1912): 586–98.

'The Contributions of Physical Activity to Human Well-Being'. *Research Quarterly* 31, no. 2, part 2 (1960).

Thomas, Jerry R. 'Physical Education and Paranoia – Synonyms'. *Journal of Physical Education, Recreation, and Dance* 56, no. 9 (1985): 20–22.

Thomas, Jerry R. 'Motor Behavior'. In *The History of Exercise Science and Sport*, edited by John D. Massengale and Richard A. Swanson. Champaign, IL: Human Kinetics, 1997.

US Department of Health and Human Services. *Physical Activity and Health: A Report of the Surgeon General*. Atlanta, GA: Centers for Disease Control and Prevention, National Center for Chronic Disease Prevention and Health Promotion, 1996.

Vertinsky, Patricia. 'Mothers of the Dance: Margaret H'Doubler and Martha Hill'. Published in this issue.

Whorton, James C. *Crusaders for Fitness: The History of American Health Reformers*. Princeton, NJ: Princeton University Press, 1982.

Wood, Thomas D. 'Some Unsolved Problems in Physical Education'. *Proceedings of the International Congress of Education of the World's Columbian Exposition*. New York: National Education Association, 1894: 621–3.

Wood, Thomas Denison and Rosalind Frances Cassidy. *The New Physical Education*. New York: Macmillan Co., 1927.

Wrynn, Alison. 'Eliza Maria Mosher: Pioneering Woman Physician and Advocate of Physical Education'. Published in this issue.

Zieff, Susan G. 'Leading the Way in Science, Medicine and Physical Training: Female Physicians in Academia, 1890–1930'. Published in this issue.

Epilogue: Retrospectus

J. A. Mangan

'If women have a will, they do it
"gainst all the watches of the world"'

(Ben Jonson, *Volpone* Act III Scene iii)

(For) sooner may one day the sea be still
Than once restrain a woman of her will. [1]

(W. Haughton, *Englishmen for my Money*)

Sport, Women, Society: Further Reflections – Reaffirming Mary Wollstonecraft is the fourth of a quartet on sport, women and society published in recent years with which I have been involved in one way or another. I mention this because, in my view, it is important to see *Sport, Women, Society: Further Reflections – Reaffirming Mary Wollstonecraft* as part of a continuing consideration of the emancipatory advance of modern woman within the framework of the momentous global expansion of modern sport with its extraordinary political, cultural, social and economic consequences.

The quartet , in order of appearance, are: *From Fair Sex to Feminism: Sport and the Socialization of Women in the Industrial and Post-Industrial Eras* [2]; *Freeing the Female Body: Inspirational Icons* [3]; *Soccer, Women and Sexual Liberation: Kicking off a New Era* [4]; *Sport, Women, Society: Further Reflections – Reaffirming Mary Wollstonecraft*. Together they represent a continuous, contextualised and contiguous commentary.

Sport, Women, Society: Further Reflections – Reaffirming Mary Wollstonecraft, edited by Roberta J. Park and Patricia Vertinsky, who need no introduction, ineluctably provides further reflections to add to earlier reflections on the relationship between sport and female liberty. There are no palms outstretched for social alms, but firm index fingers pointing out cultural realities. The tone is calmly assured: the approach is coolly transgressive. There have been sensible transgressors, of course, even before Mary Wollstonecraft.

It is worth noting Susan Kingsley Kent's useful reminder that the efforts to change both radically and dramatically the predicament of women predate that 'rare avis' Mary Wollstonecraft: 'the seventeenth century was marked by extra-ordinary change and upheaval. In every area of life – from the economy to society, to religion, to politics, to the family – traditions, customs and eternal verities faced challenge and resistance'. [5] At the heart of the struggle was power. The concern was nothing less than a reconceptualization of the gender construction of society and a reassessment of the nature of men and women and the roles they played. [6] While the struggle for parity was of a woven anachroid complexity, the nidus was uncomplicated: the reasonable demand for collective and personal self-realisation. The issue was then, and is now, the questioning of unreasonable and proscriptive authority.

It is too often forgotten that we walk down previously trodden paths. The courageous Mary Wollstonecraft herself walked in the footsteps of others. What is different today, however, is the world stage on which the struggle takes place. With the rise to global significance of protean modern sport politically, culturally, socially and economically, as stated above, has been constructed a new arena in which the confrontation takes place. To be orphaned by history is not an asset. George Eliot was incorrect when she proclaimed in *The Mill on the Floss* that 'the happiest women like the happiest nations have no history.' [7] This quartet shows just how inadequate her observation was. Contemporary history has proved her wrong. It has provided the platform for social change. Recent centuries have witnessed the gradual increase in the happiness of many women – and involvement in sport has played its part.

The Introduction to *Fair Sex to Feminism* contained a justifiably disgruntled comment that prior to the 1980s well researched, argued and written political, cultural and social studies of sport were few and far between – less than a child's handful. To add insult to injury the few substantive historical studies there were dealt mostly with men and 'those dealing with women ... were virtually non-existent.' [8] Even fewer considered women and involvement in sport in its political, cultural and social settings; a smarting wound.

Furthermore, while social historians had turned their attention up till then to neglected groups particularly the urban poor, ethnic minorities and the female sex and had considered increasingly female complaints, sexual control and childbirth, little attention had been directed 'specifically to sport, recreation and leisure as a source of pleasure, an instrument of control or a symbol of emancipation.' [9] Salt was rubbed deeper into the wound by the further observation in *Fair Sex to Feminism* that even in the exceedingly sparse enquiries undertaken, the emphasis had been invariably on middle and upper class women. In both sorrow and anger the comment continued: 'Little or no attention has been directed to the pastimes of working class women ... little has been done as yet to present a comprehensive picture which cuts across class lines.' [10]

Has there been much change? How relevant to the present is this sober caveat?

> Historians of women must never be blinded by illusions of sisterly solidarity, and so neglect distinctive class differences in gender context. There was even less semblance of gender identification in the world of women's sport than in that of men. Whereas in the world of men's sport, by the late-nineteenth century, one can see in the spread of common team games from the middle to the working class some signs of a drawing together of the forms of recreations of various classes, support for women's team games remained markedly more middle-class and public

school oriented. Within the privileged female population social snobbery and group segregation continued to dictate even more strongly than within the corresponding male one that different sports should be followed in different settings by different classes. Women had no desire to associate on the playing field with people they would never have entertained in their drawing rooms. [11]

While disillusioned realism suffused the pages of the Introduction to *Fair Sex to Feminism*, later cautious optimism surfaced. Admonitions about the arduous advance of female emancipation through sport were sensibly repeated in *Soccer, Women, Sexual Liberation* – 'women's entrance into modern sport has too frequently been characterised by condescension and confrontation by necessary forced entry and grudging accommodation'. [12] Attention was drawn equally sensibly in *Freeing the Female Body* to inspirational women in recent times, who 'through a re-evaluation, reconstruction and rehabilitation of their bodies and women's bodies in general, have influenced and determined, directly and indirectly and to a greater or lesser extent, the status of many modern women of the modern 'global village'.' [13]

However, we are all spectators of the, sometimes attractive and sometimes unattractive, 'ceaseless gavotte of continuity and change.' [14] There is always an abacus of human gain and loss, a calculation of the negative and positive. The proselytizer's understandable inclination is to suck on an empirical comfort blanket of bright colours. It is a constant temptation. But, in the interests of analytical adequacy, further warnings should be made to add to that made earlier. They have been made elsewhere [15] already but their significance merits repetition.

Olwen Hufton is critical of the work of the influential Alice Clark on seventeenth century Englishwomen, in which she compared the wives of farmers and artisans 'with the useless woman of later literature, conspicuous for her lack of meaningful activity, and she laid the responsibility for this metamorphosis at the feet of encroaching capitalism. She also idealized the working home of the seventeenth century, where she assumed husband and wife toiled as partners, and compared this situation with the later harshly severed world of work and home. Clark was in many ways writing the predicament of many of her contemporaries into the script. More dangerously, to advance her thesis of the serial decline from healthy activity to idleness and or exploitation (depending on class) she had recourse to prescriptive literature and assumed that the ideology was strong enough to produce the reality.' [16] Hufton could also be read to advantage with reference to the actual complexity of male and female relationships. She has warned of the dangers, both implicit and explicit, of reading 'ego documents' - autobiographies, memoirs, letters, diaries, lawsuits and such like – which have been exploited extensively to reveal the constraints of culture on the lives of individual women. These dangers include the difficulty of transferring 'this approach on to a broader canvas without straying into the realms of conjecture' with the associated risks to which some social historians, she claims, have fallen prey, of over-speculation, the creation of the 'generic' woman and man and corresponding versions of womanhood and manhood, at the expense of the experiences of real people.

Then there is the further risk that in some cases the search for polarised gender attitudes and the associated belief that individuals were made not born, have tended to discount biological differences between women and men and led to an insistence on gender solely as a cultural construct. Finally, there is the risk that 'in attempting to understand ... cultural rules, insufficient attention has been given to the material constraints which determined the lives of the vast majority of people' – women *and* men. In recorded history most of both sexes have been oppressed. [17]

Commentators on the triadic relationship between sport, women and emancipation could also usefully consider the arguments Maria Formes has made with reference to gender and imperialism but which have a far wider applicability. She asserts that gender historians are primarily concerned with power as it is exercised between the sexes [18] and view it as the main source of an understanding of all historical relations. [19] Unfortunately, Formes states, in studies of imperialism and gender, in fact, 'the complexity of colonial relationships between the sexes has been inadequately considered.' [20] Greater subtlety of approach is required to capture the reality of these relationships. There is truth in her observation. Equally dangerous for the historian is polemical commitment to the villain versus heroine model of explanation with women triumphing over the circumstances contrived by men to maintain a status quo of superiority and inferiority. Such polarization, to use a meaningful expression of Formes, can mask the complexity and fluidity of social experience, and, it may be added, the realities of human interaction. Thus it can be the case that analysis on occasion still shirks sophistication. There is a pressing need to break free of a too easily accepted gravitational field. To renew the metaphor, the full dismemberment of gender interaction still awaits dissection.

The complexity of relationships between the sexes self-evidently applies to modern sport, female emancipation and power. One danger of any discussion of this relationship certainly is 'to fall prey to the weaknesses of a rigid dichotomous approach involving, for example, women as victims and men as oppressors. Clearly simplistic and too pervasive stereotyping of this kind is to be avoided in the interests of reality. Another danger is the tendency for men to recede into the background and become '*monolithic* supporting players' to women-centred studies. The danger of such simplifications are obvious: naïve male stereotyping, reduction of complex realities and inter-relationships and the failure, calculated or careless, to fully assess women's actual power, covert, and overt, in male and female relationships whatever the *ostensible* formal, institutional, cultural and political framework'. [21] Incidentally Forbes, like Hufton, also points out that relationships between women and women are not always those of accord, harmony and support; evident to the realist but not always to the idealist! There is a clear need, remarks Forbes, to recognise that feminisms are as much about power as they are about rights, 'power over other women as much as men'. [22]

A word of warning also uttered earlier and repeated here. Care must be taken to avoid polemical extremism and political simplism. Power, past and present, can be presented simplistically and female powerlessness can be proclaimed ingenuously. In short, perspective, balance and accuracy should be pursued carefully. To subvert analytical sloppiness should be the aim. In the groves of academe appropriate subtlety is a *sine qua non*. It can more frequently capture life than distort it. Thus , to make the point again without apology, any inclination towards an analytically naïve subscription to 'heroines and villains' fundamentalism must be disowned. The actual world of the domineering and manipulative members of both sexes must be confronted frankly and the political, social and cultural contours of the human landscape accurately drawn. In the cold words of Emily Bronte, 'the Tyrant grinds down [the] slaves ... and they crush those beneath.' [23] The observation embraces men and women! A strong Thesean thread is still needed to find the way out of the gender maze.

Many social movements carry within themselves the seeds of their own destruction: 'it is as well also to be aware of the fact that freedom is not an inexorable linear progression. At the present time when young women drink alcohol increasingly free from social inhibition or restriction – a fact that is causing medical concern due to the associated rise in female alcoholism – the comment of the French diarist Henri Misson on women in London in the eighteenth century to the effect that they held their own with men in drinking bouts' is both interesting, illuminating and topical. [24] Pop-alcohol versus putting the shot is no contest! Furthermore, the conclusion to the Epilogue of *Freeing the Female Body* stated, 'as for the analysis of the body, so too for the analysis of power, a pluralistic approach, *among other things* would involve an extensive and extended inquiry into the means by which *women's* power through the body is achieved – in the realm of sexuality, for example, how this is enhanced, how this is maintained and how this is retained. It will then become increasingly clear that tendencies to simplistic dichotomous analyses of power and powerlessness in the past and the present, increasingly will be found wanting.' [25] Thus, some consider that one subject begging for fuller enquiry is the sexualisation of the young female in western cultures, urged through a plethora of modern media means to be sensually 'hot' rather than physically fit, a point Natasha Walker, in her recent *Living Dolls* 'which ponders the conundrum that at a time when feminism ought to be home and dry girls just want to look like tarts,' [26] makes with both force and fear. Despairing observers lament that too many girls want to look and act like binge-inclined, plastically enhanced Jordans, rather than self-disciplined, gold-achieving Amy Thompsons. [27] They are encouraged, according to an acerbic comment of brutal bluntness, by celebrities like Hilary Swank at the 2010 Oscar Award Ceremony: 'her sense of taste and style had deserted her utterly ... did we really want to see as much of it [her body] as was displayed in that navel-skimming mankini tribute gown? It was the night that Swank really stank, sartorially at least.' [28]

For some like the well-named Cassandra Jardine using a savage expression of Martin Amis, sometimes we seem to be worshipping 'two bags of silicone'. She too is of the view that Natasha Walker's 'backward progress' from *The New Feminism* to *Living Dolls* reveals optimism replaced by pessimism, and she is at one with Dorica

Shields who cannot comprehend that so many young women wish to emulate surgically enhanced celebrities and why they should want look like Jordan rather than yearn for the dignity of Meryl Streep and why young girls should make others miserable by endlessly criticising each other for failing to match up to plasticised shapes and air-brushed images in magazines and on screens.[29] It all seems a long way for many from the hoped for feminist prelapsarian Eden. For them the pressing issue is one of demeaning sexual exhibitionism born out of a preoccupation not with health but with a louche, acebral self-indulgence with appearance which blocks the path to healthy dignity and pleasure through sport. For them Obliquity appears to be the debased fashion. Are such critics misguided in their concern? Are we now close to the cultural celebrity crudity envisaged in the sardonic lines of Roger Woddis in *Nothing Sacred*:

> Decent standards melt like butter,
> Cricket is becoming crude;
> Ah, my friend, an Oh Calcutta!
> Soon they'll play it in the nude! [30]

Is Michelene Wander correct when she says, 'The concealed pockets of the psyche contain undesirable and unlooked for change, one being the freedom of the woman-object to strip, to sell the object commodity at any price however demeaning.' Without any doubt the female body is still a subject for discussion about ideological manipulation, social determinism and cultural control, but now, perhaps, at some distance from playing-fields and arenas.

> Your nose is pressed against the glass,
> the object suddenly finds herself peeping
> at herself ... the feminine voyeur finds her
> identity as pornography. The emancipated
> woman sees herself as naked buttocks bursting
> out of black suspenders ...

In short, she watches herself as an object. [31] 'This doesn't make transformation simple,' Wander adds. 'It mystifies with a giant kaleidoscope. We lose ourselves and one another in the reflected images of unrealisable desires. We walk into a world of distorting mirrors. We smash the mirrors. Only pain convinces us we are there. But there is still more glass.' [32]Are we entering a Post-Feminism Pornographic Projection Period? Some clearly think so.

Finally, it is interesting that when violence threatened the future of the famous public schools of mid-Victorian England sport became the antidote to degenerate behaviour, few commentators mention it as a solution even in part to the vulgarity of some modern young women.

On a more sanguine note, while one claim for *Fair Sex* was that it dealt with sport 'as a source of tension, as a means of both sexual antagonism and conciliation, as an illustration of both continuity and change', that it demonstrated that 'history of sport is as much political as it is social' and that power was all too often the central issue. It still is the central issue as *Sport, Women, Society: Further Reflections – Reaffirming Mary Wollstonecraft* makes clear, but it makes it equally clear that increasingly this power is shared, however imperfect our modern cultures remain. [33] The collection also attractively complements *Inspirational Icons: Freeing the Female Body* in its exploration of the contributions and achievements of women in a variety of historical and geographical contexts and provides and seeks to broaden under-standing 'about the background, motivations and achievements' of dedicated women … in a variety of different areas and for different purposes.' [34] Another emancipatory milestone has been passed with its additional revisions and counter-narratives [35] The milestone stands boldly on the democratic road from past to present. *Sport, Women, Society: Further Reflections – Reaffirming Mary Wollstonecraft* like the other publications in the quartet, to quote from Roy Porter's magisterial *Enlightenment*, presents us with women who are the direct outcome of 'the Enlightenment's secular value system to which most of us subscribe' [36] and 'which upholds the unity of mankind and basic personal freedoms and the world of tolerance, knowledge, education and opportunity.' [37] In pursuit of these meritorious ideals 'emancipationists of the female body, with justice on their side and passion in their prose' [38] have properly challenged convention.

The Introduction to *Fair Sex* was conceived in optimism but concluded with realism that it was 'exploratory, tentative and incomplete' and that 'there is still much to learn about the relationship of women, recreation and leisure not merely to political, social and cultural ideologies but to urban development, evolving work patterns, changing educational opportunities, public health improvements and social class patterns throughout the world.' It ended, however, with a clarion call: 'The status of women, relationships between the sexes and attitudes to child rearing are mirrored in the recreational, leisure and sporting opportunities available to women and it is hoped that this contribution to social historical studies will stimulate inquiry into such issues and progressively deepen our understanding of the place of women in the cultural heritage of modern society.' [39] *Sport, Women, Society: Further Reflections – Reaffirming Mary Wollstonecraft* has answered the 'call' but the perceptive will be aware that the route to full subtlety of the scrutiny of power, women and sport in the totality of the oppression of both men and women points to the inevitable appearance of a quintet. The gender ocean still has hidden depths.

In conclusion, a literary parable for all time. In her autobiography, Harriet Martineau, the Victorian novelist, describes the inspiration for her 'audacious' authorship – her idolised brother. The modest outcome was an article signed 'V' in the Unitarian periodical, the *Monthly Repository*, on the topic of 'Female Writers in Practical Divinity'. On publication, another brother, unaware that she had written the piece, requested her appraisal of it. She was silent: he was bemused. Eventually she confessed her authorship. To her surprise and delight her brother declared, '… leave it to other women to make shirts and darn stockings; and devote yourself to this!' [40] She went home 'in a sort of dream, so that the squares of the pavements seemed to float before my eyes. That evening made me as an authoress.' [41] *Sport, Women, Society: Further Reflections – Reaffirming Mary Wollstonecraft*, too, reminds us of an essential obligation: ability should always be encouraged and talent should be assisted – in both women and men in sport and beyond sport. In short: 'All of us do not have equal talent, but all of us should have the equal opportunity to develop our talents.' [42] *Sub-specie aeternitatis*

Notes

[1] Quoted in Dalbiac, *A Dictionary of Quotations*, 123.
[2] Ibid., 232.
[3] See Mangan and Park, eds. *From 'Fair Sex' to Feminism: Sport and the Socialization of Women in the Industrial and Post Industrial Eras.* London: Frank Cass, 1987.
[4] Mangan and Hong, *Freeing the Female Body.*
[5] Hong and Mangan, Soccer, *Women, Sexual Liberation.*
[6] Kent, *Gender and Power in Britain 1640 –1990*, 4.
[7] Ibid.
[8] Quoted in Dalbiac, *A Dictionary of Quotations*, 257.
[9] Mangan and Park, *From 'Fair Sex' to Feminism*, 1.
[10] Ibid., 2–3.
[11] Ibid., 3.
[12] McCrone, 'Class, Gender and English Women's Sport', 161.
[13] Fan and Mangan, *Soccer, Women, Sexual Liberation*, 1.
[14] Mangan and Fan, *Freeing the Female Body*, 237.
[15] Collins, *History, Religion and Culture: British Intellectual History*, 11.
[16] See Mangan, 'Epilogue: Prospects for the New Millennium: Women, Emancipation and the Body', passim.
[17] Ibid., 240.
[18] Ibid., 239.
[19] Ibid., 238.
[20] Ibid., 241.
[21] Ibid., 240.
[22] Ibid., 239.
[23] Ibid., 241.
[24] *Quoted in Gross, The Oxford Book of Aphorisms*, 112.
[25] Mangan, 'Epilogue: Prospects for the New Millennium: Women, Emancipation and the Body', 240.
[26] Ibid., 248.
[27] The London quality broadsheet *The Daily Telegraph* in the Spring of 2010 contained a number of articles and reports expressing concern about the sexualisation of modern young women.
[28] While these were not deeply researched they drew a number of widely read popular publications and the personal experiences of concerned commentators.
[29] See, for example, Melanie McDonagh, 'Sex is constantly in front of the children', *The Daily Telegraph*, 22 February 2010, 22.
[30] Amy Thompson was an English gold medallist at the recent Vancouver Winter Olympic Games.
[31] See 'Liz Hunt on Wednesday', *The Daily Telegraph*, 10 March 2010, 24.
[32] Wadis, 'Nothing Sacred', 292–3.
[33] Wandor, *The Body Politic*, 28.

[34] Ibid.
[35] Ibid.
[36] See Cassandra Jardine, 'It started with girl power and has sunk into mindless hedonism', *The Daily Telegraph,* 12 January 2010, 27.
[37] Mangan and Park, *From 'Fair Sex' to Feminism,* 8.
[38] Editors' Proposal for consideration for publication, 2.
[39] Ibid.
[40] See the Series' Editor's Foreword by J.A.Mangan to *Freeing the Female Body,* IX.
[41] Quoted in Sutherland, *The Oxford Book of Literary Anecdotes,* 218–9.
[42] Quoted in Tripp, *The International Thesaurus of Quotations,* 185.

References

Collins. S, *History, Religion and Culture: British Intellectual History.* Cambridge: CUP, 2000.

Dalbiac. Phillip Hugh, (ed.), *A Dictionary of Quotations.* London: Thomas Nelson, n.d.

Fan Hong and J.A. Mangan, Soccer, *Women, Sexual Liberation: Kicking Off a New Era.* London: Frank Cass, 2004.

Gross. John, *The Oxford Book of Aphorisms.* Oxford: OUP, 1987.

Hunt, Liz, 'Liz Hunt on Wednesday' *The Daily Telegraph,* 13 March, 2010.

Jardine, Cassandra, 'It started with girl power and has sunk into mindless hedonism', *The Daily Telegraph,* January, 2010.

Kent, Susan, *Gender and Power in Britain 1640–1990.* Routledge 2000.

Mangan, J. A. 'Epilogue: Prospects For the New Millennium: Women, Emancipation and the Body'. In *Freeing the Female Body: Inspirational Icons,* edited by J. A. Mangan and Fan Hong. London: Frank Cass.

Mangan. J.A., and Fan Hong, *Freeing the Female Body: Inspirational Icons.* London: Frank Cass, 2001.

Mangan, J. A., and Park, Roberta J., eds. *From 'Fair Sex' to Feminism: Sport and the Socialization of Women in the Industrial and Post Industrial Eras.* London: Frank Cass, 1987.

McCrone, Kathleen, 'Class, Gender and English Women's Sport c. 1890–1914', *Journal of Sports History,* 18 (1991).

McDonagh, 'Sex is constantly in front of the children', *The Daily Telegraph,* February, 2010.

Roberts, Laura, 'Young girls are being sexualised says Fiona Bruce', *The Daily Telegraph,* March, 2010.

Sutherland, James, *The Oxford Book of Literary Quotations.* Oxford: Clarendon Press, 1975.

Trapp, Rhoda, Thomas (ed.) *The International Thesaurus of Quotations.* New York; Thomas.Y. Crowell, 1970.

Wadis. Roger, 'Nothing Sacred.' In *The New Oxford Book of Light Verse,* compiled by Kingsley Amis, Oxford: OUP, 1979.

Wander, Michelene, *The Body Politic: Women's Liberation in Britain,* London: Stage 1. 1972.

Index

Page numbers in **Bold** represent figures.

INDEX

INDEX

Routledge
Taylor & Francis Group

International Review of Sport and Exercise Psychology

EDITOR-IN-CHIEF:
Aidan Moran, *University College Dublin, Ireland*

ASSOCIATE EDITORS:
Cathy Craig, *The Queen's University of Belfast, Northern Ireland*
John Kremer, *The Queen's University of Belfast, Northern Ireland*
David Lavallee, *Aberystwyth University, UK*
Tadhg MacIntyre, *University of Ulster, Northern Ireland*
Nanette Mutrie, *Strathclyde University, UK*

Supported by an International Editorial Board

International Review of Sport and Exercise Psychology is a scholarly, peer-reviewed journal which aims to publish substantial critical reviews of the research literature in sport and exercise psychology. Typically, these reviews will evaluate relevant conceptual and methodological issues in the field and will attempt to provide a critique of the strengths and weaknesses of separate empirical studies that address common themes or hypotheses. Ideally, they should present the authors' summary of, and conclusions about, the current state of knowledge of the topic of interest as well as an assessment of relevant unresolved issues and future trends. Manuscripts containing reviews of research literature on theories, topics and issues that are at the interface with mainstream psychology are especially welcome.

To submit a paper to ***International Review of Sport and Exercise Psychology*** please visit
http://mc.manuscriptcentral.com/rirs

 Routledge
Taylor & Francis Group

Journal of Sports Sciences

Published on behalf of the British Association of Sport ad Exercise Sciences

2008 Impact factor: 1.625, Ranking 28/71 (Sport Sciences)
©2009 Thomson Reuters, *Journal Citation Reports*®

EDITOR-IN-CHIEF:

Alan Nevill, *University of Wolverhampton, UK*

The *Journal of Sports Sciences* publishes articles of a high standard on various aspects of the sports sciences covering a number of disciplinary bases, including anatomy, biochemistry, biomechanics, psychology, sociology, as well as ergonomics, kinanthropometry and other interdisciplinary perspectives. In addition to reports of research, review articles and book reviews are published. The emphasis of the journal is on the human sciences, broadly defined, applied to sport and exercise.

To view free articles please visit **www.tandf.co.uk/journals/rjsp** and click on News & Offers.

To sign up for tables of contents, new publications and citation alerting services visit **www.informaworld.com/alerting**

 updates
Taylor & Francis Group

Register your email address at **www.tandf.co.uk/journals/eupdates.asp** to receive information on books, journals and other news within your areas of interest.

 Powered by
informaworld

For further information, please contact Customer Services at either of the following:
T&F Informa UK Ltd, Sheepen Place, Colchester, Essex, CO3 3LP, UK
Tel: +44 (0) 20 7017 5544 Fax: 44 (0) 20 7017 5198
Email: subscriptions@tandf.co.uk

Taylor & Francis Inc, 325 Chestnut Street, Philadelphia, PA 19106, USA
Tel: +1 800 354 1420 (toll-free calls from within the US)
or +1 215 625 8900 (calls from overseas) Fax: +1 215 625 2940
Email: customerservice@taylorandfrancis.com

View an online sample issue at:
www.tandf.co.uk/journals/rjsp